For Bill,
Grace to you and peace!
Fr. Gene

# DINING
## *in the*
# KINGDOM
### *of*
# GOD

*the origins of the eucharist according to luke*

## EUGENE LAVERDIERE, SSS

**LITURGY TRAINING PUBLICATIONS**

## Acknowledgments

All scripture texts in this work are taken from the New American Bible, copyright © 1970; Revised New Testament, copyright © 1986, Confraternity of Christian Doctrine. All rights reserved.

Copyright © 1994, Archdiocese of Chicago: Liturgy Training Publications, 1800 North Hermitage Avenue, Chicago IL 60622-1101; 1-800-933-1800; FAX 1-800-933-7094. All rights reserved.

This book was edited by David A. Lysik with assistance from Sarah Huck and Jennifer McGeary. It was designed and illustrated by Mary Bowers and typeset by Kari Nicholls in Futura and Sabon.

Printed in the United States of America.

ISBN 1-56854-022-1
DINING
$11.95

*To Uncle Willy*
*Father William LaVerdiere, sss*
*Priest and Religious of the Blessed Sacrament*
*1902 – 1991*

# Preface

It was a great meal.

There was fresh spinach —lots of it — and potatoes, milk, homemade bread and an orange. There must have been something else, but I do not remember.

What I remember is the monks streaming in through the cloister and quietly taking their places at long, narrow tables, like you see in Cistercian monasteries all over the world, like you imagine at Citeaux and Clairvaux with Bernard, Alberic and Stephen Harding, taking seriously Christ's call to conversion.

Everyone ate modestly and in silence.

That was Friday, February 19 of this year, 1993. I was giving a set of conferences on St. Paul at the Abbey of Our Lady of Gethsemani, and I was invited to join the monks for meals in the monastic dining room.

What I remember most of all is standing quietly at my place on entering the dining room, knowing a peace few people ever know, waiting for the blessing prayer. We had just come from chanting the Divine Office.

Breaking the silence, one of the monks intoned the prayer: "Blessed is the one who shall feast in the kingdom of God." I held my breath. Everything inside me responded: "Now and forever."

The monk actually chanted the blessing:

Blessed is the one who shall feast in the Kingdom of God

And all the other monks chanted in response:

Blessed is the one who shall feast in the Kingdom of God

Then we spoke the Lord's Prayer.

The blessing, of course, came from Luke's gospel, from Luke 14:1 – 24, the story of a sabbath meal with Jesus at the home of a Pharisee. Jesus had just finished saying how everyone — including the poor, the crippled, the lame and the blind — was to be invited to the dinner, not just friends, relatives and wealthy neighbors. It is then that one of those at table with him exclaimed: "Blessed is the one who will dine in the kingdom of God." (14:15)

The monks' chant brought back memories of childhood, of picking berries in the fields and woods of Maine, where I grew up, and bringing the berries — stawberries, blueberries, raspberries and blackberries — home to the family. Mom cleaned them, and we enjoyed them with milk. That was most certainly dining in the kingdom of God!

There were also walks to church and school, the snow crunching underfoot in the morning cold of Lent, breakfast and books in hand. First there was Mass and then our catsup and egg sandwiches in the church-school hall. I sat with Claudette. Gary was still too small, and Peter was but a newborn. After Mass, we filed into school. That too was dining — feasting! — in the kingdom of God!

Then I remembered having lunch with Uncle Willy, Mr. Burke, Mr. Twiname and Mr. Schwarz in the executive dining room on the twelfth floor at B. Altman's on New York's Fifth Avenue. I had never been on a private elevator before. Nor had I ever seen so many forks, knives and spoons at one place setting. I watched Uncle Willy and did as he did all through the meal. Feasting in the kingdom of God!

"Blessed is the one who will feast in the kingdom of God." The scripture verse was selected by Brother Chrysogonus (Father Chrysogonus Waddell), as was the chant notation, contributing to Gethsemani's effort to renew the prayers for meals in the refectory.

After reviewing the history of such prayers, Brother Chrysogonus noted; "I could not help but be impressed with the sheer *amplitude* of most of the refectory prayer formularies.

Often enough, the prayers take on the form of a fully structured Office, complete with psalmody. All this is rather difficult to explain if it is merely a question of 'blessing the food.' My own feeling is that, in practice, the theological foundations lie deeper. The important thing seems to be less that the food gets blessed than that the brethren gather for a meal in common."[1]

Brother Chrysogonus's observation is amply borne out by the study of meals with Jesus in Luke's gospel. A meal is not so much about food as it is about people. In all meals it is the guest list, not the menu, that matters. Blessings and prayers, liturgical and non-liturgical, have to do with the people who have come together to share the meal. That is what we hear in the words of Jesus, and that is what we hear from the participant who exclaimed, "Blessed is the one who will dine in the kingdom of God."

Brother Chrysogonus concluded, "The community meal, then, takes on an ecclesial dimension of deep religious import. Would it be going too far to suggest that the family meal is as much an 'epiphany' of the local church as is the common celebration of Sext or Compline? Thus our praying together in the refectory takes on the nature of a *community celebration* in the deepest sense of the word."[2]

The community meal, like the family meal, is certainly an epiphany, a manifestation, of the church community. Like all prayer, it participates in the community eucharist, where meals, even the most ordinary, reach their highest expression in sacramental self-offering and communion. Every Christian meal reveals aspects of the kingdom of God, where guests are welcomed, people share with one another, broken covenants are renewed and all are reconciled.

The eucharist reveals all of these aspects of the kingdom of God as well as its universality. All, including the poor, the crippled, the lame and the blind, are invited to the table of Lord. "Blessed is the one who will dine in the kingdom of God."

The kingdom of God is already in our midst (Luke 17:20), but it is also to come, as Jesus taught his disciples in the Lord's Prayer: "Thy kingdom come." We, the church, have a responsibility in that. To fulfill our responsibility we pray to the Father of all for the bread we need in order to make the kingdom of God more and more present: "Give us each day our daily bread." (Luke 11:2–4)

Just as Christian family and community meals participate in the eucharist and reveal important aspects of it, the eucharist itself participates in the heavenly table of the Lord, anticipating it, revealing it and promoting it.

Meals permeate the entire fabric of Christian life. Little wonder Luke saw Jesus' Last Supper as announcing the kingdom of God (22:16, 18). Little wonder he saw every other meal with Jesus as part of the origins of the eucharist and as revealing its implications for the life of the church.

In offering this book, I wish to thank the members of my family: my mom and dad, Laurier and Gladys; Sister Claudette, MM, currently the President of the Maryknoll Sisters; Brother Gary, SSS, for many years the manager and art director of *Emmanuel* magazine; and Peter, who saved the honor of the family and moved it into its next generation. Family meals have always been special in our family. The family table was a family school, teaching all those things that matter most in life.

On the academic and professional side, I am indebted to a great many people. For the present work, I wish to single out my colleagues at the University of St. Mary of the Lake, in Mundelein, Illinois, where from 1990–1993 I have held the Margaret and Chester Paluch Chair of Theology. I am also indebted to my colleagues at Catholic Theological Union in Chicago, at the Summer Sessions of the University of San Francisco, and at the National Office of the Society for the Propagation of the Faith in New York.

I wish to thank in a special way the members of a little commission of Blessed Sacrament Religious to which I have belonged for the past five years, Erasto Fernandez (India), Joviano de Lima Junior (Brazil) and Alberto Occhioni (Italy). We have met periodically in different parts of the world to share our work on the eucharist and inquire into its implications for various cultures and social situations. I am deeply indebted to the members of the commission as well as to all those who took part in our work.

I also wish to thank the editors at Liturgy Training Publications for judicious, critical and very helpful advice, and my secretary, Mary Maloney, for carefully reading the manuscript and assisting in its preparation for publication.

I dedicate this book to Uncle Willy, who took me to lunch in the executive dining room at B. Altman and Company. I was 15 years old then and he was 50, seven years younger than I am now.

Uncle Willy was a most extraordinary priest and religious, a Blessed Sacrament Father in the fullest sense of the term, one who really knew about dining in the kingdom of God. As Uncle Willy grew older and as I grew up, we became very close. For several years we had adjoining rooms in the community at St. Jean Baptiste parish in New York.

Whenever I returned from preaching or teaching, Uncle Willy would ask, "How did you do? How did it go?" It was sometime in his last year or two, in his late 80s, when his ministry was reduced to a few letters, that I noticed a change. Instead of asking, "How did you do?" he was asking, "How did we do?"

The demands of our ministry often kept us far apart. Since February 17, 1991, we are always together.

And so, I need to ask, "Uncle Willy, how are we doing?"


May 8, 1993
Mundelein Seminary
University of St. Mary of the Lake

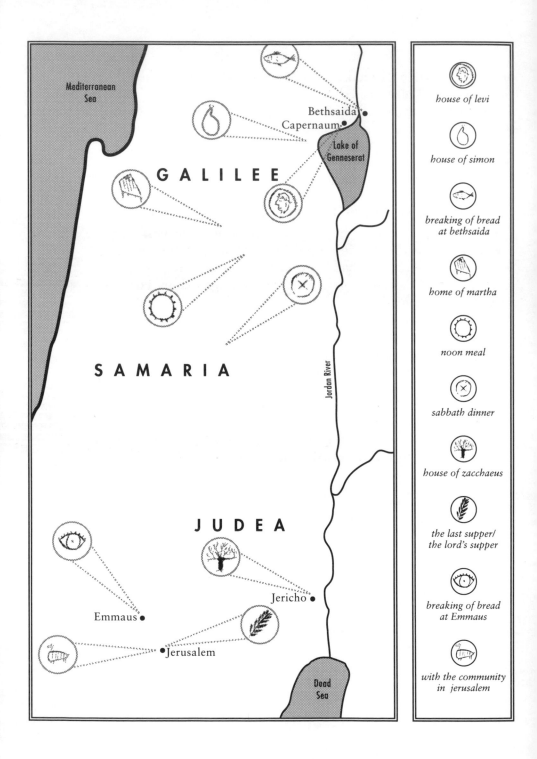

Mediterranean
Sea

Bethsaida
Capernaum

Lake of
Genneserat

G A L I L E E

S A M A R I A

Jordan River

J U D E A

Jericho

Emmaus

Jerusalem

Dead
Sea

*house of levi*

*house of simon*

*breaking of bread
at bethsaida*

*home of martha*

*noon meal*

*sabbath dinner*

*house of zacchaeus*

*the last supper/
the lord's supper*

*breaking of bread
at Emmaus*

*with the community
in jerusalem*

# The Eucharist in Luke's Gospel

Then he took the bread, said the blessing, broke it, and gave it to them, saying, "This is my body which will be given for you; do this in memory of me." And likewise the cup after they had eaten, saying, "This cup is the new covenant in my blood, which will be shed for you." (Luke 22:19 – 20)

We know that story very well. It is how the eucharist[1] began. It is also what we do each time we celebrate eucharist.

The early Christians also knew that story, if not in the exact words of Luke, in words very close to his. The story of Jesus taking bread, giving thanks and breaking it was told in their eucharistic celebration, as it is in ours.

**A Gospel Event**[2]    Recalling the story of the eucharist, Luke drew on a liturgical tradition that was already old and venerable in the mid-80s of the first century, but still very much alive in the liturgical assemblies of Gentile Christianity. Inserting this tradition into Jesus' farewell discourse at the Last Supper, Luke thereby related it to the passion-resurrection and to the whole story of the gospel. In the Gospel of Luke, the eucharist is a *gospel* event.

Paul quoted the same tradition some 30 years earlier in the First Letter to the Corinthians. At that time the tradition already had a good 15-year history of being received and handed down (see 1 Corinthians 11:23 – 25). For Paul, too, the eucharist was a gospel event, and when it lost its gospel quality, as it did at Corinth, Paul did everything he could to restore it (see 1 Corinthians 11:17 – 34).

Through Paul, the eucharistic tradition can be traced to the community of Antioch, where Paul was formed as a Christian and nurtured as the future missionary to the Gentiles. It is there at Antioch — where "the disciples were first called Christians" (Acts 11:26) — that the eucharistic tradition in Luke 22:19 – 20 and in 1 Corinthians 11:23 – 25 was developed, along with what is perhaps our oldest creed: "Christ died for our sins in accordance with the scriptures; . . . he was buried; . . . he was raised on the third day in accordance with the scriptures; . . . he appeared to Kephas, then to the Twelve." (1 Corinthians 15:3 – 5) From the very beginning, in the earliest tradition, the eucharist was known and experienced as a gospel event.

Today we talk about the liturgical tradition in Luke 22:19 – 20 as the institution of the eucharist, and we receive it and pass it on as the words of consecration. Very few think of the eucharist as a gospel event, the high point of Jesus' life, and *a compendium of the whole gospel.*

For many Christians, including Catholics, the eucharist is an isolated non-event, tangential to the gospel and barely connected with Jesus' ministry. This is to the detriment of both gospel and eucharist. Gospel that does not find expression in the eucharist is greatly impoverished. Eucharist that is cut off from the gospel is pastorally ineffective. We are very far from those vibrant beginnings when Paul and Luke knew they could proclaim the gospel more effectively by telling what Jesus did and said at the Last Supper.

Many factors contributed to the present situation. Some are very complex, but one is quite simple. It is the way we isolate the origins of the eucharist from the rest of Jesus' life and ministry, even from the passion-resurrection. When we think of the eucharist, we think of the Last Supper and Jesus' eucharistic words. We pay little attention to its context in the story of the passion, let alone the whole gospel. Isolated in our perception of its origins, the eucharist becomes equally isolated in the life of Christians today. And the New Testament, which should help us integrate the eucharist into our lives, ends up reinforcing its isolation.

*Institution and Origins*   How did we come to have such a narrow focus? Part of the answer is connected with the word "institution." It was centuries before Christians referred to the eucharist as something "instituted." In the New Testament, Paul and the synoptic gospels spoke of it as something given to us by Jesus and as something coming from him. They presented the eucharist as what Jesus did at the Last Supper, and they retold its story in the liturgy, but they did not speak of it as "instituted" by Jesus.

Like the New Testament writers, the Fathers of the church associated the eucharist with Jesus' Last Supper and his command that the apostles do this in memory of him. Witness, for example, Justin Martyr (c. 150) as he explains and provides the background for the celebration of eucharist: "For, in the memoirs which the apostles composed and which we call 'gospels,' they have told us that they were commissioned thus: Jesus took bread and having given thanks, said: 'Do this in memory of me; this is my body'; and in a like manner he took the cup and, having given thanks, said: 'This is my blood,' and he gave these to them alone."[3] They also saw the eucharist as an integral part of the passion story.[4] Referring to John 19:34, they even spoke of the sacraments issuing from the wound in the side of Christ. St. Augustine, for example, interpreted the blood and water as symbolic of the sacraments of initiation.[5]

One who came close to speaking of the eucharist as "instituted" was Pope Leo the Great (440–461), when he referred to Jesus founding the new Pasch and establishing the sacrament of his body and blood.[6] The background for Pope Leo's teaching was the monophysite controversy over the real incarnation of Jesus. Pope Leo argued for a real incarnation from the reality of Christ's presence in the eucharist,[7] a doctrine based on what Jesus *did* at the Last Supper and how the event was presented and interpreted in the New Testament. In Pope Leo's terms, Jesus founded or established the eucharist at the Last Supper, an event inseparable from the rest of the passion-resurrection.

Discussion about the actual institution of the eucharist began between the ninth and the eleventh centuries in the great controversies over the "real presence" of Christ in the eucharist. In order to affirm the real presence, the church appealed to Jesus' institution of the eucharist at the Last Supper.[8] But in doing so, it still tended to focus on what Jesus *did* at the Last Supper, not just on the words he spoke.

A similar concern about the real presence and Jesus' institution of the eucharist can be seen among the great thirteenth century theologians, notably St. Thomas Aquinas.[9] But the extremely narrow focus that influences today's experience of eucharist developed later, at the time of the Reformation and the Council of Trent[10] in the controversies surrounding the eucharistic consecration and transubstantiation. At this point, the debate tended to identify what Jesus *did* at the Last Supper with what he *said*, thereby focusing the origins of eucharist even more narrowly on the words of institution.

In the twentieth century, eucharistic controversies have ranged over a wide spectrum of issues, including the importance and the actual need of the eucharist in an ecclesial community. In all of these controversies, what matters ultimately is what Jesus *did* at the Last Supper. As Johannes Betz indicated: "The institution of the supper by the historical Jesus is decisive for all eucharistic practice and dogma."[11]

Recognizing the importance of what Jesus did, however, need not entail narrowing one's focus and isolating a moment of institution from the rest of the Last Supper, or isolating the Supper from the passion-resurrection and the rest of Jesus' life. As Betz further indicated, Jesus summed up his whole messianic being and work in his Last Supper. "Hence the supper must not only be explained in the light of the entire life of Jesus, it is this entirety in symbolic compression."[12]

Important as the notion of institution has been in doctrinal and theological controversies, it constitutes an unfortunate starting point for general catechesis and for pastoral reflection on the eucharist in the New Testament, especially in Luke's gospel, which is so conscious of telling a continuous, unfolding story, from the annunciation of John's birth (1:5–25) to the ascension of Jesus (24:50–53). The word "institution" almost automatically narrows our field of vision to the Last Supper and even more narrowly to what Jesus said when he gave the bread and the cup to his apostles.

With a vision so stringently focused, it is very easy to isolate the Last Supper from everything that leads up to it and even from the passion-resurrection. When that happens, recourse to the New Testament is of little help for connecting the eucharist with the rest of life and making it a gospel event. For this we need to speak of the *origins,* rather than the institution, of the eucharist.

What then does Luke's gospel say about the origins of the eucharist? How is the eucharist part of Luke's gospel? How is it related to the Last Supper? How is the Last Supper related to the other meals in Luke's gospel? How are the meals related to other themes, such as journey? And how is the eucharist related to the gospel of Jesus Christ? These are the questions we need to answer in order to make of the eucharist a gospel event, as we find it in earliest tradition, in St. Paul, in Luke's gospel and in the rest of the New Testament.

**Gospel and Eucharist**   There is only one gospel, the gospel of Jesus Christ, telling the good news of the savior's life, death and resurrection.[13] As a memorial of the death and resurrection of Jesus Christ and as the Lord's Supper, the eucharist is at the very heart of that gospel.

At first, the gospel was communicated live through personal presence, word and deed in the preaching, healing, reconciling and teaching ministries of the early church. The gospel also was communicated in the eucharist, where presence, deed and word come together in a unique gospel event. Paul made this very clear: "For as often as you eat this bread and drink the cup, you proclaim the death of the Lord until he comes." (1 Corinthians 11:26) From the beginning, the eucharist was indeed a gospel event.

*The Written Gospel*  Eventually, the living and spoken gospel was written down, giving us the gospels according to Matthew, Mark, Luke and John: four distinct expressions of the one gospel of Jesus Christ. Each of these gospels drew on the church's experience of the eucharist for presenting the meaning and implications of the gospel for Christian life in the church of their time. Each gospel situated the eucharist in a larger narrative, showing how it related to every aspect of Christian life.

In many ways, the four written gospels are very similar.[14] This allows three of them — Matthew, Mark and Luke, whose story lines run parallel to one another — to be aligned in columns showing their threefold development at one glance. The eucharist is an integral part of that synoptic presentation. A similar parallelism, though not as pronounced, can be shown for all four gospels, and again the eucharist is part of that parallelism. A parallel arrangement shows how the eucharist remains one and the same even when it is adapted for different pastoral situations.

Though the gospels are similar in many ways, each one is also unique and very different from the others. New situations and changing times called for different emphases and more effective ways of presenting the gospel story. The challenges facing Matthew were not the same as those facing Mark, and both differed from those facing Luke.

Each gospel is unique in the way it draws on the church's heritage and presents the traditional gospel of Jesus Christ. Each makes a special contribution regarding the person, mission and teaching of Jesus, the call and ministry of the disciples, the challenges confronting the church, and even the setting in which the gospel story unfolds. In Mark, for example, the gospel story is set mainly in the countryside around the Sea of Galilee. In Luke, the story often is transposed into an urban setting.

Each gospel also makes a unique contribution to our understanding of the eucharist and to the way it inspires, energizes and challenges the Christian community. Writing for Christians of Gentile origin, Luke was bound to emphasize many facets of the eucharist that were quite different from those in Matthew, who wrote for Christians of Jewish origin; the same can be said for Mark and for John. Written for Christians severely tested by strong apocalyptic tendencies, the Last Supper account in the Gospel of Mark emphasized the community's involvement in the passion of Christ. Written for Christians challenged by growing protognostic tendencies, the eucharistic emphasis in the Gospel of John was on the flesh of Jesus, the Son of Man.

*According to Luke*  This book is about the eucharist as presented in only one of those four written gospels, the Gospel of Luke. Luke wrote during the 80s of the first century for communities established in the 50s and 60s, during the great Pauline missions. Luke may be the person the letter to the Colossians refers to metaphorically as Paul's "beloved physician" (Colossians 4:14; see also Philemon 24). In the two-volume work commonly referred to as Luke-Acts, Luke shows great skill as a storyteller and writer. He appears to have benefitted from a good Hellenistic education. Later, on becoming a Christian, he also acquired an extraordinary grasp of the biblical world as presented in the Septuagint, a Greek translation of the Hebrew Bible with some additional books.[15]

The purpose of this book is to spell out Luke's special contribution to the meaning of the eucharist and to indicate some of the questions it raises for us. It also suggests possible implications Luke's work might have for the life of the church today. In the process, we shall meet Luke at his storytelling best.

Luke introduced his gospel as "a narrative of the events that have been fulfilled among us" (1:1). As a narrative, his gospel is a story. It is a story of events conceived in divine promise and brought forth in a history of salvation. The eucharist is part of that story, a special motif woven into its tapestry of gospel events promised and fulfilled.

Luke means to tell those events "just as those who were eye-witnesses from the beginning and ministers of the word have handed them down to us" (1:2). The roots of Luke's gospel lie deep in traditions received and passed on by pastoral ministers who saw the gospel unfold. Luke's presentation of the eucharist is equally traditional and pastoral.

After careful research, like one well-versed in the historical arts of the time, Luke decided to write down those events "in an orderly sequence" (1:3). So, too, with the eucharist, whose story begins early in the gospel and is carefully related to the greater story of Jesus and his disciples as it moves toward its climax in the passion, resurrection and ascension.

Luke's purpose in telling the story was that readers and listeners might "realize the certainty of the teachings" they had "received." His purpose, therefore, was not to reveal new things — although there are many things in Luke's gospel for which we have no other source — but to reveal the truth and solid ground of things already known. The same applies to Luke's presentation of the eucharist, whose truth is inseparable from that of Christ and the gospel. Luke means not to tell new things about the eucharist but to help us see how well-grounded it is along with what it means and what it asks of us.

Such also is the purpose of this book, not to tell new things about the eucharist but to show more clearly the things Luke has made known to us, approaching them in an orderly fashion and with a sensitivity to pastoral tradition so that the eucharistic promise might continue to be fulfilled. For this I shall explore the eucharist's place in the gospel, examine its meaning and implications for those engaged in salvation history, and see how it challenges today's eucharistic assemblies and their participants.

**A Story of Meals and Journeys**    The Gospel of Luke tells the story of the eucharist in a story of meals and journeys with Jesus, Son of God and Son of Man. Unlike foxes who have dens and the birds of the sky who have nests, Jesus the Son of Man "has nowhere to rest his head" (9:58). His entire life is thus one great journey in which meals and simple hospitality play a critical part for him as well as for his followers. Jesus, his disciples, all who would follow later, and the church itself are a people on a journey, a people of hospitality, both offered and received. The eucharist is the supreme expression of that hospitality, sustaining them on their journey to the kingdom of God.

This appreciation of meals and journeys is reflected in the gospel narrative as it tells the story of Jesus and his followers (5:1 – 11), those chosen to be the Twelve (6:12 – 16), and a large number of women, some of them quite prominent (8:1 – 3), all engaged in a great journey to God (9:51 — 24:53). While on that journey, Jesus is presented as a prophet, the savior who is Christ and Lord, dining with his disciples — both men and women — and with the Twelve, together with tax collectors, Pharisees, scribes and a host of others.

*Journeys in Luke*    There are many important journeys in Luke's gospel.[16] Even the prologue has its journey of Mary, already pregnant with Jesus, to her relative Elizabeth (1:39 – 56); the journey of Joseph and Mary to Bethlehem, the city of David,[17] where Jesus was born (2:1 – 40); and that of Jesus and his parents to Jerusalem for Passover when Jesus was about twelve years old (2:41 – 52).

In the sections with the historical and theological background for Jesus' mission (3:1 — 4:13) and the beginnings of his ministry (4:14 – 44), Jesus returns from his baptism (3:21 – 22) and a period of testing in the desert (4:1 – 13) to Galilee, where he taught in the synagogues (4:14 – 15), and to Nazareth, "where he had grown up" (4:16 – 30). Later he goes down to Capernaum (4:31 – 44), where people try to prevent him from leaving, and he reveals the divine necessity that he go "to the other towns" and "proclaim the good news of the kingdom of God." This is the purpose for which he was sent (4:43).

In the gospel's first large section, with its story of the origins of the church in the ministry of Jesus (5:1 — 9:50), the Twelve and the others accompany Jesus as he journeys "from one town and village to another, preaching and proclaiming the good news of the kingdom of God" (8:1 – 3). Later he sends them out on their own "to proclaim the kingdom of God and to heal [the sick]" (9:1 – 6) as he himself had done and shown them to do.

But as great as these journeys are, none of them compares with the journey to Jerusalem, the city of the ascension (9:51). This final journey, which takes up fully 15 of the gospel's 24 chapters, is a geographical journey (9:51 — 19:44), but one whose ultimate destination lies beyond every earthly city and place (24:50 – 53). Jesus' journey to Jerusalem and the ascension is a journey to God, his true Father (2:49) and the one to whom he turns regularly in prayer (10:21 – 22; 11:2, 13; 22:42; 23:46). Jesus' great journey to Jerusalem is a life journey, telling the story of the destiny of the church in the ministry, passion, resurrection and ascension of Jesus.

*Meals in Luke*    Luke's gospel contains many stories of meals with Jesus.[18] There are ten in all, beginning with a banquet at the home of Levi (5:27 – 39) and ending with a meal in Jerusalem with the Eleven and those gathered with them just before the ascension (24:36 – 49). One of those meals tells the story of the Last Supper, long associated with the institution of the eucharist (22:14 – 38).

While no meal is actually told of in the prologue, the story of Jesus' birth during the journey of Joseph and Mary to the city of David situates the Christian meal at the very heart of the gospel (see 2:10). When hospitality is denied them in David's city, Mary reclines Jesus in an eating trough (2:7), symbolically offering her child at the table of the manger.[19] The sign of the child lying in the manger would reveal him to the shepherds as Savior, Messiah and Lord (2:11 – 12). The first to hear the gospel, the shepherds would also be the first to make its message known (2:16 – 17).

Mary's gesture and the sign of the child lying in the manger have profound implications for all meals taken with Jesus, but most especially for Jesus' last Passover, when Jesus, the one denied hospitality at birth, offered hospitality on the eve of his passion and death, his final rejection in the city of David (22:1 – 38).

The part of the gospel with the background of Jesus' mission (3:1 — 4:13), like the prologue, does not speak of meals with Jesus, but it does refer to fasting, hunger and the temptation or test *(peirasmos,* see 4:2, 13) that comes with them, as well as the inadequacy of bread alone, the need for God's word, and the nourishment it provides (4:1 – 4).[20]

Like the journey of desert temptation or testing, which announces and prepares the later journeys — in particular the great journey to God — Jesus' actual test in the desert points ahead to the tests connected with the other meals told in the gospel (5:1 — 24:53). Every meal does indeed present a test, but none compares with that of the Last Supper, when the test of the passion begins to unfold, and Jesus complements the table of his bread and wine with the table of his teaching (22:14 – 38).

The story of the beginnings of Jesus' ministry in Galilee, first at Nazareth and then at Capernaum (4:14 – 44), a double paradigm for Jesus' life, passion and death, has Jesus entering the house of Simon and healing his mother-in-law, who was afflicted with a severe fever. Healed, she immediately rises up and begins to serve those present (4:38 – 39).[21] The Greek term used for serving is the verb *diakoneo,* which refers to service at table, but not exclusively, for service at table is only part of a larger service associated with hospitality and concern for one's guests. Like the birth and temptation stories, this is not actually a meal story, where Jesus' teaching is always emphasized, but it does introduce the important theme of service that will be developed in several meals with Jesus and will be a central theme in the account of the Last Supper.

**Table I**

**The Ten Meals with Jesus in the Context of Luke's Gospel**

1:1–4      Preface: Narrative of events fulfilled in our midst
1:5—2:52    Prologue: Ultimate origins and ultimate destiny
3:1—4:13    Historical background and preparation
4:14—24:53 The story of Jesus

  Beginnings in Galilee   4:14–44

  Origins of the church in Jesus' Galilean ministry   5:1—9:50
      5:1—6:11  The call to discipleship
        **Banquet at the house of Levi   5:27–39**
      6:12—8:56  Establishing the community of Twelve
        **Dinner at the house of Simon the Pharisee   7:36–50**
      9:1–50  The mission of the Twelve
        **The breaking of the bread at Bethsaida   9:10–17**

  Life of the church in Jesus' journey to Jerusalem   9:51–24:53
      9:15—13:21  Setting out on the journey
        **Hospitality at the home of Martha   10:38–42**
        **Noon meal at the home of a Pharisee   11:37–54**
      13:22—19:48  Proceeding to Jerusalem
        **Sabbath dinner at the home of a Pharisee   14:1–24**
        **Hospitality at the house of Zacchaeus   19:1–10**
      20:1—21:38  In the Temple at Jerusalem

      22:1—24:53  Passion, resurrection and ascension
        **The Last Supper   27:7–38**
        **The breaking of the bread at Emmaus   24:13–35**
        **With the community in Jerusalem   24:36–53**

Of the ten meals with Jesus, all are important, starting with the three told in the story of the origins of the church in Jesus' ministry (5:1 — 9:50), namely:

1) the banquet at the home of Levi (5:27 – 39)
2) the dinner at the home of a Pharisee (7:36 – 50)
3) the breaking of the bread in Bethsaida (9:10–17).

Equally important are the four meals in the story of the great journey on the way to Jerusalem and the passion, resurrection and ascension (9:51 — 21:38). This second series includes:

1) the hospitality offered at the home of Martha (10:38 – 42)
2) a second dinner at the home of a Pharisee (11:37 – 54)
3) a third such dinner, this one a sabbath meal (14:1 – 35)
4) the hospitality extended by Zacchaeus (19:1 – 10).

Important too are the two meals after Jesus' death and resurrection, just before the ascension, where the great journey ends. These include:

1) the meal at Emmaus at the home of two disciples (24:13 – 35)
2) the meal with the entire community in Jerusalem (24:36 – 49).

But important as these meals clearly are, none of the nine compares with the Passover meal in the city of David, where Jesus, the one denied hospitality at birth (2:7), offers hospitality before he dies (22:14 – 38). As told by Luke, this final meal of Jesus' historical life recapitulates all those meals that came before and anticipates those that will come after. It is the ultimate meal, told as both the Last Supper and the Lord's Supper, and it is the meal to which we turn for the sharpest and fullest presentation of the eucharist.

The gospel's many meals are an integral part of Luke's story of the great journey, both in its Galilean preparation — where the disciples are called, established as the Twelve, formed and initiated into the mission (5:1 — 9:50) — and in its actual unfolding on the way to Jerusalem and the ascension (9:51 — 24:53). Like the great journey, which is more a life journey in the company of Jesus than a geographical journey, the meals with Jesus provide more than physical nourishment. They ensure spiritual health and strength for the Christian journey. Luke's story of journeys provides a basic setting for his story of meals, making each one a pause that challenges, forms and transforms regarding the most basic values for Christian living in community and on mission.

Much of Jesus' teaching took place during meals. Indeed, meals appear to have been the privileged place for Jesus' teaching. Of their very nature, meals provided an excellent setting for surfacing the various problems and issues in the community as well as for serious conversation. In view of the importance of meals in the life of the community, the meal itself was often the subject of Jesus' teaching at dinner. Such is the case in the dinner at the home of a Pharisee (7:36 – 50), in the hospitality at the home of Martha (10:38 – 42), and even at the Last Supper (22:14 – 38). In every instance, however, the meal issue, while seemingly narrow, epitomizes a much larger issue affecting the life of the community.

Some of Jesus' most memorable teaching on meals was given in the form of parables. Several of these were told during meals, for example, the parable concerning those choosing the places of honor at table (14:7 – 11) and the parable of the great feast to which few of those invited came (14:15 – 24). Most meal parables, however, were given in a setting other than a meal. These include the parable of the friend appealing for three loaves (11:5 – 8), the parable of the lost son, popularly known as the prodigal son (15:11 – 32), and the parable of the rich man and Lazarus (16:19 – 31).

*A Story of Meals* Each of the ten meal stories, like so many of the stories in Luke's gospel, is a complete story in itself. Each has its own particular setting and cast of characters, among whom Jesus is usually, but not always, the principal guest. At the Last Supper Jesus is both the host and the one providing the service. Each story also raises a particular issue, question or problem, which Jesus addresses with a brief dialogue, a short discourse or a simple saying.

Each story is succinctly told and sparing in details, like a parable, avoiding everything superfluous but including everything needed for the story's literary development. Withdrawn from Luke's gospel, each meal story is a compact little episode, similar in some respects to the others but also truly unique, like children born of the same parents or paintings done by the same artist.

Complete and satisfying as each individual meal story may be, all ten of them were written in their present form to be part of a much larger story, the Gospel according to Luke. No meal speaks in isolation from its context in the gospel — its literary environment — and each is related to the other meal stories that are part of that same environment. Each contributes to a larger unit, which itself has a place and function in the literary unfolding of the gospel as a whole.

Withdrawn from its context, a story loses a good part of its meaning. It is like a flower that loses much of its beauty when plucked from the garden or taken from the arrangement for which it was selected. This is true of all the meal stories in Luke. Two examples, the banquet in the home of Levi (5:27–39) and the dinner in the home of a Pharisee (7:36–50), will illustrate.

The banquet at the home of Levi (5:27–39), which is part of a larger unit on the call to conversion and the following of Jesus (5:1 — 6:11), finds much of its meaning in those themes and it contributes significantly to their development. As part of the larger unit, the meal in Levi's home presupposes the three previous stories, where Jesus calls Simon Peter to follow him (5:1–11), cleanses the leper (5:12–16) and heals the paralytic (5:17–26). The meal at Levi's home shows how dining with Jesus is also a healing event (5:31) and a call to conversion (5:32).

Apart from the stories of the leper and the paralytic, Jesus' saying about the need for a physician remains apropos, but strictly speaking it is no longer required. It could easily be dropped or replaced by another saying with an entirely different set of images. Apart from the call of Simon Peter, "a sinful man," as he himself confesses (5:8), Jesus' saying about calling sinners to conversion remains significant but it no longer is seen as the most basic issue for the following of Jesus.

A similar case can be made for the story of the dinner in the home of a Pharisee (7:36 – 50). Withdrawn from its context, it is a story of a Pharisee's inattentiveness and lack of understanding and of a woman's love for Jesus and of the forgiveness of sins. When the same story is seen in its larger context (6:12— 7:50), which has Jesus establishing the Twelve as the foundation of a new people, it shows how the community founded on the Twelve must be open to both men and women and how this affects the composition of the assembly and the meals of the community.

By contributing to greater gospel units, and through them to the whole gospel, the meals are also related to one another in a developing story of meals. This can be seen not only from their place in the flow of the gospel and their relationship to the great journey to God, but also from the sub-themes in the meal stories themselves, notably the call to conversion, the welcome accorded sinners, the presence of women, the quality of hospitality and the value of service. Introduced in one story, a theme may be developed in a later story and developed yet further in an even later one. So it is with the theme of service, which is introduced when Jesus heals Simon's mother-in-law (4:38 – 39), and is developed in the meal at the home of Martha (10:38 – 42), but receives its fullest development in the story of the Last Supper (22:14 – 38).

The ten meal stories in Luke's gospel fall into two basic categories, those that are influenced by the Hellenistic symposium and those that express simple hospitality. The two categories are very different from each other.

*The Symposium*    The Hellenistic symposium is well known from images on Greek vases and monuments, as well as from many references to symposia in Greek literature.[22] The symposium was a social event normally associated with people of considerable means, who lived in fine urban houses or great country villas. A symposium was a formal event, carefully planned and prepared, with considerable attention given to the menu and even more to the guest list.

Those who participated in a symposium did so by the special invitation of the host, who offered the symposium in the dining room of his home or in a suitable space where dining couches could be set up for himself and the guests. A symposium might even be held in a summer dining area, possibly outdoors in a garden when the weather permitted. Among the dining couches, one close by the host in a place that facilitated conversation was reserved for the guest of honor. Service at a symposium was provided by slaves or household servants, usually male.

Wherever Roman culture dominated, a dining arrangement with three dining couches, each large enough for at least three guests, tended to replace the older Hellenistic arrangement providing for individual couches. The three couches, set up on three sides of a rectangle, formed what was called a *triclinium*. By early New Testament times, this name also was applied to the party or group of those who dined in a *triclinium* and even to a dining room that was set up with couches in *triclinium* style.

Once the guests had arrived and been welcomed, the symposium began with a dinner, a banquet that could be more or less sumptuous. This dinner part of the symposium, for which the Greek term was *deipnon*, was served on individual dining tables set up before each dining couch. Beverages were not served during the *deipnon* (save perhaps for water) but only in the second part of the symposium, after the dining tables had been removed. This second part, called in Greek a *sumposion*, a word meaning drinking party, was the symposium proper, but it early lent its name to the whole event. It was only then, in the symposium proper, that wine was served while the host led his guests in a conversation that allowed the guest of honor, often a distinguished and learned man, to expound on a particular topic. This practice of engaging in a such a conversation at a symposium gave rise to a particular literary genre,[23] best exemplified by Plato's *Symposium* and Xenophon's *Symposium*.

Symposia did not always involve dialogue and discourse. In place of the learned discussion, a performance was sometimes presented for the entertainment of the guests. The performance might include poetry reading, instrumental music, singing, dance, mime or even acrobatics.

Women, children and slaves did not ordinarily participate in a symposium, at least not in the dinner, or *deipnon*. As a reclining banquet, the symposium was for free people only, that is, adult males. At times, women, boys and slaves were brought in during the second part of the symposium for the drinking feast but their purpose was to serve as prostitutes or the like. A reclining banquet could become quite depraved.

By welcoming everyone to the eucharistic symposium — including women, children and slaves — the early Christians opened themselves to accusations of gross immorality and of subverting the social order. The Christians were, in fact, very countercultural, but appear not to have been daunted by negative reactions and the conflicts that resulted.

Five of the meals in Luke's gospel reflect certain aspects of the Hellenistic symposium, namely, the banquet at the home of Levi (5:27 – 39),[24] the three dinners taken at the home of a Pharisee (7:36 – 50;[25] 11:37 – 54;[26] 14:1 – 35[27]), and the Last Supper (22:14 – 38),[28] which was also a Passover meal and the meal at which Jesus gave his farewell discourse.

These five meals may reflect — if only minimally — the literary genre that sprang from the symposium. Every example of literary symposium in existence, including the symposia written by Plato and Xenophon, is quite long and is always a work that stands on its own, unlike meal stories in Luke, which are very short and are part of a larger narrative. Besides, in a literary symposium each of the guests is given the opportunity to speak. In the Lukan stories, such dialogue is reduced to a minimum, and Jesus' teaching tends to be highlighted in the form of a short discourse. For each of the five meals, however, it is helpful to keep the literary genre in mind as part of the background.

*The Hospitality Meal*   The hospitality meal is especially well known from biblical literature, with its wonderful images of desert and domestic hospitality. The first is the story of Abraham and Sarah and the three mysterious guests they welcomed and served in the shade of Mamre's terebinth: "When [Abraham] saw them, he ran from the entrance of the tent to greet them; and bowing to the ground, he said: 'Sir, if I may ask you this favor, please do not go on past your servant. Let some water be brought, that you may bathe your feet, and then rest yourselves under the tree. Now that you have come this close to your servant, let me bring you a little food, that you may refresh yourselves; and afterward you may go on your way.'" (Genesis 18:1 – 5)[29]

A second and equally wonderful scene of hospitality follows shortly after: "The two angels reached Sodom in the evening, as Lot was sitting at the gate of Sodom. When Lot saw them, he got up to greet them; and bowing down with his face to the ground, he said, 'Please, gentlemen, come aside into your servant's house for the night, and bathe your feet; you can get up early to continue your journey.' But they replied, 'No, we shall pass the night in the town square.' He urged them so strongly, however, that they turned aside to his place and entered his house. He prepared a meal for them, baking cakes without leaven, and they dined." (Genesis 19:1 – 3)

Extending and receiving hospitality was a traditional value deeply embedded in all the cultures of the Eastern Mediterranean. A meal, however simple, was considered hospitality's primary expression. The importance of this underlies Jesus' parable in Luke 11:5 – 8, where someone goes to a friend at night pleading for three loaves of bread, which he needed because a friend of his had just arrived from a journey.

Hospitality was expected of everyone, even the poorest of the poor, and it could be offered in the humblest dwelling. The friend in Jesus' parable who had to beg because he had no bread to offer was not a rich man. Neither was his friend who could not get up without awakening the children. Unlike the symposium, this simple hospitality meal was not a planned event; its preparation was impromptu, as when a friend comes in during the night from a journey.

Simple hospitality, which always included a meal and the breaking of bread together, did not require a large, formal dining room. A hospitality meal was more in the nature of an ordinary domestic meal, made different only by the presence of a guest. It could be taken and shared in any appropriate space, including the shop where the family did business, or whatever living space was considered home. After all, few people could afford a dining room.

One did not need an invitation to receive and enjoy hospitality. Some form of relationship, such as friendship or having a friend in common, was all that was needed. Nor were women and children excluded from sharing in the hospitality meal, no more than from a domestic family meal where a wife ate with her husband, and children with their parents.

Slaves, on the other hand, who were not invited to the domestic meal, were excluded from taking part in a simple hospitality meal.[30] This exclusion underlines Luke's parable of the master and the slave in Luke 17:7 – 10. When the slave came in from working in the field, no one expected the master to say: "Come here immediately and take your place at table." A slave was expected to serve his master while the master ate and drank. Only later was the slave permitted to take his own meal.

The early Christians were just as countercultural in the area of simple hospitality as in their formal dining. In both instances, the big issue for Luke's gospel had to do with the question once asked Jesus by a lawyer: "Who is my neighbor?" (10:29) Jesus responded with the parable of the good Samaritan, one who at one time would not have been recognized as one's neighbor (10:30 – 37). For Christians, one's neighbors included all human beings, even slaves.

Five of the meals in Luke's gospel reflect the tradition of simple hospitality meals embedded in the culture of the New Testament world. These include the breaking of the bread in the city of

Bethsaida (9:10–17), the hospitality offered at the home of Martha (10:38–42) and that given later in the home of Zacchaeus (19:1-10), as well as the two meals after Jesus' resurrection—the one at Emmaus (24:13–35) and the one in Jerusalem (24:36–49) just before the ascension. Whereas at Bethsaida Jesus is the host, in the four other meals he is the guest.

Luke's gospel contains five meal stories reflecting the influence of the Hellenistic symposium and five meal stories reflecting the simple hospitality of the time. Drawn from early tradition, these stories are an integral part of the gospel of Jesus Christ. Retold by Luke, they are also part of his narrative of "events that have been fulfilled among us" (1:1). But how are these meals related to the eucharist?

**Luke and the Origins of the Eucharist**   When the hour came, Jesus took his place at table with the apostles. He had eagerly desired to eat this Passover with them before he suffered. This was their last Passover together; the next time Jesus ate the Passover, it would be fulfilled in the kingdom of God. Taking a cup, he gave thanks and asked the apostles to share it among themselves. This was their last cup together before he died. Jesus would not drink of the fruit of the vine until the kingdom of God came. This was indeed the Last Supper (see 22:14–18).

Luke's unique emphasis on the Last Supper as truly the last is very significant for the way he viewed the origins of the eucharist. This Last Supper was surely the most important meal with Jesus in the entire story of the gospel, but it was not the only supper. As the Last Supper, it was the last in a long series of suppers together. And there had been many.

As Luke tells it, the first meal was in the home of a tax collector named Levi (5:27–39). This happened not long after the followers were called, but before they were appointed as the Twelve (6:12-16) and sent out as apostles (9:1–6). Of the many meals that followed in Jesus' ministry, six others were distinctive enough to merit telling in Luke's gospel.

From the point of view of Luke, therefore, the Last Supper came as the last in a series of eight; it was a climactic meal recapitulating the previous seven. It was also the first in a new series of three, announcing and anticipating the day of fulfillment when Jesus would eat and drink again in the kingdom of God. All the previous meals had done the same, each in its own way, but never so explicitly. Fulfillment came after Jesus' resurrection in "the breaking of the bread," long a part of the life of the Lukan communities, and the "Lord's Supper," described by Paul in the First Letter to the Corinthians.

After telling of the Last Supper, Luke therefore continued to tell of the Lord's Supper (see 22:19–20). Parting the curtain of the passion and resurrection, Luke followed up his account of the Last Supper with the liturgical text that was familiar to all from their celebration of the Lord's Supper: "Then he took bread, gave thanks, broke it, and gave it to them saying, 'This is my body which will be given for you; do this in memory of me.'" (22:19)

Even if Luke had gone no further, it would have been enough. The communities would have understood. The Last Supper and the Lord's Supper, like the death and the resurrection of Jesus, were one great event. But Luke did go on, first summarizing the cup action, "And likewise the cup after they had eaten," and then very solemnly presenting the words of Jesus: "This cup is the new covenant in my blood, which will be shed for you." (22:20) The Lord's Supper marked the beginning of a new covenant.

As the Last Supper, the climactic meal of Jesus' life was part of his historical life and ministry. From its vantage point at the end it looked back to the beginning, recapitulated all the previous meals with Jesus, and fulfilled Israel's historic Passover. As the Lord's Supper, the same meal event belonged to Jesus' risen life and the life of the church. From its position at the beginning, it looked forward to future meals with the risen Lord, and to a long story of meals climaxing in a heavenly banquet in the kingdom of God.

So it is that in Luke's gospel, the one story of the Last Supper and the Lord's Supper (22:14–38) is the first in a new series of three meals. It is followed by the meal with the disciples at Emmaus (24:13 – 35) and the meal with the assembled community in Jerusalem (24:36 – 49) just before the ascension. This new series is short, but it assured that the Last Supper and the Lord's Supper would never be able to be separated from one another. Besides, it would have its sequel in Luke's second volume, the Acts of the Apostles.

As the final meal of Jesus' life, the Last Supper unfolds on the doorstep of the passion. As the first meal of the new covenant, the Lord's Supper stands on the threshold of the resurrection. It belongs to the story of the passion, and it belongs to the story of the resurrection.

Like the passion, the Last Supper comes at the climax of a long story. In that story, with its account of Jesus' life and ministry, lie the origins of the passion and the Last Supper. Without that history the two are cut off from life and all the challenges and conflicts that led to them. Severed from the life of Jesus and his followers, the passion story and the Last Supper make no sense.

Like the resurrection, the Lord's Supper comes at the beginning of a long story. That story, with its account of the risen Lord and the Christian community, spells out the implications of the resurrection and the Lord's Supper. Without that history, the two are cut off from the life of the church, along with the challenges and commitments of its journey to the kingdom of God. Severed from the Lord's presence in the life of the church, the resurrection story and the Lord's Supper make no sense.

These reflections on the Last Supper and on the Lord's Supper, the relationship of the supper to the passion and resurrection and to the rest of the gospel raise the question of whether it is even proper to speak of the institution of the eucharist. Does not Luke's history of salvation, unfolding in one continuous story, demand or at least invite another approach?

The word institution suggests the act of a moment or a singular event, distinct from all the others in the life of Jesus. As the epitome of Jesus' life, death and resurrection and a compendium of the gospel, the Last Supper and Lord's Supper is clearly the only meal in the gospel that qualifies as that act or event. But would not the Last Supper and Lord's Supper be better grasped if we spoke of the *origins* of the eucharist rather than its institution?

Finding the origins of the eucharist in a long history of meals with Jesus does not mean that every meal in Luke's gospel is eucharistic. What it does mean is that *the origins of eucharist lie in a long and complex series of events that has the Last Supper and Lord's Supper as their climax.* The origins of eucharist also include the post-resurrection meals that flow from the Last Supper and Lord's Supper. All those meals may not be celebrations of eucharist, but they all have something to say about the eucharist. Each meal symbolizes the eucharist, preparing for it or pointing back to it in some way. Having its origins in a history of meals also shows how the eucharist is intimately related to the gospel and to every aspect of Christian living, both in community and on mission.

From a Christological point of view, there are three basic kinds of meals in Luke's story of the origins of the eucharist:

1) meals at the table of Jesus the prophet
2) the meal at the table of Jesus the Christ
3) meals at the table of Jesus the Lord.

Who Jesus is makes all the difference. It is one thing to eat with Jesus the prophet and join in his prophetic vision. It is another to eat with Jesus the Christ and share in the memorial of his death and resurrection. It is still another to dine at the table of Jesus the Lord.

Those who eat with Jesus the prophet accept being challenged by him even as they show solidarity with him and take on his prophetic mission. Those who eat with Jesus the Christ accept being challenged anew and being transformed by his passion and resurrection. By renewing their baptismal commitment to die and rise with Christ, they join Jesus the Christ in transforming the world. Those who dine with Jesus the Lord join him as Lord of all and reach out with him to human beings of both sexes and of every race, culture and nation, welcoming them to one table of salvation.

Because the gospel was written from a Christian vantage point in the 80s of the first century, every meal reveals Jesus as prophet, Christ and Lord. It is all a matter of emphasis. Before the passion, emphasis is on Jesus as prophet. At the Last Supper it is on Jesus as Christ. And on the first day of the week, it is on Jesus as Lord.

*At the Table of Jesus the Prophet*    The meals with Jesus the prophet[31] form two distinct series. The first series includes the three meals in Jesus' Galilean ministry and is part of the story of the origins of the church (5:1 — 9:50). The second series includes the meals on the great journey before the events of the passion and resurrection (9:51 — 21:38). They are both part of the story of the church's unfolding destiny.

In every one of these meals, Jesus acts and speaks as a prophet. That is what people expected when he was at table in the home of Simon the Pharisee: "If this man were a prophet, he would know who and what sort of woman this is who is touching him, that she is a sinner." (7:39) That is also how the disciples of Emmaus described him: "a prophet mighty in deed and word before God and all the people" (24:19). Speaking of his mission, Jesus himself declared: "Yet I must continue on my way today, tomorrow, and the following day, for it is impossible that a prophet should die outside of Jerusalem." (13:33) With Jesus' prophetic presence dominating each of these meals, they can accurately be described as prophetic meals.

At the same time, Jesus is not an ordinary prophet or "one of the ancient prophets" who "has arisen" (9:8, 19). As Peter confessed, Jesus was the Christ of God (9:20), but it was not yet time for this to be manifested (9:21), not even in the breaking of the bread for the 5,000 (9:10 – 17). Even so, Jesus' solemn announcement of his passion and resurrection (9:22, 43 – 45; 18:31 – 33) oriented his entire prophetic message and activity toward his manifestation as the Christ in the Passover mystery (22:14 – 38).

The meals with Jesus the prophet are consequently oriented to the meal with Jesus the Christ. They were also written in light of Jesus' risen state and his title as Lord of all. In Luke, the title

Lord is Jesus' title *par excellence*. It appears three times, for example, in the meal at the home of Martha (10:38 – 42). Here, as elsewhere in Jesus' prophetic ministry, the title Lord may be honorific, but in a translucent way it allows the light of Jesus' future risen state to shine through.

The three prophetic meals in Jesus' Galilean ministry focus on three of the most basic issues in Christian life. They relate the eucharist to the call to discipleship among the followers of Jesus, the inclusiveness of the church as the community of the Twelve, and the Church's mission to gather the hungry for the breaking of bread.

In the first, which is situated in the house of Levi the tax collector (5:27 – 39), the meal is forcefully defended as a healing event calling sinners to conversion *(metanoia)*. This first meal suggests that pastorally the eucharist is first of all an evangelizing event, a prophetic call to repentance.

At the second meal, that held at the home of Simon the Pharisee (7:36 – 50), Jesus defends a woman, a sinner whose great love showed that she had been pardoned and was already a true disciple of Jesus the prophet. This second meal suggests that the eucharist is also a reconciling event, a prophetic demonstration of charity's universal welcome.

At the third meal, which takes place in the city of Bethsaida (9:10 – 17), the Twelve were overwhelmed by a crowd of 5,000 and wanted to send them away, but Jesus had the Twelve nourish the crowd with five loaves and two fish. This third meal shows how the eucharist is a missioning event, challenging the Twelve with the mission of Jesus.

The four prophetic meals in the great journey on the way to the passion and the Last Supper focus on ministerial issues and on attitudes in the community of disciples and the life of the church. They relate the eucharist to *diakonia* (service), inner purification, attitudes toward oneself and others, the gift of salvation and the behavior that flows from it.

At the first meal, at Martha's home, Martha feels overburdened by the demands of hospitality (10:38 – 42). Her problem, however, is that she is neglecting what really matters. This story shows how attending to the person of the Lord and listening to his word are the things with which we cannot dispense at eucharist.

At the second meal, in the home of a Pharisee, the Pharisee notes that Jesus has not observed the prescribed ritual purification (11:37–54). In response, Jesus speaks of the primacy of inner purification over external ritual. This second story shows that the quality of participation in the eucharist depends on such matters as loving concern for our neighbor and love of God.

The third meal takes place at the home of a leading Pharisee, who usually invites only his friends, relatives and wealthy neighbors (14:1–24). Jesus reverses the ordinary codes of behavior for guest and host. This third story shows how all self-serving and exclusive attitudes have no place at eucharist.

The fourth meal is at the home of a wealthy tax collector named Zacchaeus, who overcomes considerable odds to see Jesus (19:1–10). Jesus responds to his efforts, announcing that he will come to his home. This fourth story shows that a eucharist that welcomes Jesus is a salvific event.

*At the Table of Jesus the Christ*   The meals with Jesus the prophet lead to the meal with Jesus the Christ:[32] the Last Supper and Lord's Supper (22:14–38). This, too, is a prophetic meal in which Jesus acts and speaks very much as the prophet, challenging the Twelve on key issues. But at this meal, Jesus' prophetic role is fulfilled in his mission as the Christ.

The disciples of Emmaus spoke of Jesus as the Nazarene, "a prophet mighty in deed and word before God and all the people" (24:19). With this view of Jesus, they could not make sense of the events of the passion. Jesus did not deny that he was a prophet, but he did show them how as prophet he was also the Christ, and as such was meant to suffer and so enter into glory (24:26).

Applied to Jesus, the title Christ is inseparable from his passion-resurrection, an event both singular and decisive for Jesus, his disciples, the church and all human beings. For the early

Christians the title was associated with baptism, the decisive event whereby a person "died with Christ" to "live in newness of life" and one day "be united with him in the resurrection" (Romans 6:3 – 5).

Like the passion-resurrection, baptism is an event that is both unique and unrepeatable. It is a Christian's personal appropriation of Jesus' passion-resurrection. The eucharist also is a unique event. As with Jesus' death-resurrection and baptism, there is nothing truly comparable to it. It is, however, repeatable, but always in relation to the passion-resurrection and baptism. The eucharist is the memorial of that singular and unrepeatable event that is the death and resurrection of Jesus Christ. The eucharist is also an event in which Christians recall and apply the grace and commitment of their baptism in ever new situations throughout their lives.

At eucharist, then, we are very much at the table of Jesus the Christ, called to Christian solidarity in offering our lives that all might live. As the climactic meal of Jesus' prophetic ministry, the Last Supper challenges us where we fall short in our solidarity with Christ, in our baptismal commitment and in our failure to live it in our mission, relationships and ministry. As a meal with Jesus the Christ, the eucharist continues the transformation begun in our baptismal event.

*At the Table of Jesus the Lord*    Besides the meals at the table of Jesus the prophet and the meal at the table of Jesus the Christ, there are also the meals at the table of Jesus the Lord.[33] These meals associate us with the person of Christ living forever with God in glory (24:26), but also as present to the disciples and the church in the Lord's Supper and the breaking of the bread. The title is the one used to welcome the returning disciples of Emmaus to Jerusalem: "The Lord has truly been raised and has appeared to Simon!" (24:34) Jesus the prophet (24:19) is the Christ (24:26), and Jesus the Christ is the Lord (24:34).

The title of Christ presents Jesus in relation to an event, that of his passion-resurrection. His role as a prophet, on the other hand, was related not to a particular event but to a state of existence, an ongoing historical state affecting every event in his life. Jesus' title as Lord also refers to an ongoing state, begun in the event of his passion-resurrection and abiding through all eternity.

As Lord, Jesus transcends all the limitations of his earthly existence, including the most basic limitation of all, which is death. As Lord, Jesus is "Lord of All" (Acts 10:36). This means that those who gather at the table of the Lord join in solidarity with the Lord of All. With the Lord of All, they consequently feel the urgency to reach out to all and welcome all human beings to a table with places for all. That table is none other than the table of the kingdom of God.

The post resurrection meals at table with Jesus the Lord bring Luke's story of meals with Jesus, the great journey to God, and the gospel itself to a close. The first of them coincides with the Last Supper (22:14 – 38), which we have been calling the Last Supper and Lord's Supper. The Last Supper is consequently the first expression of the Lord's Supper, to which all are invited, as well as the memorial of Christ's passion-resurrection and the climactic meal in Jesus' prophetic ministry.

The second meal at table with Jesus the Lord is the story of the disciples of Emmaus (24:13 – 35). The disciples had not learned the prophetic lesson of the passion and so could not recognize the person of Jesus the Lord. The horizon of their understanding and expectations needed to be broadened. Only then would they recognize the risen Lord in the breaking of the bread. The story, an amazing synthesis, shows how eucharist is related to many facets of life in the new era inaugurated by Jesus' passion-resurrection.

The third meal at table with Jesus the Lord is situated in Jerusalem (24:36 – 49), just before the ascension (24:50 – 53). It shows the assembled community, with Jesus eating in their midst and teaching them. The story shows how the eucharist is related to the church's mission to all nations, beginning with Jerusalem.

In the following chapters we shall examine each of these meals in turn, beginning with the two series of meals at the table of Jesus the prophet, continuing with the meal at the table with Jesus the

Christ and concluding with the meals at the table of Jesus the Lord. In each instance, we shall see how the meal contributes to Luke's story of the origins of the eucharist and how it may challenge us today.

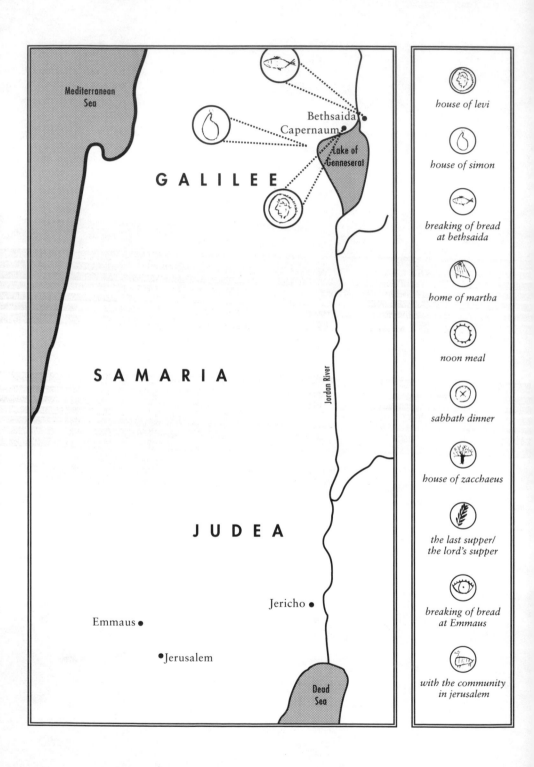

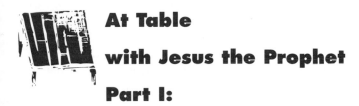

## Chapter II

# At Table
# with Jesus the Prophet
# Part I:
# In the Galilean Ministry

*L*uke's story of the eucharist begins with the origins of
the church in Jesus' Galilean ministry (5:1 — 9:50).
Before this, Luke tells of Jesus' ultimate origins and destiny
(1:5 — 2:52) and of the historical background for his mission and ministry (3:1 — 4:13). He also offers a brief synthesis of Jesus' life — from his return to Galilee to the
ascension — in stories of its dramatic beginnings at
Nazareth and Capernaum (4:14 – 44). These earlier parts
of the gospel, like the short preface before them (1:1 – 4),
are introductory, providing a literary, theological and biblical setting for the story of the origins and destiny of the
church, which begins with the call of Simon Peter
(5:1 – 11) and climaxes in Jesus' passion, resurrection and
ascension (22:1 — 24:53). In the earlier parts of the
gospel, Luke's concern is mainly Christological. Beginning
with the call of Simon Peter and his partners (5:1 – 11), it
is ecclesiological as well.

With symbolic language, such as repeated references to the manger (2:7, 12, 16), and with various allusions to hunger and the hungry, meals and nourishment, and service at table (1:53; 3:11; 4:3 – 4, 25 – 26, 39), the earlier parts of the gospel also provide a literary, theological and biblical setting for the eucharist. The actual story of the eucharist, however, like that of the church, formally begins when Luke moves beyond the predominantly Christological concerns of 4:14 – 44 and integrates the origins of the church in the life, mission and ministry of Jesus (5:1 — 9:50).

The eucharist comes from Christ, and there is no understanding it apart from Christology. But because the eucharist belongs to the church, there is no understanding it apart from ecclesiology. In Luke, the story of the eucharist is part of the story of the church, and the origins and development of the eucharist parallel the origins and development of the church.

Luke tells of the origins of the church (5:1 — 9:50), beginning with Jesus and the disciples in Galilee. He presents the story in three large units (5:1 — 6:11; 6:12 — 8:56; 9:1 – 50), each with its own general theme, highlighted by an introductory passage concerning the disciples (5:1 – 11; 6:12 – 16; 9:1 – 7).

The theme for the first large unit (5:1 — 6:11) is the *call to discipleship*. It is introduced by the call of Simon Peter and his partners (5:1 – 11). The theme for the second unit (6:12 — 8:56) is the *constituting* of those called to be disciples as *the community of the Twelve*. It is introduced by the establishment of the Twelve (6:12 – 16). The theme for the third large unit (9:1 – 50) is the *mission* of those called to be disciples and constituted as the community of the Twelve. It is introduced by the sending of the Twelve on mission (9:1 – 7).

Luke's story of the origins of the church includes three stories of meals, one for each large unit. The stories of meals develop the unit's dominant theme in relation to the origins of the eucharist. But like all the stories of meals in Luke's gospel, including the Last Supper, the three meals in this section are not meant so much to tell about the eucharist as to show what the eucharist tells about the church and Christian life. In doing this, they do indeed tell us a great deal about the eucharist, but indirectly. They help us see how the eucharist is related to three constitutive aspects of the church: its foundation in the call of Jesus, its constitution as the community of the Twelve and its purpose in the mission of the Twelve. The meal stories show how these aspects also are constitutive of the eucharist.

The eucharist *makes* the church — not abstractly but very concretely. It makes the church a community of evangelization, universal reconciliation and mission. Conversely, the church makes the eucharist — and just as concretely. It makes the eucharist an event of evangelization, universal reconciliation and mission.

For the first and third stories, the great feast in the house of a tax collector named Levi (5:27 – 39) and the breaking of bread with a crowd of 5,000 at Bethsaida (9:10 – 17), Luke followed Mark quite closely. From the elements he dropped, retained, developed or added, we gain a fairly good idea of Luke's intention in telling the story. In both cases, he maintained the story's traditional flavor and most of its elements. But while incorporating these stories into the greater story of the origins of eucharist, he also adapted them to the situation and the needs of the Lukan communities. In many ways the stories remain the same, but in many other ways they are strikingly different.

For the second story, the dinner in the house of a Pharisee named Simon (7:36 – 50), we are not so fortunate. The story is related to one told in Mark (14:3 – 8; see also Matthew 26:6 – 13) and a tradition preserved and developed in John (12:1 – 11), but these merely provided Luke with a point of departure, hardly enough to call a source. As told by Luke, the story is so new that it is very easy to miss its relationship to the stories in Mark and John. To uncover the Lukan intention and its place in the story of the origins of the eucharist, we shall therefore rely mainly on Luke's use of vocabulary, the story's internal unfolding, its context in the gospel and its literary relationship to other stories in Luke.

## A Great Banquet at the House of Levi (Luke 5:27 – 39) [1]

*"I have not come to call the righteous to repentance but sinners."*

(Luke 5:32)

The first of the meals at the origins of eucharist is a great feast in the house of a tax collector named Levi. The story is about the call to follow Jesus and about what the call implies. There was a huge difference between the attitudes and values of the Pharisees and scribes and the attitudes and values expected of Jesus' disciples. The difference surfaced in a variety of contexts but especially at meals for which the various parties came together. Sharing a meal implies solidarity and communion and is bound to uncover any incompatibility or conflict among the participants.

The story of Levi and the dinner at his house is a story of eucharist and evangelization. It shows how the eucharist, at its most basic level, calls the participants to conversion and challenges them with the demands of following Christ. As an evangelization event, the eucharist calls sinners, indeed everyone, to repentance. The Greek word for repentance, *metanoia*,[2] refers to a profound conversion, a change in attitudes and behavior, required and brought about by communion and solidarity with Jesus at table. Attending to Jesus' call to *metanoia* makes a great difference for both the celebration of the eucharist and for the life of the church. But everything depends on who is recognized as a sinner. For Jesus, no one is righteous. All are in need of repentance.

**Context and Tradition**   This feast at the house of Levi comes very early in Jesus' Galilean ministry, in the section introduced by the call of Simon Peter and his partners, James and John (5:1 – 11). The section develops what it means to be a people called to follow Jesus (5:12 — 6:11). The story of the meal in Levi's house is the first of two where Jesus eats in the house of a tax collector.[3] The second is on Jesus' way to Jerusalem (9:51 — 19:48), at the house of Zacchaeus, the chief tax collector in Jericho (19:1 – 10). These are the only two stories of Jesus dining with tax collectors in Luke's gospel. But he surely dined with tax collectors on other occasions as well, often enough to invite accusations that he was a glutton and a drunkard (7:34), and to draw criticism from the Pharisees and the scribes (15:1 – 2).

In the section presenting the church as a people called to *meta-noia* (5:1 — 6:11), the meal immediately follows Jesus' cleansing

---

**Table II: Setting for the banquet at the house of Levi**

5:1 — 6:11 **The Call to Discipleship**

The call of Simon Peter and his partners   5:1 – 11
The cleansing of a leper   5:12 – 16
The healing of a paralytic   5:17 – 26
A great banquet at the house of Levi   **5:27 – 39**
   **5:27 – 28**   The call of Levi
   **5:29**       A large crowd of tax collectors
   **5:30**       The Pharisees' complaint
   **5:31 – 32**   Jesus' response
   **5:33 – 39**   Discourse on feasting and fasting;
                new wine in fresh wineskins
Procuring food on the Sabbath   6:1 – 5
Curing on the Sabbath   6:7 – 11

---

of a leper (5:12 – 16) and the healing of a paralytic (5:17 – 26). On seeing the faith of the paralytic and of those lowering him through the roof tiles on account of the crowd, Jesus declared the paralytic's sins forgiven (5:20). To the Pharisees this was blasphemy. Only God could forgive sins (5:20)! Responding, Jesus associated the forgiveness of sins with the healing of paralysis. If Jesus had the power to heal the paralytic, he also had the authority to forgive sins (5:22 – 24). Jesus drew a similar parallel at the feast in Levi's house: The people in need of a physician are the sick, not the healthy (5:31). In the same way, Jesus came to call sinners to repentance, not the righteous (5:32).

The relationship between sinners and Jesus' call to follow him had already been introduced in Simon Peter's response to the extraordinary catch of fish. "Depart from me, Lord," he exclaimed, "for I am a sinful man." (5:8) Peter's sinfulness did not stop Jesus from calling him. From then on, Peter and his partners would be catching human beings (5:10). Past sinfulness did not prevent Jesus from dining with tax collectors and sinners. Dining with Jesus was a celebration of repentance and forgiveness. The story of Levi and the Pharisees situates the call to discipleship in the context of eucharist. Like Peter, all who thought themselves righteous, including the Pharisees and their scribes, had to acknowledge themselves as sinners. In the eucharist, Jesus called them to repentance and discipleship.

The great feast in the house of Levi was loosely patterned on a Hellenistic symposium, a formal meal followed by wine and conversation. In the literary tradition associated with such meals, a question or significant issue usually surfaced either during the course of the meal or soon after, as the wine was being served. The question or issue became the topic for a dialogue among the participants or for a discourse given by the guest of honor.

Luke's story of the feast in the house of Levi was drawn from Mark 2:13 – 22, where it appears as two distinct stories, Mark 2:13 – 17 and 2:18 – 22, each with its own setting.[4] In Mark, the first story tells of the call of Levi (Mark 2:13 – 14) and the controversy that arose while they were at table (Mark 2:15 – 17). Seeing that Jesus was eating with sinners and tax collectors, the scribes and the Pharisees brought the matter to his disciples, "Why does he eat with tax collectors and sinners?" The second story tells of an independent controversy about fasting (Mark 2:18 – 22). "Why," people asked Jesus, "do John's disciples and the disciples of the Pharisees fast, but your disciples do not fast?"

Luke's gospel joined these two stories together and showed how the two controversies were actually two facets of the same basic controversy. Jesus' response showed how in both 5:31 – 32 and 5:34 – 39 it was a matter of the old and the new. Jesus called his followers to repentance *(metanoia)*, to a transformation of their old attitudes, relationships and way of living into a radically new set of attitudes and relationships, along with a very different way of life. The old and the new were totally incompatible, as became very obvious when those who adhered to the old and those who espoused the new came together for the meal.

The new Lukan form of the story streamlined the two stories in Mark. Elements that were important for Mark's theology and literary development but were not germaine to Luke's theological purpose were simply eliminated. Other elements were refocused and some were expanded. The final result is a well-unified story with the spotlight on Jesus' message to the Lukan communities.

The story's new emphasis on the discourse of Jesus highlights some of the characteristics of a symposium. As told, however, the great feast in the house of Levi is not a true literary symposium, which is a fairly long and independent piece of literature. We might perhaps think of it as minisymposium.[5] Outside of Luke's gospel, however, there is scant precedent for minisymposia forming part of a larger story. Therefore, it seems preferable to read this first meal story as loosely patterned on actual symposia. In the Hellenistic world, symposia had an important place in the life of the wealthy, and stories about symposia would normally have circulated even among those who never reclined for one in a formal dining room.

It is very likely that the images of symposia, the stories told of them and the symposia themselves were influenced by the developing tradition of the literary symposium. Nature and history provide the inspiration for art, but art then transforms our view of nature and history.

**The Setting: The Call of Levi**    The story begins with an introductory episode, situated not in Levi's house but at the customs post (5:27 – 28):

> After this he went out
> and saw a tax collector named Levi
> sitting at the customs post.
> He said to him, "Follow me."
> And leaving everything behind,
> he got up and followed him.

The call of Levi, like that of Simon and Andrew and of James and John in Mark 1:16 – 20, and of Levi in Mark 2:13 – 14, is patterned on the call of Elisha in 1 Kings 19:19 – 21. In such stories the event provides a capsule summary of the person's life. Levi's whole life could be summed up in terms of his position as a tax collector, of Jesus calling him and of him leaving everything to follow Jesus.

Luke drew the story of Levi's call from Mark 2:13 – 14, but presented it much more simply. Gone is the reference to Jesus going out again *(palin)* beside the sea (Mark 2:13), an introductory note connecting Levi's call with the calls of Simon and Andrew and of James and John (Mark 1:16 – 20).

Gone too is Mark's reference to the gathering of a large crowd and to Jesus' teaching them (Mark 2:13). In Mark, these events associated the call of Levi with Mark's motif of the growing crowd (see Mark 1:28, 32 – 33, 37, 45; 2:1 – 4) and the theme of Jesus' teaching with authority — not as the scribes (Mark 1:22), but with an entirely new teaching (Mark 1:27). These elements were directly related to Mark's concerns in this part of the gospel, presenting the call of Levi and the meal at his house as an example of Jesus' new teaching with authority.

Mark's concerns, however, were not those of Luke, who reduced Mark's remarkably rich introduction to a simple one: "After this he went out." Luke also simplified and refocused Mark's presentation of Levi. In Mark we learn that Jesus "saw Levi, son of Alphaeus, sitting at the customs post." In Luke, Jesus "saw a tax collector named Levi sitting at the customs post" (5:27). Luke was interested not so much in the person and identity of Levi as in associating him with tax collectors and the large crowd of them that would later share in the great feast in his house.

This simplification of the introductory elements focuses the story of Levi's call on the call itself, while deemphasizing it as a distinct episode, stripping away everything that would distract from its main function, which is to introduce the meal story (5:29 – 39). In telling of the tax collector's call, Luke added that Levi left everything behind. Leaving everything behind is a Lukan concern (see 9:3, 57 – 62; 10:4; 14:33). In the present context it associates the call of Levi to that of Simon Peter and his partners, who also left everything behind and followed Jesus (5:11). For Levi, leaving everything behind meant leaving his way of life as a tax collector along with the concerns and preoccupations it involved — all this as a necessary prerequisite for *metanoia* (5:32).

**The Great Banquet**   After the call of Levi, the setting for the story moves from the customs post to the house of Levi, with a great banquet Levi hosted for Jesus. It is in that setting, the meal in Levi's house, that Jesus continued his ministry, calling people to follow him. The story emphasizes the presence of a large crowd of tax collectors and others invited to the banquet (5:29):

> Then Levi gave a great banquet for him in his house,
> and a large crowd of tax collectors and others
> were at table with them.

Mark's gospel left it unclear whether Jesus was dining in the house of Levi or Levi in the house of Jesus. The expression, "while he was at table in his house" (Mark 2:15), could apply to either.[6] Luke eliminated this ambiguity, making it quite plain that Jesus attended a banquet given for him in Levi's house.

We can understand how Jesus' attendance at such a banquet could have been a source of misunderstanding and difficulty for many. To dine with people, especially in their homes, was to show solidarity with them. Joining Levi and a large crowd of tax collectors at a banquet in the house of a tax collector meant Jesus was truly *with* them.

We note also that Mark described the participants as "many tax collectors and sinners" at table with Jesus (Mark 2:15). Luke eliminated Mark's reference to sinners. For Luke, the participants were simply "a large crowd of tax collectors and others."

That the banquet was given for Jesus does not necessarily mean it was given in his honor, as would normally have been the case before Levi's conversion. When Levi gave the banquet for Jesus, he already was a follower, one who had left everything to follow Jesus. It was as a follower, not as a tax collector, that he gave the banquet and thereby joined Jesus and took an active part in his mission and ministry. Levi's principal purpose in giving the banquet was not so much to honor Jesus as to enable Jesus to invite tax collectors and others to *metanoia,* so they could become his followers along with Levi. The very presence of the tax collectors and others at the same table with Jesus and Levi indicates a readiness on their part to be *with* them.

**The Pharisees' Complaint**   We next learn that besides the large crowd of tax collectors, some Pharisees and their scribes also were at the banquet. This is quite surprising because the Pharisees reproached the disciples for eating with tax collectors and sinners (5:30):

> The Pharisees and their scribes
> complained to his disciples, saying,
> "Why do you eat and drink with tax collectors
> and sinners?"

The Pharisees and their scribes were among the "others" included at the banquet with the large crowd of tax collectors. Historically there is very little likelihood that some Pharisees would actually have been present. The Pharisees were noted for separating themselves from everyone they considered unrighteous.

From a literary point of view, we consequently need to ask who these Pharisees represent in Luke's story.

In the 80s, when Luke wrote his gospel, the Pharisees were undergoing a rapid transformation into what would become rabbinical Judaism. The Pharisees of Jesus' time were fast disappearing and the Lukan communities, unlike the Matthean community, had little contact with them. The Pharisees, however, who played a significant role in the story of Jesus, had left a strong mark on the Christian memory.

The presence of the Pharisees at the banquet Levi gave for Jesus shows a certain readiness to join in solidarity with Jesus. As elsewhere in Luke's gospel, this makes sense only if those referred to as "the Pharisees" were actually Christians with attitudes reminiscent of the Pharisees at the time of Jesus. This would suggest that in some or even many of the Lukan communities there were those who thought themselves righteous and who judged others unrighteous. These Christian Pharisees were ready to be with Jesus and the disciples, but they objected to the presence of the tax collectors, whom they considered unrighteous.

The notion that the Pharisees at Levi's banquet were members of the Christian community is supported by the way the Pharisees did not address their complaint to Jesus but to his disciples. Nor did their complaint have to do with Jesus personally eating and drinking with tax collectors, as was the case in Mark 2:16. In Luke, what the Pharisees objected to was that Jesus' *disciples* were eating and drinking with tax collectors and sinners. The story's focus is on situations in the life of the church rather than on Jesus' historical life and ministry.[7] Luke thus provided the story with an environment similar to that of his readers, who dined in the home of a disciple hosting them for "the breaking of the bread."

**Jesus' Response**  The Pharisees and the scribes may have addressed their complaint to Jesus' disciples, but it is Jesus who responded.

Jesus' two-part reply opens with a general saying and concludes with an application to the purpose of his mission (5:31 – 32):

> Jesus said to them in reply,
> "Those who are healthy do not need a physician,
> but the sick do.
> I have not come to call the righteous to repentance
> but sinners."

Jesus' reply presupposes that everyone is sick and in need of a physician. No one is righteous. All, including the Pharisees and their scribes, are sinners. All need to repent. As in the case of the tax collectors, the presence of the Pharisees and their scribes at Jesus' banquet ought to indicate a willingness to repent. Later in the gospel, the contrast between the attitudes of the Pharisees and those of the tax collectors regarding sin and righteousness is very graphically presented in Jesus' parable of the Pharisee and the tax collector (18:9 – 14).

**Feasting and Fasting**   The Pharisees countered with an even more basic objection, questioning the propriety of Jesus' disciples eating and drinking in the first place. This time they addressed themselves directly to Jesus (5:33):

> And they said to him,
> "The disciples of John fast often and offer prayers,
> and the disciples of the Pharisees do the same;
> but yours eat and drink."

Jesus responded with a mini-discourse, introduced by a question and followed up by a prophetic announcement (5:34 – 35):

> Jesus answered them,
> "Can you make the wedding guests fast
> while the bridegroom is with them?

But the days will come,
and when the bridegroom is taken away from them,
then they will fast in those days."

The wedding guests and the bridegroom are transparent images for the disciples and Jesus in the days of his being with them. The days of fasting announce the passion and the periods of persecution awaiting the community. In those days, Jesus' disciples would fast. Jesus' response presents fasting as a symbolic sharing in the passion of Jesus. Concretely, it would be one of the ways they would take up their cross daily and follow him (9:23).

Jesus then continued with two parables showing why he and his disciples ate and drank while others did not (5:36 – 39):

And he also told them a parable.
"No one tears a piece from a new cloak
to patch an old one.
Otherwise, he will tear the new
and the piece from it will not match the old cloak.
Likewise, no one pours new wine
into old wineskins.
Otherwise, the new wine will burst the skins,
and it will be spilled,
and the skins will be ruined.
Rather, new wine must be poured
into fresh wineskins."

The two parables provided good reasons why, unlike others, Jesus and his disciples ate and drank. The Christian way of life was not a matter of patching up an old way of life, including that of John the Baptist's disciples, with some new teaching. The old and the new were incompatible. Nor could the Christian way of life be poured into the wineskins of an older way of life. This would both destroy the old way and spill the new. What Jesus' disciples did, whether feasting or fasting, represented new wine and it needed fresh wineskins.

In providing justification for the disciples' eating and drinking, the two parables also invited the Christian Pharisees to examine their understanding of the Christian way and assess their position regarding it. Jesus' double-edged response appears especially apt if the Pharisees were in fact voicing not a polemic with disciples who did not belong to their community but a conflict internal to the Christian community.

Jesus ended the mini-discourse with a third parable, throwing an entirely new light on the situation (5:39):

> "[And] no one who has been drinking old wine
> desires new,
> for he says, 'The old is good.' "

It must have been very difficult for the Pharisees in the community of Jesus' disciples and later on for those in the early church to put aside the old wine in favor of the new.[8] The first and second parable spoke of why Jesus and his disciples did as they did — why they ate and drank. The third parable spoke of why the Pharisees in the community found it so difficult to change.

Luke's story of the great feast in the house of Levi deals with many issues. It speaks to those community members who, thinking themselves righteous, object to the presence of others whom they consider to be sinners at the breaking of the bread. In the various ancient cultures underlying the New Testament, dining with someone indicated solidarity with that person. For the Pharisees in Luke's story, the disciples were demonstrating solidarity with tax collectors and sinners by joining them at table. It did not occur to them that the tax collectors and "sinners" were professing solidarity with the disciples, rather than the reverse.

Responding to the Pharisees, Jesus called everyone to *metanoia,* including those who thought they were righteous. The dinner in the house of Levi shows Jesus prophetically challenging the Christian Pharisees and their scribes. As the first meal in Luke's story of the origins of eucharist, the meal in Levi's house presents the eucharist as a moment of evangelization, calling every participant to conversion. Here is the eucharist at its most basic in relation to the life of the church.

Jesus' teaching was both new and authoritative, not like that of the Pharisees and scribes who challenged the disciples. The eucharist is indeed new wine, and it needs new wineskins.

## A Great Dinner at the House of Simon the Pharisee (Luke 7:36–50) [9]

The Pharisees and their scribes complained to Jesus' disciples, "Why do you eat and drink with tax collectors and sinners?" (Luke 5:30) Jesus responded that he had "not come to call the righteous to repentance but sinners" (5:32). This exchange took place at the great banquet in the house of a tax collector named Levi. After an encounter such as this, we would not expect a Pharisee to invite Jesus for dinner. But as always, the gospel is full of surprises: A Pharisee named Simon invited Jesus to dine at his house.

*"Her many sins have been forgiven; hence, she has shown great love."*

*(Luke 7:47)*

The first story related the eucharist to evangelization and showed how the eucharist calls sinners to repentance *(metanoia)*. This second story relates the eucharist to reconciliation and shows how the eucharist asks those who repent to welcome one another as followers and disciples of Jesus.[10] The eucharist is an event in the life of the church demanding that it truly be and act as the community of the Twelve.

The first story showed the Pharisees and the scribes rejecting the most basic presupposition for *metanoia,* namely, that everyone is a sinner and in need of repentance. In this, they struck at the very nature of the church as a sinful people continually called to repent and follow Christ. For the Pharisees the meal was vitiated, or at least flawed, by the presence of "tax collectors and sinners," and so they questioned its value. Instead of feasting, Jesus' disciples should have been fasting (see Luke 5:33).

The meal was indeed flawed, but not fatally. The flaw was in the Pharisees themselves, not in the rest of the assembly. Speaking prophetically to the Pharisees and their scribes, Jesus challenged them to do what his disciples did: eat and drink with tax collectors and those they considered sinners. More than that, Jesus called them to do what the tax collectors did: recognize that they, like the others, were sinners and needed to repent.[11]

This second story shows a Pharisee refusing what ought to be an immediate outcome of genuine conversion *(metanoia)* and forgiveness *(aphesis):* reconciliation. The Pharisee's attitude and behavior contrasted with that of a woman, a sinner who had accepted Jesus' call, had repented and been forgiven. Instead of extending proper hospitality, the Pharisee questioned whether Jesus was indeed a prophet. Those who really accept Jesus' call, who do repent and are forgiven, welcome one another without regard for past sinfulness. Reconciled in the community of the Twelve, they, like the woman at Jesus' feet, show great love when they come together for a meal with Jesus and his followers.

**Context and Tradition**　The story of the dinner at the house of a Pharisee (7:36 – 50) is situated in Jesus' Galilean ministry in the section introduced by the call, choice and appointing of the Twelve (6:12 – 16). The entire section tells the story of the community of the Twelve (6:17 — 8:56).[12] Like the other stories in this section, the purpose of the meal in Simon's house is to spell out exactly what it means for the church to be established as the community of the Twelve.

For ancient Israel, being the community of the Twelve meant transcending tribal distinctions and forming one people, a chosen people, distinct from all others surrounding it. For the church this means transcending every distinction, including not only tribe but race, ethnicity, nationality, class, sex and peoplehood itself to form a new people.

The sign of the new Christian family was its meal, an event challenging every vestige of division and failure of hospitality. The Christian meal implied a tremendous reversal of accepted values.

Such a reversal was announced earlier in Jesus' sermon on the plain (6:17–49) as part of a dramatic series of blessings and woes:

> Blessed are you who are now hungry,
>> for you will be satisfied. (6:21a)
> But woe to you who are filled now,
>> for you will be hungry. (6:25a)

---

### Table III: Setting for the dinner at the house of Simon the Pharisee

**6:12—8:56   Establishing the Community of the Twelve**

Choice and naming of the Twelve   6:12–16
Ministry and Sermon on the Plain   6:17–49
Healing a centurion's slave   7:1–10
Raising a widow's only son   7:11–17
Jesus and John the Baptist   7:18–35
A dinner at the house of Simon the Pharisee   **7:36–50**
   **7:37–38**   A woman who is a disciple
   **7:39**      Jesus, a true prophet?
   **7:40–47**   Forgiveness, source of great love
   **7:48–50**   Reconciliation, faith and salvation
Women who followed Jesus with the Twelve   8:1–3
Parables, purpose and explanation   8:4–18
Calming a storm at sea   8:19–21
The true family of Jesus   8:22–25
Healing the Gerasene demoniac   8:26–39
Daughter of Jairus; woman with a hemorrhage   8:40–56

The beatitude is reminiscent of Jesus' inaugural presentation in the synagogue at Nazareth, proclaiming in the words of Isaiah that he was sent "to bring glad tidings to the poor" (4:18; see Isaiah 61:1). It was reflected also in Jesus' call of Levi and the welcome accorded tax collectors and others at table with him in Levi's house. The woe was anticipated in Jesus' challenge to the Pharisees and the scribes, who thought themselves righteous and withdrew from those called by Jesus to *metanoia*. Thinking themselves righteous, the Pharisees and the scribes were now filled, but they would be hungry. Recognizing themselves sinful, the tax collectors were now hungry, but they would be satisfied.

The meal at Simon's house is the first of three to be taken in the house of a Pharisee (see Luke 11:37–54; 14:1–24). The second and third come later, on the way to Jerusalem (9:51 — 19:48) in the great journey of Jesus and his followers to the passion, resurrection and ascension (9:51 — 24:53).

Within the section on the church and the community of the Twelve (6:12 — 8:53), the meal comes right after Jesus' response to John's inquiry regarding his messianic mission (7:18–23) and Jesus' testimony concerning John as more than a prophet, indeed as God's messenger, like Elijah preparing his way (7:24–35). By rejecting John's baptism, the Pharisees, the scholars of the law and others rejected the whole plan of God for them. For his fasting, people thought John to be possessed by a demon. For his eating and drinking, they thought the Son of Man "a glutton and a drunkard, a friend of tax collectors and sinners" (7:34). But as Luke says, wisdom would be vindicated by all her children (7:35).

The Pharisees had already compared Jesus unfavorably with John at the meal in Levi's house, but at the time nothing was said of their rejecting John's baptism. Indeed they had presented their own disciples as religious people who fasted as did John's disciples (5:33). In his testimony to John (7:18–35), Jesus unmasked their hypocrisy.

With the story of the Pharisee who loved little and the woman who loved much, Luke shows how in fact "wisdom is vindicated by all her children" (7:35). The role of the woman in Luke 7:36–50 points ahead to the rest of the section (8:1 – 53), in which Luke highlights the place and role of women in a church constituted as the community of the Twelve.

Like the banquet in the house of the tax collector named Levi, the dinner in the house of the Pharisee named Simon was modeled to a certain extent on Hellenistic symposia.

For the story of Levi, Luke had a source in Mark, who also told of the call of Levi and followed its story with a banquet taken with tax collectors. For the dinner in Simon's house, Luke had no written source: The story was developed by Luke from a few elements in Mark's story of a meal at the home of Simon the leper (Mark 14:3 – 9) and a tradition underlying John's story of a meal with Lazarus (John 11:2; 12:1 – 11).

In both Mark and John, the meal takes place in Bethany shortly before the passion. In Mark, the meal is actually told as part of the passion story. Both Mark and John also feature an anointing of Jesus by a woman. There are enough common elements here to say that Luke's story is related to the one in John as well as to the one in Mark. But Luke develops these elements with great originality, resulting in an almost entirely new story. (Luke will again draw on the tradition underlying John 11:2 and 12:1 – 11 for the story of Martha and Mary in 10:38 – 42.)

**The Setting: At Table in the House of a Pharisee**  The story begins with the setting (7:36):

> A Pharisee invited him to dine with him,
> and he entered the Pharisee's house
> and reclined at table.

In the great dinner at Levi's house, Jesus challenged the Pharisees and their scribes to recognize their personal need for conversion. By agreeing to dine in the house of a Pharisee, Jesus showed solidarity with him and his guests, as he had shown to Levi the tax collector and his guests.

Into this setting the story introduces a woman and describes
her extraordinary gesture toward Jesus (7:37 – 38):

> Now there was a sinful woman in the city
> who learned that he was at table
> in the house of the Pharisee.
> Bringing an alabaster flask of ointment,
> she stood behind him at his feet weeping
> and began to bathe his feet with her tears.
> Then she wiped them with her hair, kissed them,
> and anointed them with the ointment.

The woman's gesture, so striking in every detail, acts as a cata-
lyst, giving direction and unity to the rest of the story. We note
that this woman brought an alabaster flask, as did the woman
who anointed Jesus in the house of Simon the leper (Mark
14:3 – 9). Luke retained this traditional note as an expression of
the woman's great respect for Jesus the prophet, but dropped its
connection with Jesus' death and burial.

The woman placed herself behind Jesus at his feet. The image
is quite clear. In a Roman-style dining room, Jesus and the others
at table would have been reclining with their heads toward the
serving area in the center of the room and their bodies and legs
extending back toward the wall. The woman thus approached
Jesus from along the wall and placed herself at his feet.

The image, however, must not be taken literally. The expression
"to be at someone's feet" means being someone's disciple. It
refers to one's personal and spiritual posture in relation to a
respected teacher and has nothing to do with physical posture.
The same image appears later in the gospel in the description of
Mary, in the story of Martha and Mary (10:38 – 42).[13]

If being at Jesus' feet was a symbol for the woman's being a
disciple, it follows that her weeping and bathing Jesus' feet with
her tears, wiping them with her hair, kissing them, and anointing
them with ointment were also figurative. The woman showed

that she was more than an ordinary disciple. Her behavior indicated that she was extremely dedicated.

**Reaction of Jesus' Host**  Surprisingly, Jesus did not respond to the woman and her gesture. His host, however, was quite taken aback by it, and even more surprised by the fact that Jesus did nothing to stop her. But he kept the reaction to himself, saying nothing openly (7:39):

> When the Pharisee who had invited him saw this
> he said to himself,
> "If this man were a prophet, he would know
> who and what sort of woman this is who is touching him,
> that she is a sinner."

With this, we have come to the heart of the story. The narrative of the woman's striking gesture was included in the story of the events at the Pharisee's house in order to provide a context for both the Pharisee's reaction and ultimately for Jesus' response. As a participant in the story, the Pharisee remained blind to the symbolic meaning of her gesture. Privy to its meaning, the reader immediately senses the enormous difference in the quality of discipleship shown by the woman and that shown by the Pharisee. It is the Pharisee's reaction to the woman's gesture, and not the gesture itself, that moves Jesus to respond.

**Jesus' Response**  A brief opening dialogue now focuses our full attention on the story's main personage, Jesus' host, the Pharisee, whose name, Simon,[14] we are told for the first time (Luke 7:40):

> Jesus said to him in reply,
> "Simon, I have something to say to you."
> "Tell me, teacher," he said.

Jesus had Simon's full attention as he began to speak. First he told a parable about two people who were in debt, concluding with a question to Simon and drawing him reluctantly into the parable (7:41 – 43):

> "Two people were in debt to a certain creditor;
> one owed five hundred days' wages and the other
>   owed fifty.
> Since they were unable to repay the debt,
> he forgave it for both.
>  Which of them will love him more?"
> Simon said in reply,
> "The one, I suppose, whose larger debt was forgiven."
> He said to him,
> "You have judged rightly."

Jesus' parable about a creditor forgiving debts reveals the personal nature of debts in the various cultures represented in the New Testament.[15] Paying and forgiving debts were not just matters of justice. Rather, because incurring a debt placed someone in *personal* debt, debts could never be fully repaid. They could be forgiven by the creditor, but then the one who was absolved incurred a permanent debt of gratitude. In Jesus' parable, that gratitude is expressed in the form of love. The greater the debt forgiven, the greater the gratitude, and the greater the love shown. As Simon the Pharisee responded, one could expect the degree of love to be proportionate to the debt that was forgiven.

With Simon drawn into the parable, Jesus led him to interpret it as his own personal story, as it were, from inside the parable. Calling Simon's attention to the woman, Jesus contrasted the lavish welcome she had provided with the poor welcome Simon had given him (7:44 – 46):

> Then he turned to the woman and said to Simon,
> "Do you see this woman?

When I entered your house,
  you did not give me water for my feet,
  but she has bathed them with her tears
  and wiped them with her hair.
  You did not give me a kiss,
  but she has not ceased kissing my feet
  since the time I entered.
  You did not anoint my head with oil,
  but she anointed my feet with ointment."

Jesus concluded his response by pointing out what her lavish welcome and the Pharisee's contrasting lack of welcome said about love and forgiveness (7:47):

"So I tell you, her many sins have been forgiven;
  hence, she has shown great love.
  But the one to whom little is forgiven, loves little."

The Pharisee was forgiven little, so he loved little. Perhaps it was that he had less to be forgiven. More likely, it was that he repented less and as a result was forgiven less, and so showed less love than the woman did.

It is not that the woman's love led to or brought about the forgiveness of her sins but that her love flowed from her being forgiven. Having been forgiven much, she loved much. We were led to expect a similar application to Simon, the Pharisee who loved little, but instead Jesus presented a saying, a generalization, inviting all listeners and readers to place themselves in the Pharisee's position and ponder Jesus' message as addressed to him. With that, we have all joined Simon inside the parable and are invited by Jesus to interpret it as our personal story.

Simon the Pharisee thus becomes every Christian. In Luke's telling of the story, it is not so much Simon, the particular Pharisee with whom Jesus dined, that Jesus addresses. Rather it is everyone in the Lukan communities and every reader of the gospel whose attitudes and behavior are embodied by Simon the Pharisee — everyone, that is every Christian, who refuses to welcome and be reconciled with one who has repented and been forgiven.

A similar message returns later, in Luke 15:1 – 32, when Pharisees complain about Jesus' welcoming sinners and eating with them. At that point, Jesus responds with three parables, that of the lost sheep that is found, that of the lost coin that is found and that of the lost younger brother who is found. The Pharisees are mirrored by the older brother who refused his father's invitation to welcome his repentant younger brother in a feast of reconciliation.

**Jesus Addresses the Woman**　The story ends with Jesus addressing the woman for the first time and declaring her sins forgiven. Once again Jesus' gesture raises the question of his identity, this time among the others at table. Ignoring their question, Jesus speaks to the woman a second time and relates her repentance, forgiveness and love to her faith and the larger context of salvation and peace (7:48 – 50):

> He said to her,
> "Your sins are forgiven."
> The others at table said to themselves,
> "Who is this who even forgives sins?"
> But he said to the woman,
> "Your faith has saved you; go in peace."

Jesus' concluding words to the woman, "Your faith has saved you; go in peace," may have been associated with an early Christian baptismal liturgy (see Mark 5:34; 10:52; Luke 8:48; 17:19; 18:42). If so, they carried a powerful message, evoking the baptismal experience of all who knew that liturgy. The relationship between hospitality, reconciliation and salvation would be taken up again in the story of Zacchaeus (19:1 – 10). With the woman who anointed Jesus, salvation is directly related to the woman's faith. With Zacchaeus, salvation is related to the welcome Jesus received at his home.

Like the great feast in the house of Levi, the dinner at the house of Simon the Pharisee deals with many issues. Here was a Pharisee, in Luke's terms a sinner, who had responded to Jesus' call for *metanoia,* a Christian who was unable to welcome and be reconciled with another Christian who had accepted the call to *metanoia.*

The fact that in Luke 7:36 – 50 the person involved was a woman may have led Luke to select her for this story, because Luke was careful to include both men and women in the gospel story. However, her being a woman is not the main point in this story. In the Lukan communities, it was quite normal for women to be present at table with Jesus and other disciples. What is significant is that the woman was recognized as a sinner. For the Pharisee, once a sinner always a sinner. Repentance made no difference with respect to someone's life in the community or their joining in the breaking of the bread.

As in the story of Levi, Jesus is again the prophet. This time Jesus challenges a Pharisee who questions his prophetic credentials. He calls on the Pharisee to welcome the woman at his table as a disciple who has repented and been forgiven. Her lavish expression of love showed her to be a better disciple than the Pharisee, even if he did play host to the community for the breaking of the bread.

The feast at the house of Levi, the first meal in Luke's story of the origins of the eucharist, dealt with the most basic aspect of eucharist in relation to the life of the church, that of *metanoia.* The eucharist is a call to *metanoia* and an offer of forgiveness. The dinner at the house of Simon the Pharisee deals with another very basic aspect of eucharist, one that flows directly from eucharistic metanoia and forgiveness, namely reconciliation. Of its very nature, the eucharist is a sacrament of reconciliation, prophetically calling all its participants, indeed all who are invited to its banquet, to be one in love.

Wherever it is celebrated, the eucharistic feast is an event of evangelization, a call to *metanoia*. Again, wherever it is celebrated, the eucharist is also an event of reconciliation, a call to love another in peace.

## The Breaking of the Bread at Bethsaida (Luke 9:10–17)[16]

*"Give them some food yourselves."*

*(Luke 9:13)*

At the banquet in the house of Levi (5:27–39), we heard Pharisees ask Jesus' disciples why they ate and drank with tax collectors and sinners.

Then, at another dinner — this one in the house of a Pharisee named Simon (7:36–50) — Jesus' host questioned his authenticity as a prophet. If Jesus were truly a prophet, would he allow a woman known as a sinner to bathe his feet with her tears, anoint them with ointment and wipe them with her hair? Surely he would know what sort of woman this was who was touching him!

We now come to a very different meal. At the first two, Jesus was a special guest at a formal dinner, a symposium, which Jesus turned into a prophetic symposium. In this third meal, Jesus himself is the host welcoming an extremely large crowd for a banquet situated somewhere in the city of Bethsaida.[17] Unlike the earlier meals, there is no mention of a house or home, or any other specific location. But then this meal is in a section of the gospel devoted to mission (9:1–50), and perhaps this is the way it should be for a meal symbolic of the church's missionary journey. Jesus himself was known not to have a personal home. As he declared at the start of the great journey to Jerusalem, "Foxes have dens and birds of the sky have nests, but the Son of Man has nowhere to rest his head." (9:58)

For the symposium, Jesus and the other guests received a special invitation. For the banquet at Bethsaida, there were no special invitations. Because everyone was invited, special invitations were not needed. The crowds had come to be taught and healed by Jesus, and they stayed late into the day until it was time to eat and find lodging. Jesus would offer them hospitality.[18] He would be their host at a banquet served by the Twelve.

In Luke's story of meals with Jesus, this is the first of five described as hospitality meals.[19] In the biblical world, as in most of the world today, hospitality always includes the offering and sharing of food and drink. But providing hospitality for 5,000 people was not something one normally expected to do. At the previous meals, the main concern was with the guests and the implications of dining with tax collectors and sinners. The concern now moves away from the precise composition of the guest list to the overwhelming number of participants. For the first time, the focus is also on food and its meager quantity, as well as its extraordinary nourishing quality when it is generously shared.

This third meal is a great hospitality event welcoming hungry thousands for the breaking of bread. It is here at a dinner hosted by Jesus that Luke first introduces key expressions from the early Christian liturgy: "Then *taking* the five *loaves* and two fish, *and looking up to heaven, he said the blessing over them, broke them, and gave them* to the disciples to set before the crowd." (9:16) The next time we hear such expressions will be at the Last Supper (22:19), where again Jesus will act as host. Some of the same expressions will also reappear in the story of the breaking of the bread with the two disciples of Emmaus (24:30).

The banquet at the house of Levi showed the eucharist as an evangelizing event calling sinners to repentance. The dinner at the house of Simon presented the eucharist as a reconciling event in which those who repent and are forgiven reveal great love for Jesus and one another. The breaking of the bread at Bethsaida presents the eucharist as a mission event: Those who were called to repentance and were reconciled are sent to nourish the hungry with the bread of Christ. By its very nature as an assembly of the Twelve, the eucharist constitutes the first realization of that mission.

Taken together, the three meals present the eucharist as a prophetic event challenging the church as a people called to repentance (5:27 – 39), reconciled as a community of the Twelve (7:36 – 50) and sent on mission (9:10 – 17). In this first series of meals, the breaking of bread at Bethsaida — with its liturgical expressions from the early Christian eucharist — comes as the first climax in Luke's story of the origins of eucharist.

At Levi's house, the disciples were guests along with Jesus, and the Pharisees challenged them for eating and drinking with tax collectors and sinners (5:30). Jesus defended the disciples and challenged the Pharisees in return (5:31 – 32). At Simon's house, a woman came as a disciple placing herself at Jesus' feet. When Simon questioned Jesus' authenticity as a prophet because he allowed someone known as a sinner to touch him, Jesus defended her and confronted the Pharisee with his own lack of love.

At the breaking of the bread in Bethsaida, the Twelve were present, though not as guests nor precisely as host. The host was Jesus, but the Twelve were associated with Jesus, and it is through their ministry that Jesus nourished the 5,000. Jesus thus shared his role of host with the Twelve. It is for this mission, to nourish the crowds with bread blessed and broken by Jesus, that the disciples were called to repentance and reconciled in the community of the Twelve.

Like the first and second meals, this third meal is not without its challenges. This time the challenge comes not from the Pharisees but from the apostles asking that Jesus dismiss the crowd. As Jesus did earlier with the Pharisees, he returned the challenge to its source, this time to the Twelve, and through them to the apostolic community and the church to our own day.

**Context and Tradition**  With the breaking of the bread in the city of Bethsaida, we come to the first climax in Luke's story of the origins of the eucharist. The second will come at the Last Supper. The story is told in the concluding section of Jesus' Galilean ministry (9:1 – 50), just before the great journey to Jerusalem.[20] In many ways, the section also serves as an introduction for the journey narrative (9:51 — 24:53), announcing many of its most prominent themes and spelling out what it means for the community of the Twelve to be missionary.[21]

As part of the mission section (9:1–50), the meal comes right after a passage giving various views on Jesus' identity (9:7–9). Was he John the Baptist raised from the dead? Was he Elijah?

---

**Table IV: Setting for the breaking of the bread at Bethsaida**

9:1–50   **The Mission of the Twelve**

The mission of the Twelve   9:1–6

Who is Jesus?   9:7–9

The breaking of the bread at Bethsaida   **9:10–17**

   **9:10**  Jesus and the apostles withdraw in private

   **9:11**  Jesus welcomes the crowd
            and teaches about the Kingdom of God

   **9:12**  Disciples want to dismiss the crowd

   **9:13–17**  Jesus, host at the table of the Kingdom

Jesus, the Messiah of God   9:18–21

First announcement of the passion and resurrection   9:22

Denying oneself, taking up the cross daily   9:23–27

The Transfiguration   9:28–36

Healing a boy, an only child   9:37–43

Second announcement of the passion   9:44–45

Who is the greatest in the kingdom?   9:46–48

One not in our company invoking Jesus' name   9:49–50

Was he one of the ancient prophets who had arisen? Herod was certain Jesus was not John, whom he had beheaded, but then just who was Jesus? Part of the purpose of the breaking of the bread at Bethsaida was to answer the question of Jesus' identity. But unlike the various opinions circulating, it *shows* who Jesus is instead of merely *saying* who he is or associating him with a biblical figure.

Immediately after the breaking of the bread, the question of Jesus' identity was taken up again, this time with Jesus himself asking who the crowds said he was. The reply was the same as before. Some thought he was John the Baptist, others Elijah, and still others one of the prophets who had arisen (9:18 – 19). The breaking of the bread had revealed very little to the crowds about Jesus' identity. But then, when Jesus asked the disciples who they said he was, Peter replied, "The Messiah *[Christos]* of God." (9:20) There was no contesting Peter's answer. Still, Jesus "rebuked them and directed them not to tell this to anyone" (9:21).

From the breaking of the bread, Peter and the disciples saw that Jesus was the Christ of God. However, they had yet to learn what it meant for Jesus to be the Christ, and most especially that "the Son of Man must suffer greatly and be rejected by the elders, the chief priests, and the scribes, and be killed and on the third day be raised" (9:22). The breaking of the bread could be understood properly and reveal Jesus' true identity only in relationship to his passion-resurrection. At this point in the gospel, the disciples were not able to understand this and were afraid to ask (see 9:43b – 45). Even after Jesus' passion-resurrection, the disciples of Emmaus would not understand. In order to understand, their minds would have to be opened to the message of the prophets. Only then would they recognize him, really know him, in the breaking of the bread (24:13 – 35).

The introduction for this section of the gospel showed Jesus sending the Twelve on mission to proclaim the kingdom of God and to heal (9:1 – 6). They were to take nothing for the journey, neither walking stick, nor sack, nor food (literally "bread," *artos),* nor money, nor a second tunic. Instead they were to accept the hospitality that was offered them. Having returned from their journey, still without bread or money, they would learn what hospitality was all about.

In the breaking of the bread at Bethsaida Jesus would show them that for Christ's followers hospitality was not just a matter of giving out bread and money. As Jesus indicated earlier when the devil tempted him to command a stone to become bread, "One does not live by bread alone" (4:4; see Deuteronomy 8:3). The meal Jesus hosted for the 5,000 at Bethsaida shows how the eucharist contains the most basic challenges of the Christian mission.

Luke's source for the breaking of the bread at Bethsaida was the first of two such stories in Mark (6:30–44; 8:1–9),[22] but as Luke had done for the banquet at the house of Levi, he simplified Mark's story, changed some of its elements and introduced some new elements. Mark had given the story a fairly elaborate introduction: "The apostles gathered together with Jesus and reported all they had done and taught. He said to them, 'Come away by yourselves to a deserted place and rest a while.' People were coming and going in great numbers, and they had no opportunity even to eat. So they went off in the boat by themselves to a deserted place." (Mark 6:30–32) The corresponding elements in Luke are much simpler: "When the apostles returned, they explained to him what they had done. He took them and withdrew in private to a town called Bethsaida." (9:10)

Luke eliminated Mark's growing-crowd motif, as he did earlier when introducing the banquet at the house of Levi (5:27). He also moved the event from the countryside to the city of Bethsaida. Describing how Jesus welcomed the crowd, Mark stressed how deeply moved Jesus was on seeing them like sheep without a shepherd, and he showed how Jesus became shepherd to them by teaching them many things (6:34). Luke merely mentioned that Jesus received the crowds, and he stressed what Jesus taught them: "He received them and spoke to them about the kingdom of God, and healed those who needed to be cured." (9:11) In Mark, what mattered was *that* Jesus taught them. In Luke, what mattered was *what* Jesus taught them.

Taught about the kingdom of God and healed of everything that prevented them from entering it (see 9:6), the crowd was now ready to dine in the kingdom of God. At the breaking of the bread in Bethsaida, Jesus was host at the table of the kingdom of God.

**The Setting: Jesus Receives the Crowd**   The story begins as the apostles[23] return from their missionary journey (see 9:6). They had gone from village to village proclaiming the good news of the kingdom and curing diseases everywhere (9:6; see 9:2). On returning, they explained to Jesus what they had done (9:10). Jesus then took them to Bethsaida, and the crowds followed him there. The story's opening verses introduce the personages, indicate the setting and situate the event in the ministry of Jesus (9:10 – 11):

> When the apostles returned,
> they explained to him what they had done.
> He took them and withdrew in private
> to a town [literally "city," *polis*] called Bethsaida.
> The crowds, meanwhile, learned of this
> and followed him.
> He received them
> and spoke to them about the kingdom of God,
> and healed those who needed to be cured.

By withdrawing in private with the apostles, Jesus indicated that he had very special teaching for them. But the crowd learned of Jesus' whereabouts and followed him. Although aimed specifically at the apostles, Jesus' teaching would be given in the midst of large crowds in the city of Bethsaida. The opening verses give no hint of anything like a symposium. Rather, the themes of journey and mission suggest a meal of hospitality.

The disciples had received hospitality as they traveled about, proclaiming the good news of the kingdom of God and healing the sick (see 9:1 – 6). They would now learn how to extend it. Both the receiving and the giving of hospitality were essential for apostles whose lives would unfold as one great missionary journey.

**The Twelve Respond**   When evening came, Jesus was still teaching and healing those in need. The apostles saw the way he welcomed the crowds, but they did not see its implications for them as his followers and apostles. They went up to Jesus and asked him to send the crowd away in order to provide for themselves. When Jesus answered that they should themselves give the crowd something to eat, they objected that they had ridiculously little food, unless they went and bought some, and this was not a small crowd (9:12 – 14a):

> As the day was drawing to a close,
> the Twelve approached him and said,
> "Dismiss the crowd
> so that they can go to the surrounding villages and farms
> and find lodging and provisions;
> for we are in a deserted place here."
> He said to them,
> "Give them some food yourselves."
> They replied,
> "Five loaves and two fish are all we have,
> unless we ourselves go and buy food for all these people."
> Now the men there numbered about five thousand.

The expression, "as the day was drawing to a close *[he de hemera erxato klinein]*," signals meal time, as does a like expression in the story of Emmaus (24:29). Overwhelmed by the demands of hospitality, the Twelve took the initiative and asked Jesus to dismiss the crowd to see to their own lodging and nourishment.

In Greek, the word for "finding lodging" is *kataluo*, a verb which is associated with hospitality. The same verb is used in the story of Zacchaeus when those surrounding Jesus grumble that he has gone to stay *(katalusai)* at the house of a sinner (19:7).

The noun derived from this verb, *kataluma,* is the "inn" in the story of Jesus' birth (2:7) and the "guest room" in that of the Last Supper (22:11).

By asking Jesus to dismiss the crowd, the Twelve were denying them hospitality and asking Jesus to do the same, just as the people of Bethlehem had denied hospitality to him when Mary and Joseph came to there (2:7). But instead Jesus — the one denied hospitality — would *offer* hospitality both here in the breaking of the bread (9:16) and at the Last Supper (22:11).

The reference to a "deserted place" *(eremos topos)* is very striking in the geographical context of the city of Bethsaida. At first, we might be tempted to consider it as a poorly digested element from Mark's story (Mark 6:35), with no particular meaning in Luke. But literarily, it associates the city of Bethsaida with the desert experience of the exodus, which lies in the background of this whole section of the gospel. In the transfiguration, Moses and Elijah appearing in glory would speak of the exodus *(exodos)* that Jesus would fulfill in Jerusalem (9:31). Wherever "the breaking of the bread" is done, it is always a desert meal, like the daily bread God provided the people of Israel in the formative days of their desert journey.[24]

Jesus did not accept that the crowd be dismissed. "Give them some food yourselves," he ordered them. Here lay Jesus' prophetic challenge. Although the Twelve had hardly any food at all — they had been told not to bring any bread on their journey — Jesus ordered them to give food to the crowd. In John's gospel, Jesus had food to eat of which the disciples did not know (see John 4:32). Here in Luke, it is the disciples themselves who had food to eat of which they did not know, enough to nourish a crowd of 5,000 "men."

The Greek term used for "men" is not the inclusive term *anthropoi,* but *andres,* which usually means men as distinguished from women. However, at times it is also used generically to refer to both men and women. Given Luke's sensitivity to include women throughout the gospel, we may safely assume that the crowd of 5,000 included women.[25]

**Preparations for the Dinner** Jesus now gave directives for preparing the dinner. In these directives, Jesus focused entirely on the arrangements for those who would share in it (9:14 – 15):

> Then he said to his disciples,
>
> "Have them sit down in groups of [about] fifty."
>
> They did so and made them all sit down.

The translation (RNAB) at this point is not very helpful.[26] What the Greek text actually says is, "Have them recline on dining couches by fifties *[kataklinate autous klisias (osei) ana pentekonta]*." The image is of people coming for a formal banquet, a symposium, for which people reclined. Luke's telling of the preparation is much simpler than that of Mark: "So he gave them orders to have them sit down in groups on the green grass. The people took their places in rows by hundreds and by fifties" (Mark 6:39 – 40).

Up to this point in the story, there still had been no indication that this was to be a symposium.[27] Nor do we find any influence coming from the Hellenistic literary form associated with the symposium. The breaking of the bread at Bethsaida quite clearly represents a hospitality meal. A symposium would have been impossible in a desert place, even in the city of Bethsaida.

Still, Luke insists on associating the meal with Hellenistic symposia. Setting all considerations of verisimilitude aside, Luke describes the meal preparations in terms of a symposium, indeed of 100 symposia, each for a community of about 50 people. The image is of a gathering of local church communities from throughout the eastern Mediterranean world, about 100 communities, gathered not only as a church but as a church universal. Here was a symposium of symposia, assembled with the Twelve at the table of Jesus the prophet, a meal fit for the kingdom of God.

Jesus had been speaking about the kingdom of God (9:11). He had also instructed the Twelve apostles to do the same (9:2), and they did, proclaiming the good news everywhere. The hospitality meal revealed in deed what Jesus and the Twelve taught in word.

At Jesus' table in Bethsaida, the crowds would dine in the kingdom of God.

The meal preparations follow a pattern that reappears in the preparations for Jesus' entry into Jerusalem (19:28 – 35) and in the preparations for the Last Supper (22:7 – 13). First, Jesus gives instructions, and then we are told the disciples fulfilled them. Literarily, this may seem repetitive, but rhetorically it is very effective, enabling listeners to follow developments step by step.

**The Breaking of the Bread**    The story now reaches its climax, as Jesus breaks bread and gives the loaves to the disciples to distribute to the crowd, now reclining on dining couches by parties of fifty. The expressions used are mainly liturgical, with a few modifications introduced to adapt these liturgical expressions to the context of the present story (9:16):

> Then taking the five loaves and the two fish,
>
> and looking up to heaven,
>
> he said the blessing over them,
>
> broke them,
>
> and gave them to the disciples
>
> to set before the crowd.

The actions of Jesus definitively associated this event with the eucharist. Referring to a few expressions from the beginning of a liturgical narrative for the eucharist sufficed to evoke the whole event. The principal adaptations made for the sake of the story include the reference to the five loaves— while the liturgical text speaks of bread in the singular — and Jesus' giving the loaves to the disciples to set before the crowd — in the liturgical text the loaves are intended for the disciples themselves (22:19; see also 24:30).

We note also that Jesus blessed the loaves and the fish (see Mark 8:7),[28] whereas in 22:19 he gave thanks. In the first case, the act is directed to the objects Jesus blessed. Looking up to heaven, he called down God's blessing on the five loaves and the fish. In the second, the act is addressd to God, the source of every gift.

In the story's introduction, the Twelve (9:1, 12) were referred to as "the apostles," highlighting their role as missionaries (9:10). Now in the actual breaking of the bread, they are referred to as "the disciples," highlighting their position as pupils at the table of Jesus the prophet. Jesus taught them to extend the hospitality of the kingdom of God. The bread, blessed, broken and given was the bread of the kingdom.

**The Bread Broken**  We have reached the story's denouement. Amazingly, all had eaten their fill, and there was bread left over besides (9:17):

> They all ate and were satisfied.
> And when the leftover fragments were picked up,
> they filled twelve wicker baskets.

Those who ate numbered 5,000. The bread Jesus gave through the intermediation of his disciples was enough to nourish the assembly of the whole church, present as local communities but sharing beyond their local boundaries. The term here translated as "the leftover fragments" is *klasmaton,* the perfect passive participle in the genitive plural of the verb *klao,* meaning to "break." The participle means "broken" and modifies "loaves," in the singular, "bread." A translation indicating they gathered what was left over of the "bread broken" would be more adequate and would invite theological reflection. The bread gathered remained bread that was broken by Jesus.

What was gathered of the bread broken filled twelve baskets, a transparent allusion to the Twelve. The church of the Twelve draws the nourishment it offers from the bread broken by Jesus. The mission of the Twelve and of the church was to continue Jesus' proclamation of the gospel of the kingdom of God as well as Jesus' offer of hospitality at the table of the kingdom.

Like the great banquet at the house of Levi the tax collector and the dinner in the house of Simon the Pharisee, the breaking of the bread at Bethsaida shows Jesus the prophet challenging the disciples. This time his challenge speaks to their missionary responsibility as the church of the Twelve.

The breaking of the bread at Bethsaida reveals Jesus' messianic identity and relates the eucharist to the church's mission. It shows Jesus teaching the crowds about the kingdom of God, a kingdom not fully established until it embraces all human beings. An earthly kingdom, including the kingdom of David, is for a particular nation or people. The kingdom of God is for the whole human race. The breaking of the bread at Bethsaida in a great gathering of local assemblies both announces and symbolizes a meal in the kingdom of God.

The story reveals the missionary dimension of the eucharist. It tells about Jesus' challenge to the Twelve when, turning away from their mission, they asked him to send the crowd away to provide for themselves. "Give them some food yourselves," Jesus said. Jesus' command applies to the church celebrating eucharist today just as it did to the church in Luke's time.

The eucharist is a call to conversion, *metanoia* in the following of Christ: It is an event of evangelization. The eucharist also requires a loving welcome for all who embark on the way of *metanoia* in the community of the Twelve: It is an event of reconciliation. The eucharist is a proclamation of the kingdom of God: It is a missionary event, summarizing the missionary life of the church.

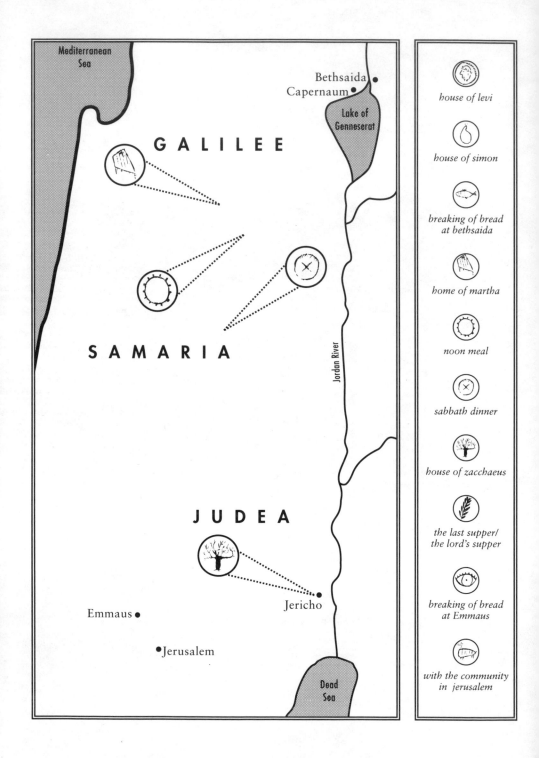

# At Table
# with Jesus the Prophet
# Part II:
# On the Way to Jerusalem

*L* uke's story of the eucharist began with three meals in the Galilean ministry (5:1 — 9:50): a great banquet in the house of a tax collector named Levi (5:27 – 39), a dinner in the house of a Pharisee named Simon (7:36 – 50), and the breaking of the bread in the city of Bethsaida (9:10 – 17). It is in Jesus' Galilean ministry that Luke set down the foundations of the church as a people called (5:1 — 6:11), constituted as the Twelve (6:12 — 8:56) and sent on mission (9:1 – 50). The meals correspond to each of these three sections telling of Jesus' Galilean ministry.

In these meals, Luke laid out the most basic aspects of the eucharist in the life of the church. The eucharist calls people to repentance *(metanoia)* in the following of Jesus (5:27 – 39), demands reconciliation *(katallage)* among those who respond to this call in the community of the Twelve (7:36 – 50), and sends them forth to proclaim the kingdom of God (9:10 – 17). At its most basic, the eucharist is consequently an event of evangelization, of reconciliation and of mission.

At each of the meals, Jesus was present primarily as a prophet challenging the community to fulfill its basic identity as a people called, assembled and sent by Jesus. The two meals at which Jesus and his disciples were guests (5:27 – 39; 7:36 – 50) were patterned on the Hellenistic symposium. The third meal, at which Jesus was the host and the apostles served (9:10 – 17) was in fact a rather impromptu hospitality meal, albeit told with some of the imagery associated with the symposium.

We now come to a second set of meals in which Jesus again acts primarily as a prophet. This new set is situated on Jesus' journey to Jerusalem. Thematically, the journey is to the ascension, whose story is told at the very end of the gospel (24:50 – 53).[1] Geographically, the journey is to the city of Jerusalem and Jesus' cleansing of the temple (19:45 – 48).[2]

The gospel's journey narrative announces the great journey of the church to the ends of the earth as told in the Acts of the Apostles. Literarily, Paul's journey to Jerusalem and Rome (Acts 19:21 — 28:31), which brings the story of Acts to a close, parallels Jesus' journey to Jerusalem (9:51 — 24:53), which brings the gospel to a close. The Galilean ministry told the story of the church in relation to its ultimate *origins* in Jesus' divine mission. The journey to Jerusalem tells the story of the church in relation to its ultimate *destiny* with Jesus in God.

There are four meals in the part of the journey leading up to Jerusalem:

> 1) a hospitality meal in the home of a woman named Martha (10:38 – 42)
> 2) a symposium-like meal in the home of a Pharisee (11:37 – 54)
> 3) a symposium-like dinner—a sabbath meal—in the home of a leading Pharisee (14:1 – 24)
> 4) a hospitality meal in the home of a chief tax collector named Zacchaeus (19:1 – 10).

The four meals reflect different situations in the daily life of the church and at each a particular issue or set of issues is raised and addressed prophetically by Jesus.

At the meal in the house of Martha, the focus is on "the one thing necessary" in the ministry of a true disciple (10:38 – 42). The noon meal in the house of a Pharisee deals with the primacy of interior purity over exterior fulfillment of obligations (11:37 – 54). At the sabbath meal in a Pharisee's house, the issue that is raised deals with the attitudes and conduct of both the guests and the host (14:1 – 24). At the house of Zacchaeus, the issues are justice and concern for the poor (19:1 – 10).

Each of the four meal stories is unique to the Gospel of Luke and reflects Luke's literary style and creativity. Two of the meals, the one in the house of Martha (10:38 – 42) and one of those in the house of a Pharisee (11:37 – 54), are associated with older traditions. The Martha and Mary story draws on a tradition preserved in John 12:1 – 11. The meal in the house of the Pharisee draws on a few elements in Mark 7:1 – 9 and on traditional sayings from a source called Q that Luke has in common with Matthew (see Matthew 23). But the meal setting for these sayings is due entirely to Luke. For the other two meals, there is no discernible source or tradition. It is very likely that Luke based these stories on some old traditions (see 1:3), and that he retold and transformed them as part of the story of the origins of eucharist in Jesus' journey to Jerusalem.

## Hospitality at the Home of Martha (Luke 10:38 – 42)[3]

The first meal on the great journey to Jerusalem was in the home of a woman named Martha. The story shows Martha "burdened with much serving" (10:40), complaining to Jesus that her sister Mary was not helping her. Responding to Martha, Jesus stated that only one thing is really necessary and that Mary, who was seated at the Lord's feet and listening to his word, exemplified what this was. The story deals with the tension that arises between ministry and discipleship. It is about the importance of being a true follower and disciple of Jesus while serving in the

*"There is need of only one thing."*
(Luke 10:42)

ministry. Without that—the one thing that is necessary—ministry loses its meaning.

The story of Martha and the hospitality offered at her home is a story of eucharist and ministry *(diakonia)*. It shows how those in ministry can be distracted by secondary considerations and diverted from what is absolutely necessary and critical to the meaning of everything else they do. Eucharist is a matter of mutual presence and communication. Eucharistic hospitality requires that those who minister recognize the Lord's presence, that they respond to the Lord's presence by being present to him in return. They do this by listening and attending to his word. Apart from this, whatever may actually be done in ministry has no Christian value.

**Context and Tradition**  The story of the meal at Martha's house comes after the journey's introduction (9:51—10:37),[4] at the very start of the first section (10:38—13:21). It is immediately followed by Jesus' teaching on prayer (11:1–13), which includes the Lord's Prayer (11:2–4). The meal at Martha's home tells of the one attitude necessary for the Christian journey to Jerusalem and the kingdom. The Lord's Prayer is the one prayer necessary for the same journey.

The introduction to the journey (9:51—10:37) did not include a meal story as such but it did refer several times to the hospitality associated with meals. First, when Jesus sent disciples ahead of him, they entered a Samaritan village to prepare for his coming there, but people would not welcome them. When the disciples asked about invoking divine vengeance on the Samaritans, as Elijah had done in 1 Kings 1:9–12, Jesus set aside their recommendation. The disciples would learn later that some Samaritans were good, and they themselves had much to learn from them about caring for their neighbor (10:25–37).

Immediately after, Jesus taught his disciples that in the service of the kingdom they had to be like the Son of Man, with no place of their own to lay their heads (9:57–62). Then, sending

**Table V: Setting for the hospitality at the home of Martha and the noon meal at the home of a Pharisee**

9:51 — 13:21    **Setting Out on the Journey**

Introduction to the journey narrative    9:51 — 10:37
Hospitality at the home of Martha    **10:38 – 42**
   **10:38 – 39**    With Martha and Mary
   **10:40**        Martha's concern
   **10:41 – 42**    Jesus' response: the one thing needed
Catechesis on prayer    11:1 – 13
Jesus' power to drive out demons    11:14 – 26
Those who are truly blessed    11:27 – 28
The sign of Jonah    11:29 – 32
Being filled with inner light, not darkness    11:33 – 36
**Noon meal at the home of a Pharisee    11:37 – 54**
   **11:37 – 44**    Woe to the Pharisees
   **11:45 – 54**    Woe to the scholars of the law
Discourse on the leaven of the Pharisees    12:1 – 59
Call to repentance    13:1 – 5
Parable of the barren fig tree    13:6 – 9
Curing a crippled woman on the Sabbath    13:10 – 17
Concluding parables    13:18 – 21

the seventy[-two] on mission, Jesus told them to bring no provisions of their own (10:4) and to stay in one house, accepting whatever hospitality, including food and drink, that was offered them (10:7 – 8). They were to concentrate on bringing peace to the households and the cities they visited, curing the sick and announcing the proximity of the kingdom of God (10:5 – 6, 9).

The story of the meal in Martha's home shows Jesus modeling the challenge he presented to those who followed him (9:57 – 62) as well as the instructions he issued to the seventy[-two] sent in pairs (10:1 – 12). The story also paves the way for the next story, a unit including Jesus' teaching of the Lord's Prayer as well as his more general teaching on prayer. This unit on prayer places great emphasis on the Christian meal, beginning with "Give us each day our daily bread" (11:3), continuing with a parable about someone begging a friend for three loaves in order to show proper hospitality to a guest just arrived at his home (11:5 – 8), and including some parabolic sayings about a father offering not a snake or a scorpion but good food to a child asking for a fish or an egg (11:11 – 12).

For the story of Martha and Mary, Luke turned to the tradition underlying John 12:1 – 11, with its story of the anointing at Bethany, as he did for the story of the dinner at the house of a Pharisee (7:36 – 50). On the earlier occasion, he relied more on Mark 14:3-9, a meal in Bethany at the house of Simon the leper, than on John 12:1 – 8, a meal in Bethany with Martha, Mary and Lazarus. This time, we find no trace of Mark 14:3 – 9.

It is not that Luke used John 12:1 – 11 as a source. The contacts between the two are too meager for that. The traditional story served rather as an inspiration and a point of departure. Both Luke 10:38 – 42 and John 12:1 – 11 tell of Jesus being welcomed and given hospitality at a meal served by Martha. Both also refer to Mary's attentiveness to the person of Jesus. In John 12:3, Mary anoints the feet of Jesus and dries them with her hair (see also 11:2, 32). In Luke, Mary sat at the Lord's feet and listened to his word (10:39). We note too that Luke, whose general tendency was to speak of towns and villages as cities, referred to the place where Martha lived as a village *(kome,* 10:38), as did John (11:1).

There are differences between Luke 10:38 – 42 and John 12:1 – 11, but all of these are related to the greater literary context in each gospel. John refers to Lazarus, but only to connect the meal story with the raising of Lazarus (John 12:1 – 2, 9 – 11; see 11:1 – 54). Lazarus has no role in the meal itself (John 12:3 – 8) and may not have been included in the traditional story of the meal. There is no mention of Lazarus in Luke 10:38 – 42. In John the story took place six days before Passover and the event was situated at Bethany. Luke makes no mention of Passover, nor does he situate the story at Bethany, which was near Jerusalem on the east slope of the Mount of Olives. In Luke's gospel, the event took place in the early part of the journey to Jerusalem, while Jesus and the disciples were still in Galilee.

When Luke drew on this same tradition in the story of the dinner at the house of Simon the Pharisee (7:36 – 50), the anointing of Jesus was the element developed and emphasized. In the meal at Martha's home, there is no mention of an anointing. Luke's entire focus is on discipleship and ministry.

**The Setting: At the Home of Martha**   The story opens with a detailed presentation of the setting. Jesus and the disciples were on their journey to Jerusalem when Jesus entered an unnamed village and a woman named Martha welcomed him to her home. A second woman was present — Martha's sister, Mary — who sat at the Lord's feet and listened to his word. As often happens, Luke's introduction, carefully situating the story in place and time and presenting its various personages, is quite long. In this case, it takes up a third of the story (10:38 – 39):

> As they continued their journey
> he entered a village
> where a woman whose name was Martha
> welcomed him.
> She had a sister named Mary [who]
> sat beside the Lord at his feet
> listening to him speak.

The introduction gives all we need in order to understand what follows. The story takes place on the journey to Jerusalem. The plural "they" tells us this is a story not just about Jesus but about Jesus and his disciples, even though his disciples have no part in what follows. The opening reference to the journey, which began in 9:51 and was referred to again in 9:56, 9:57 and 10:1, connects this particular story and what happened in Martha's house with the great journey to God.

After the opening statement, the story contains no further references to the disciples. It is as though Jesus were traveling alone. Very likely, the story of Martha and Mary was originally unconnected to the journey motif, and it is Luke himself who integrated it into the journey. The story may be about a particular event involving a few people who knew one another, but the story's message was meant for all Jesus' followers and disciples.

On their journey, Jesus and the disciples entered a village *(kome).*[5] In the tradition, the village may have been called Bethany (see John 11:1; 12:1), but here it remains unnamed, perhaps because Bethany's geographical location did not fit in Luke's plan for this journey. Leaving the village unnamed also has the advantage of universalizing it. The village Jesus entered could be any village, a place where some people live and others visit on their journey to Jerusalem.

Prior to this point in the story, every person who plays a role has been referred to by a pronoun, whether explicit or implied in the Greek verb. The first to be named is "a woman whose name was Martha." The story does not assume that anyone knows Martha, hence the indirect way of introducing her. Emphasis is on Martha not so much as an individual person but as a woman.[6]

Martha is the principal character in the story. She is the one who welcomed Jesus, presumably to her home, as a number of ancient manuscripts made explicit.[7] She is also the one who spoke to Jesus, complaining about her sister, and the one to whom Jesus responded. It is also she who had a sister named Mary, not Mary who had a sister named Martha (see John 11:1). Like the home and everything else in the story, Mary is seen in relation to

Martha. Mary, the second to be named in the story, may have chosen the better part, but it is her sister who is at the center of the story.

That Martha welcomed Jesus to her home seems quite extraordinary. Ordinarily, a man would have been welcomed by a man into a man's home, but not by a woman into a woman's home. An example from Acts helps us see how unusual it was for Martha to welcome Jesus into her home as well as to understand why, among Christians, it could be different.

There is the case of Paul, newly arrived at Philippi, where "a woman named Lydia, a dealer in purple cloth, from the city of Thyatira, a worshiper of God, listened, and the Lord opened her heart to pay attention to what Paul was saying" (Acts 16:14). This led to the woman's conversion as well as to that of her entire household. After her baptism, Lydia offered Paul, Silas and Timothy hospitality: "If you consider me a believer in the Lord, come and stay at my home" (Acts 16:15). And they did.

It is because Lydia was a believer that she felt free to invite Paul, Silas and Timothy to stay[8] at her home. The gospel reversed many of the traditional values. A believer was expected to be a person of honor and probity. The same must be presupposed in the story of Martha and Mary. Both women were friends and disciples of Jesus of Nazareth, but in Luke 10:38–42 both are presented as believers and members of the early Christian community.

Jesus is then introduced by the narrator as "the Lord," which is the title used throughout the story. Later, when Martha complained to him, she addressed him as "Lord" *(Kyrie)*. And in telling Jesus' response, the narrator again referred to him as "the Lord."

It is certainly true that in ordinary Greek usage, "lord" *(kurie)* was a normal way of addressing someone. When a personage in the story is referred to or called "lord," the title could consequently mean no more than "sir." "Lord" *(kurios)* could also be used to refer to one who was the head of a household. But in this case, Jesus was but a visitor. And Luke was writing from the stance of a Christian for whom Jesus' title, "Lord," was far more than a polite form of address. The narrator's references to Jesus as Lord reflect Jesus' status as risen Lord. Jesus the guest was nevertheless the head of the household of the church. In the context of Jesus' historical ministry, Martha may have called Jesus *kurie* in the sense of "sir," but in the words of the storyteller we immediately sense the irony in the title. Martha was saying far more than she realized!

Mary was sitting at the Lord's feet, indicating she was a disciple. As we saw earlier, it was quite extraordinary for Martha to welcome Jesus into her home. It was also quite extraordinary for Mary, a woman, to be a disciple.[9] Her position calls to mind that of the woman who came and placed herself at the feet of Jesus while he was reclining at dinner in the home of Simon the Pharisee (7:38). It also reminds us of the story of the Gerasene demoniac (8:26–39): When Jesus allowed the demons to leave the man and enter the swine, the former demoniac was seen sitting at the feet of Jesus (8:35); he had become a disciple.

As a disciple, Mary listened to the word of the Lord *(ton logon autou)*.[10] The story is part of Luke's theology of the word that came to John (3:2), raised questions about Jesus' identity at Nazareth (4:22) and drew crowds to hear him by the Lake of Gennesaret (5:1). This is the word to which Simon Peter responded when he lowered the nets even though he had caught nothing all night (5:5). As a disciple, Mary was attentive to the word of the Lord, the prophetic word of God at work in and through the Christian community.

**Martha's Complaint**   The storyteller has given us everything we need to know to appreciate Martha's plight. After a description of Martha's situation as "burdened with much serving," we hear her complaint (10:40):

> Martha,
> burdened with much serving,
> came to him and said,
> "Lord,
> do you not care

that my sister has left me
by myself to do the serving?
Tell her to help me."

Martha was burdened, distracted "with much serving" *(peri pollen diakonian)*. The Greek term for "serving" is *diakonia,* the same term that Luke used in the story about the Jerusalem community when the widows of the Hebrew-speaking members were favored over those of the Greek-speaking members (Acts 6:1 – 7). In that story, we learn that the Hebrew-speaking widows were being neglected in the community's ministry *(diakonia,* 6:1), and that the Twelve were overwhelmed by the demands of ministry *(diakonein)* at table, to the point where they were neglecting the ministry *(diakonia)* of the word (6:2, 4).

The story in Acts parallels the story of Martha and Mary. In both cases, the hosts either felt or were actually overwhelmed by the demands of the ministry. But there is a big difference between the two stories. Martha was distracted by the demands of the ministry from attending to the word as a disciple should. The Twelve were distracted by the demands of the ministry from proclaiming the word as apostles were sent to do.[11]

Martha's complaint was quite simple. From her point of view she had too much ministry to do, her sister was not helping her, and the Lord was not concerned. Her suggested solution was equally simple. If the Lord told her sister to help her, she surely would do so, since she was attending to his word. As a result, Martha would no longer have too much to do, and the Lord would have shown his concern.

**The Lord's Response**   The Lord answered Martha. Ignoring her assessment of the problem, he also ignored her solution. Instead, the Lord responded to her real problem, which was not that Martha had too much ministry but that she was neglecting the one thing that would give meaning to it all and that would put everything in perspective (10:41 – 42):

> The Lord said to her in reply,
> "Martha, Martha,
> you are anxious and worried about many things.
> There is need of only one thing.
> Mary has chosen the better part
> and it will not be taken from her."

It is the Lord who speaks, indicating the story's relationship to the Lord's Supper, but he speaks very much as the prophet who sees deeply into situations and opens his listeners eyes to see realities as they truly are. The way Jesus addressed Martha is a key for understanding his message to her. Jesus addressed Martha by name and he repeated the name. As always, such a repetition is very significant.

In the Old Testament, for example, Samuel was called by name out of a deep sleep, "Samuel, Samuel" (1 Samuel 3:10), opening his ears to the presence and word of the Lord. In the New Testament, Simon Peter was called by name when Jesus announced at the Last Supper that Satan had demanded to sift them all like wheat, "Simon, Simon" (Luke 22:31). In this case, the repetition draws attention to the importance of the announcement, as would the even more solemn but less personal expression, "Amen, Amen, I say to you." And then of course there was Saul on the way to Damascus, who also was called by name, "Saul, Saul, why are you persecuting me?" (Acts 9:4), stopping Saul in his tracks.

In each of these cases, and in others as well, the purpose of the repetition must be ascertained by the context, but all have two things in common. They focus the attention of the one called on the person calling, and they alert the one called to an important announcement.

The repetition of Martha's name was to draw her attention to the person of the Lord. Distracted by many things, she had been in no position to hear his word. Indeed, by telling Jesus what to do, she indicated she was not interested in his word, and this was her real problem from the beginning.

Jesus then spoke to her about her general state of mind. She was worried and anxious about many things *(peri polla)* in her ministry, whereas only one thing *(henos)* was needed. In her ministry Martha was neglecting the one most vital component. For this she called attention to her sister Mary, who as a disciple was sharply focused on the word of the Lord. This was the better part and it would not be taken away from her.

Note that being at the Lord's feet does not mean Mary was not working. It does mean that she was not distracted by the ministry or worried and excited about many things. Her attention was fixed on the word of the Lord, the one thing necessary, which gives meaning to every other aspect of ministry.

The story may reflect a profound change regarding the role of women in the Lukan communities of the time. Martha, busy with the service, may represent the more traditional way of those who "provided for *[diekonoun]* them [Jesus and the Twelve] out of their resources" (8:1–3). These women were followers of Jesus, but they were not recognized as his disciples in the sense that John the Baptist and the Pharisees had disciples (see 5:33; 7:18). Mary may reflect the newer development in Christian communities, which accepted women as disciples in the full sense. If this is the case, Jesus' response to Martha defended the emergence of this new development. The better part, that of being a disciple and listening to the word of the Lord, would not be taken away from Mary.[12]

Like the meals in Jesus' Galilean ministry, this first meal on the journey to Jerusalem presents Jesus as a prophetic teacher, responding to the disciples and challenging them at table. This time, he challenges a woman named Martha, who welcomed him at her home but complained about the burden of the ministry she carried with no help from her sister, a disciple.

A number of elements in the story show how it was intended to mirror life and the Lord's Supper as experienced in the early Christian community. This is the first time a meal story refers to Jesus as Lord, even as he fills the role of prophetic teacher. The description of Mary at the Lord's feet shows her in the position of a disciple of Jesus, the risen Lord. Martha's service is described in terms used to denote early Christian ministry, *diakonia* (ministry) and *diakoneo* (to minister). And of course, there is the fact that Jesus was welcomed by a woman into her home.

This fourth meal in Luke's story of the origins of eucharist tells of a classic situation for the church on its journey to Jerusalem and the fulfillment of its mission — the tension between discipleship and ministry. Jesus shows how to resolve this tension. One thing only is necessary: attention to the person and word of the Lord. Apart from this, nothing matters. It is the one element that gives meaning to all the others.

## A Noon Meal at the Home of a Pharisee (Luke 11:37 – 54) [13]

*"Did not the maker of the outside also make the inside?"*

(Luke 11:40)

We heard the Lord's response to Martha that one thing only was necessary, that her sister Mary had chosen the better part and that it would not be taken away from her (10:38 – 42). In this story of the first meal on the journey to Jerusalem, Luke told of the conflict that can arise between the demands of ministry and of discipleship, within a person as well as within a community. It was easy to neglect even the most basic values associated with discipleship while taken up with the demands of one's ministry. It was easy to resent new developments in the community allowing for a woman to be a disciple at the feet of the Lord, listening to his word.

We now come to a second meal on the journey to Jerusalem. The first meal stressed the primacy of discipleship and of listening to the word of the Lord over everything that is undertaken in the ministry. This second meal insists on the primacy of interior purity over external observance. Just as discipleship and attentive listening to the word gave value and meaning to the ministry, good interior attitudes are what give value and meaning to exterior observances.

Like the banquet at the the house of Levi (5:28 – 39) and the dinner at the house of Simon the Pharisee (7:36 – 50), this second meal at the home of a Pharisee reflects aspects of the structure of the Hellenistic symposium, which was normally expected to be genteel and certainly not contentious. But in this case, as in the two previous stories, the guest of honor was Jesus the prophet, whose after-dinner discourse challenged not only the Pharisee who had invited him but all Pharisees in general.

**Context and Tradition** Like the story of hospitality at the home of Martha, this second story on the journey to Jerusalem is in the first section of the journey (10:38 — 13:21), which is divided into two parts (10:38 — 11:54; 12:1 — 13:21). The first part deals with issues of discipleship and the way disciples respond to the word of the Lord while on the journey. The second deals with the need to be prepared for the final crisis. (See Table V, page 77.)

This meal in the home of a Pharisee comes at the conclusion of the section's first part (10:38 — 11:54). The part is thus framed by two meals: the meal at the home of Martha (10:38 – 42) and the meal at the home of a Pharisee (11:37 – 54), highlighting the importance of the meal for this entire part of the journey. It was in this part of the journey that Jesus taught his disciples to pray, "Give us each day our daily bread" (11:3), that is, give us the bread we need to extend hospitality to those on the journey (see 11:5 – 8).[14]

It was also in this part of the gospel that Jesus taught how a demon may have left someone only to return to its former home, now swept clean of the old (see 5:33 – 39), and bring back seven other spirits worse than itself, making the person's last state worse than the first (11:24 – 26). A little later in this section Jesus referred to the ministry and spoke of placing one's lamp on a lampstand, that all who enter might see its light. The lamp was like a person's eye, an interior lamp filling the whole body with light. Without this interior lamp, the whole body remained in darkness, and there was no point in placing it on a lampstand

(11:33 – 36). The context invites us to read the story of the noon meal with the Pharisee as an example of one who offered the daily bread of hospitality to those on the journey (see 11:3, 5 – 8) but whose condition became worse than it was before becoming a disciple (see 11:24 – 26), one whose interior eye was no longer sound and whose light became darkness (see 11:33 – 36).

Like the story of the previous meal in the home of a Pharisee (7:36 – 50) and that of hospitality at the home of Martha (10:38 – 42), the story is a Lukan composition inspired by various traditional elements. In particular, the story is related to Mark 7:1 – 9, where Jesus responded to the Pharisees and some scribes who complained that some of his disciples ate their meals with unclean hands. It is also related to the sayings source (Q) underlying Matthew 23, with its repeated denunciations introduced by "Woe to you, scribes and Pharisees."

Neither Mark nor Q, however, situated Jesus' teaching at a meal. The meal setting in 11:37 – 54 is due entirely to Luke, who made the story part of the origins of the eucharist, highlighting the indispensability of interior purity among all participants but especially among those responsible for hosting the meal.

**The Setting: Jesus and Ritual Purifications**   The setting for the story is the meal proper (11:37 – 38), which is briefly presented as an introduction for Jesus' discourse (11:39 – 54). It tells of a Pharisee who was Jesus' host at a noon meal in his home. It also brings up something that proved problematic for the Pharisee. Jesus did not observe the prescribed purification before the meal (11:37 – 38):

After he had spoken,
a Pharisee invited him to dine at his home.
He entered and reclined at table to eat.
The Pharisee was amazed to see

that he did not observe the prescribed washing
before the meal.

The meal took place in the dining room or dining area. The Pharisee invited Jesus to dine with him *(par' auto)* and Jesus went in to recline at table *(anepesen)*. Like the home of Martha, the Pharisee's home was situated somewhere along the way to Jerusalem (see 9:51, 56, 57; 10:1, 38; 13:22). Again, because the journey to Jerusalem was actually a journey to the ascension and to the fulfillment of Jesus' whole life and mission in God, the precise geographical location is not important. What is important is the home's relationship to the faith journey to God.

The meal was different from all the previous meals in that it took place at noon. The Greek verb used for dining is *aristao,* which refers to the noon meal, or lunch *(ariston)*.[15] Such a lunch could be quite festive. Inviting people for a symposium at noon spoke of considerable wealth and leisure, such as Jesus presupposes in his message to the host for the sabbath dinner in 14:12–14. The Greek term for an evening meal or supper would have been *deipnon* (see 14:12). A *deipnon* could also be simple, but it was usually the principal meal and could be a large banquet or *doche,* as in Luke 5:29 and 14:13.

The meal was held right after Jesus had spoken. It was connected with the long discourse in which Jesus spoke of the divine source of his power to cast out demons, and warned that after being cast out these demons could return. People had to heed the sign of Jonah and make sure that the gospel lamp that had been lit in them would not be extinguished (11:14–36).

Jesus is not referred to by name in the introductory setting, nor is his host the Pharisee. What is important for the story is that Jesus' host be recognized as a Pharisee, a personal symbol of the Pharisees Jesus would address in the discourse. As earlier in the gospel, the Pharisee who hosted Jesus, and the Pharisees he addressed, represented Christians, people who once repented and whose houses had been cleaned but had been newly sullied — worse than before (see 11:24–26). Jesus would address them prophetically, calling them to internal purity, without which external purity is worthless.

**Jesus and the Pharisees**    Jesus' discourse is given in two parts. The first, in which he addresses the Pharisees, is directly related to the Pharisees' observation that Jesus did not observe the ritual purification before eating. For this observation by the Pharisees, Luke was inspired by Mark 7:1 – 7, where the Pharisees and some scribes from Jerusalem observed that Jesus' "disciples ate their meals with unclean, that is, unwashed, hands" (Mark 7:1 – 2). Jesus' message for the Pharisees starts with a prophetic denunciation containing an exclamation, a declaration, another exclamation, a question and an exhortation given in rapid sequence (11:39 – 41):

> The Lord said to him,
> "Oh you Pharisees!
> Although you cleanse the outside of the cup and the dish,
> inside you are filled with plunder and evil.
> You fools!
> Did not the maker of the outside also make the inside?
> But as to what is within,
> give alms, and behold, everything will be clean for you."

In the story's introductory setting (11:37 – 38), Jesus was not referred to by name or title. It is only now in 11:39 that he is introduced as "the Lord" *(ho kurios),* the title so often used in this section of the gospel.[16] The title "Lord" invites the reader to transpose the story's setting beyond the ministry of Jesus into the life of the early church.

When Jesus responded to his host the Pharisee, he addressed him in the plural, "Oh you Pharisees!" In doing this, Jesus used the rhetorical form known as an apostrophe, whose addressee is symbolic and whose message is intended for all who hear it. Later in the gospel, Jesus addressed Jerusalem in the same way,

"Jerusalem, Jerusalem, you who kill the prophets and stone those sent to you . . ." (13:34 – 35).

The externalism of many Pharisees at the time of Jesus and at the time of the beginnings of Christianity gave rise to the stereo-type of the Pharisees that this discourse addresses. It is important to recognize that the stereotype did not apply to all Pharisees, who counted great religious figures among their number. One of these was Gamaliel, who intervened in the Sanhedrin on behalf of Peter and the apostles (Acts 5:34 – 39). Recall, too, that at the time of his conversion, Paul himself was a Pharisee (Acts 26:5), whom no one would have accused of externalism.

Jesus' denunciation was not intended as a blanket condemnation of Jewish Pharisees. In Luke 11, the Pharisaic stereotype applies to members of the Christian community whose externalism recalled that of the Pharisees. As elsewhere in Luke, the designation Pharisee refers not to the Pharisees of the time of Jesus, who were gradually disappearing and being absorbed into rabbinic Juda-ism, but to Christians in the Lukan communities. Jesus' apostrophe "Oh you Pharisees!" was addressed to every Christian. For those to whom it applied, the apostrophe was meant as a prophetic denunciation. For the others, it provided a prophetic warning.

Jesus' references to the cup and the dish are clearly metaphorical because they are set in contrast with the plunder and evil filling the Pharisees. Cleansing the cup and the dish, something the Pharisees insisted upon, here becomes an image for the Pharisees' own exterior purification.[17]

The Lord then raised a question, referring to the maker of the cup and the dish — the potter — but also alluding to God the cre-ator, the divine potter who fashioned the human being out of potter's clay (see Genesis 2:7). Did not the maker of the outside also make the inside? Did not the creator fashion the interior of the human being as well as the exterior?

To ensure that their interior was truly clean, Jesus called on the Pharisees to give alms. For Luke and the early Christians, alms-giving was a source of interior purification. Later in the gospel Jesus exhorts the disciples: "Sell your belongings and give alms.

Provide money bags for yourselves that do not wear out, an inexhaustible treasure in heaven that no thief can reach or moth destroy." (12:33)

After this general introduction come three "woes" (11:42 – 44):

> "Woe to you Pharisees!
> You pay tithes of mint and of rue and of every garden herb,
> but you pay no attention to judgment and to love for God.
> These you should have done, without overlooking the others.
> Woe to you Pharisees!
> You love the seat of honor in synagogues
> and greetings in marketplaces.
> Woe to you!
> You are like unseen graves over which people
> unknowingly walk."

A "woe" or curse is the opposite of a "blessed" or blessing.[18] The first "woe" is not given because the Pharisees pay tithes, but because they do so while disregarding all sense of justice and love for God. They should pay tithes, but only while attending to judgment (justice) and love of God. The second "woe" is closely related to the first. Instead of loving God, their love is focused on seats of honor in synagogues and greetings in marketplaces. As a result, and here is the third "woe," they are like unseen graves, ritually defiling those who unknowingly walk over them. Ironically, the Pharisees' preoccupation with external ritual purification makes them a source of ritual defilement for others.

**Jesus and the Scholars of the Law**    When Jesus finished addressing the Pharisees, one of the scholars of the law replied (11:45), and Jesus directed a second series of three "woes" to the scholars as well (11:46 – 52). The scholar of the law is a lawyer *(nomikos)*, a Pharisee who was a learned teacher of the law of God.[19] Just as

Jesus addressed the Pharisee who was his host as representative of all Pharisees, he addresses the learned teacher as representative of all scholars of the law (11:45–46):

> Then one of the scholars of the law
> said to him in reply,
> "Teacher, by saying this you are insulting us too."
> And he said,
> "Woe also to you scholars of the law!
> You impose on people burdens hard to carry,
> but you yourselves do not lift one finger to touch them."

The scholar of the law, one who made much of being a scholar and teacher, addressed Jesus as "Teacher," an indication of Luke's well-developed sense of irony. The scholar was right. What Jesus said to the Pharisees applied also to them, and *a fortiori*. Hence the new series of "woes." The scholars of the law imposed on others hard burdens that they themselves did not so much as touch. These burdens parallel the demands the Pharisees placed on others for ritual purity while showing no concern for their own interior purity.

This first "woe" was followed up by a second (11:47–51):

> "Woe to you!
> You build the memorials of the prophets
> whom your ancestors killed.
> Consequently,
> you bear witness and give consent
> to the deeds of your ancestors,
> for they killed them
> and you do the building.
> Therefore, the wisdom of God said,
> 'I will send to them prophets and apostles;
> some of them they will kill and persecute'
> in order that this generation might be charged

with the blood of all the prophets
shed since the foundation of the world,
from the blood of Abel to the blood of Zechariah
who died between the altar and the temple building.
Yes, I tell you,
This generation will be charged with their blood!"

As always, the story presupposes a situation in the early church. We note especially how the persecution of "the prophets and apostles" is linked to that of the ancient prophets by their fathers. Like the Pharisees, the scholars of the law were taken up with external and public recognition, and this was well demonstrated by the monuments they erected to the prophets killed by their ancestors. Because of their personal disregard for the law (11:46), they would be held responsible for the crimes of their ancestors. They were not building monuments to the prophets but to the crimes of their ancestors.

The second "woe" was followed by a third (11:52):

"Woe to you, scholars of the law!
You have taken away the key of knowledge.
You yourselves did not enter
and you stopped those trying to enter."

By their interpretation of the law and their imposition of heavy legal burdens, the scholars have made it impossible to gain true knowledge of the law. Jesus' message is aimed at particular members of the Christian community. The reference to "the key of knowledge" presupposes that such a key exists. Some may have taken it away, but Luke's gospel and those who welcomed Jesus' teaching on the way to Jerusalem were restoring the key of knowledge. Jesus' teaching in 11:37–54 is a good example of a teacher, a scholar who was not like the others, offering the key of knowledge, not taking it away.

The story of the noon meal at the home of a Pharisee, which is almost entirely taken up with the long discourse of Jesus, deals with some extremely basic attitudes for the eucharist. Eucharist requires inner purification, not just external ritual. Because eucharist is a sharing event in the community, it calls for giving alms (11:41), for sharing with the poor, both in the eucharistic assembly and outside of it. Such sharing is required by one's sense of justice and love of God, the creator of all.

The story addresses the attitudes and behavior of those who are leaders in the community, here represented by the Pharisees and the scholars of the law. They must be careful to not be a source of ritual defilement for others. It is especially at the eucharist that the church's prophetic teachers must offer the key of knowledge to all, as Jesus, the Lord, did at the luncheon symposium at the home of the Pharisee.

## A Sabbath Dinner at the Home of a Leading Pharisee (Luke 14:1 – 24) [20]

For the first meal on the great journey to Jerusalem, Jesus was welcomed at the home of a woman named Martha. The story tells about the classic tension between the demands of the ministry and those of discipleship. Addressing this tension, Jesus stressed the primacy of being a disciple and attending to the word of the Lord. For the second meal on the journey Jesus was invited to the home of a Pharisee. The story tells how the Pharisee noticed that Jesus did not observe the expected ritual purifications before eating. Jesus responded with his most severe indictment of the Pharisees, especially of their scholars, in the gospel. In his response, Jesus stressed the primacy of interior purity and justice and the love of God over external observance and public display.

We now come to the third meal on the journey, a sabbath meal at the home of a leading Pharisee. This meal shows how those participating in the meal should view themselves and relate to one another. The story is told in four units, dealing first with the right attitude toward sabbath observance (14:1 – 6), then with

*"Blessed is the one who will dine in the kingdom of God."* (Luke 14:15).

appropriate attitudes and behavior for those who were guests at the dinner (14:7 – 11), for the host in issuing the invitations (14:12 – 14), and for those who did or did not accept the invitation (14:15 – 24). The last unit consists almost entirely of the parable of the great feast, a parable about a meal told in the course of a meal. Jesus told the parable in response to a guest who exclaimed, "Blessed is the one who will dine in the kingdom of God." (14:15) This third meal, like the preceding one, shows the influence of the Hellenistic symposium.

---

**Table VI: Setting for the Sabbath dinner at the home of a leading Pharisee**

**13:22 — 17:10   Proceeding to Jerusalem**

Who will recline at table in the Kingdom?   13:22 – 30
Jesus to fulfill his purpose in Jerusalem   13:31 – 35
Sabbath dinner at the home of a Pharisee   **14:1 – 24**
   **14:1 – 6**    Healing a man from dropsy
   **14:7 – 11**   Message to the guests
   **14:12 – 15**  Message to host
   **14:16 – 24**  Response of a guest: "Blessed is the one who
                      will dine in the Kingdom of God"
Demands of discipleship   14:25 – 35
Parables: rejoicing on finding what was lost   15:3 – 32
Parables: entering the Kingdom of God   16:1 – 31
Forgiveness, faith, being a servant   17:1 – 10

---

**Context and Tradition**   The sabbath meal at the home of a leading Pharisee is in the second section of the journey to Jerusalem

(13:22 — 17:10). When the Lord comes in judgment, it will not be enough to have eaten and drunk in his company (13:26). "People will come from the east and the west and from the north and the south and will recline at table in the kingdom of God." (13:29) These words from the section's introductory unit (13:22 – 30) are taken up and developed in the parable of the great feast Jesus gave at the sabbath meal (14:16 – 24).

This section is especially rich in eucharistic teaching. It includes two additional parables with a meal as a main theme. When the Pharisees complained that Jesus welcomed sinners and ate with them (15:1 – 2), Jesus responded with three parables, that of the lost sheep (15:3 – 7), that of the lost coin (15:8 – 10) and that of the lost son (15:11 – 32). Each parable ends with a call to rejoice because what had been lost was now found. In the third parable, the father orders a great feast when the lost son returns. The focus of the parable then shifts to the older brother, who refuses to join in the feast. This echoes Jesus' parable of the great feast — that which those first invited refused to attend (14:15 – 24).

The second meal parable is that of the rich man and Lazarus (16:19 – 31). The rich man remains unnamed, but he is described as dressed in purple garments and fine linen and as dining sumptuously each day (16:19). Lazarus, by contrast, lying at the rich man's door and covered with sores "would gladly have eaten his fill of the scraps that fell from the rich man's table" (16:20 – 21). We are reminded of the younger son, who "longed to eat his fill of the pods on which the swine fed, but nobody gave him any" (15:16).

The story of the rich man and Lazarus also brings to mind Jesus' prophetic plea that the Pharisees give alms so that all things might be made clean for them (11:41). It also develops Jesus' message to the host that he invite not only his friends, brothers, relatives and wealthy neighbors to a lunch or dinner, but the poor, the crippled, the lame and the blind (14:12 – 14).

The story of the sabbath meal in the home of a Pharisee has no parallel anywhere in the New Testament. In its present form it represents a Lukan composition. As on so many other occasions,[21] Luke appears to have gathered a number of traditions that were previously unrelated and adapted them to form the literary unit given in 14:1–24. For parts of the meal, he may also have been inspired by stories told earlier in the gospel in which Jesus healed on the sabbath (see 6:6–11; 13:10–17).

**The Setting: Healing on the Sabbath**  As usual, Luke opens the story by describing the setting, which in this case is very closely related to those for previous meals, especially those shared in the homes of Pharisees (7:36–50; 11:37–54). But as with every other meal in Luke's gospel, there is something unique about this one (14:1–2):

> On a sabbath
> he went to dine at the home of one of the leading Pharisees,
> and the people there were observing him carefully.
> In front of him
> there was a man suffering from dropsy.

The meal was a sabbath meal, and its host was not just an ordinary Pharisee but a leading Pharisee, as seems quite fitting for this third and last of Jesus' meals at the home of a Pharisee. In the same way, the meal at Zacchaeus's home would be hosted not by an ordinary tax collector, but by a chief tax collector (19:1).[22] The setting for the meal is a formal dining room set up with dining couches, some of which were considered places of honor *(protoklisiai,* see 14:7–8), and at least one of which could be considered the last or lowest place *(eschaton topon,* see 14:9–10).

The dining room was in the home of a leading Pharisee (14:1), somewhere along Jesus' journey to Jerusalem (see 13:22; 17:11). The journey is actually referred to, though discreetly, in the story's opening expression, which reads, when rendered literally, "and it happened in his going" *(kai egeneto en to elthein).* Unfortunately, this introductory reference to the journey is usually lost in translation. It is important, however, because it associates what happens in the home with the journey and the fulfillment of Jesus' life and mission.

The dinner took place on a sabbath and is very likely thought of as the meal that opens the sabbath observance after sundown on a Friday evening, following the Jewish reckoning of the day from sundown to sundown. No other indication of time is given or needed. That it was sabbath, however, was critical for the story's first episode (14:2 – 6).

The setting also presents some of the participants at the meal. As usual, there is Jesus, here referred to at first by a pronoun, but soon after by his name (14:3).[23] Besides the leading Pharisee who invited Jesus *(keklekos,* 14:12), the story makes a vague reference to "they" *(autoi)* — "and they were observing him" — and indicates that "a man suffering from dropsy" *(hudropikos,* 14:2) was in front of Jesus.

As the story unfolds, we learn that "they" includes the scholars of the law and the Pharisees (14:3), recalling those Jesus addressed in the previous meal (11:37, 45). The pronoun "they" also includes those reclining *(keklemenoi,* 14:7), that is, the invited guests and Jesus' fellow guests *(hoi sunanakeimenoi),* many of whom must have been Pharisees. But "they" also includes the fellow guest who exclaimed, "Blessed is the one who will dine in the kingdom of God." (14:15) Not all who were observing Jesus carefully were of the same mind.

**Jesus, the Scholars of the Law and the Pharisees**   The story's introductory setting places everyone in position for what follows. A man suffering from dropsy was in front of Jesus. People were observing Jesus closely, as people did in 6:6 – 11: "The scribes and the Pharisees watched him closely to see if he would cure on the sabbath so that they might discover a reason to accuse him." (6:7) Jesus was known to heal people, even on the sabbath (6:10). Would he once again heal on the sabbath? Such was the situation for this first episode (14:3 – 6):

Jesus spoke to the scholars of the law
 and the Pharisees in reply, asking,
"Is it lawful to cure on the sabbath or not?"
But they kept silent;
so he took the man and,
after he had healed him,
dismissed him.
Then he said to them,
"Who among you,
if your son or ox falls into a cistern,
would not immediately pull him out on the sabbath day?"
But they were unable to answer his question.

This is not the first time the issue of Jesus' healing on the sabbath arose,[24] but this is the first time it arose at a sabbath meal. The issue is well expressed in Jesus' question to the scholars of the law and the Pharisees: "Is it lawful to cure on the sabbath or not?" In 6:6 – 11, Jesus asked the scribes and the Pharisees, "I ask you, is it lawful to do good on the sabbath rather than to do evil, to save life rather than to destroy it?" (6:9) They did not answer, understandably, because Jesus had humiliated them before on the very same question (13:17).

After healing the man, Jesus challenged the scholars of the law and the Pharisees concerning their own behavior, as he did in the previous meal story (11:37 – 54). Jesus questioned them directly. Which of them would not rescue a son — let alone a son, even an ox! — on the sabbath day? His question may have been inspired by a similar question in 13:10 – 17: "Hypocrites! Does not each one of you on the sabbath untie his ox or his ass from the manger and lead it out for watering?" (13:15)

Earlier when Jesus asked, "Is it lawful to cure on the sabbath or not?" the scribes and the Pharisees remained silent. Now, when Jesus asked what they themselves would do in a sabbath emergency, "they were unable to answer."

The basis for Jesus' response comes from the nature of a meal and of the sabbath itself. A meal, of its very nature, expresses solidarity among the participants, a solidarity expressed and confirmed in the breaking of bread. But the sharing that flows from solidarity, which Luke calls *koinonia* (Acts 2:42), includes not only food but everything required to ensure well-being, even healing when necessary. Luke affirmed this connection between dining and healing from the start, at the meal in the house of Levi, where Jesus used a healing metaphor to justify dining with tax collectors and those referred to by the Pharisees as sinners: "Those who are healthy do not need a physician, but the sick do." (5:31)

The basis for Jesus' response lies also in the nature of the sabbath, whose observance is not an end in itself. The purpose of the sabbath was to protect life and health (see Mark 2:23–28; Luke 6:1–5). By healing the man suffering from dropsy on the sabbath, Jesus was fulfilling the purpose of the sabbath and expressing meal solidarity with the person who was ill.

**Jesus and the Invited Guests**  The second episode addresses an issue regarding the guests and the choice of places at table. Observing that some of the guests were choosing places of honor, Jesus responded with a parable and a saying (14:7 – 11):

> He told a parable to those who had been invited,
> noticing how they were choosing the places of honor
>   at the table.
> "When you are invited by someone to a wedding banquet,
> do not recline at table in the place of honor.
> A more distinguished guest than you
> may have been invited by him,
> and the host who invited both of you
> may approach you and say,

'Give your place to this man,'
and then you would proceed with embarrassment
to take the lowest place.
Rather, when you are invited,
go and take the lowest place
so that when the host comes to you he may say,
'My friend, move up to a higher position.'
Then you will enjoy the esteem of your companions
    at the table.
For everyone who exalts himself will be humbled,
but the one who humbles himself will be exalted."

The parable contrasts two situations. In the first, a guest loses face. Guests who choose the best places for themselves risk being asked to yield their place to someone of greater dignity and go down to the lowest place. In the second situation, a guest is honored by the host and enjoys the esteem of his companions at table. Guests who take the lowest place are apt to be called to a higher place by their host. Note that for Jesus, it was a bad thing to seek superior position and honor in the assembly. On the other hand, it was a good thing to be honored and esteemed by others (14:8 – 10).

The parable is typical of Luke, the only gospel writer to include Jesus' listeners in the parable: "When you are invited by someone to a wedding banquet. . . ." Recall Luke's little commentary on the Lord's Prayer (11:5 – 13), when Jesus asked, "What father among you would hand his son a snake when he asks for a fish? Or hand him a scorpion when he asks for an egg?" (11:11 – 12) In this meal's first episode, Jesus did the same when he responded to the scholars of law and the Pharisees: "Who among you, if your son or ox falls into a cistern, would not immediately pull him out on the sabbath day?" (14:5)

The saying, "Everyone who exalts himself will be humbled, but the one who humbles himself will be exalted" (14:11), calls to mind Mary's song of praise, the Magnificat (1:46 – 55), the great reversals of the beatitudes (6:20 – 26), as well as Jesus' teaching concerning the greatest in the kingdom (9:46 – 48). The theme would again return at the Last Supper, when the apostles argued about which of them was the greatest (22:24 – 30).

**Jesus and the Host**   In the story's third episode, Jesus addresses the host concerning the guest list and who should be invited to a dinner (14:12 – 14):

> Then he said to the host who invited him,
> "When you hold a lunch or a dinner,
> do not invite your friends or your brothers or your relatives
> or your wealthy neighbors,
> in case they may invite you back
> and you have repayment.
> Rather, when you hold a banquet,
> invite the poor, the crippled, the lame, the blind;
> blessed indeed will you be
> because of their inability to repay you.
> For you will be repaid at the resurrection of the righteous."

Instead of inviting friends, brothers and sisters and wealthy neighbors, the host should invite the poor, the crippled, the lame and the blind. The true family of Jesus includes all who hear the word of God and act on it (8:19 – 21). Jesus' true family — the true Christian family — extends to the poor, the crippled, the lame and the blind, indeed to all who hear the word of God and act on it. In Jesus' parable, the word of God corresponds to the host's invitation to the banquet. Those invited act on it by accepting the invitation and joining their host and the other guests in the banquet.

The poor, the crippled, the lame and the blind are those who have been abandoned by others and are helpless, like Lazarus, languishing on the rich man's doorstep (16:19 – 21), and the man stricken with dropsy, whom others would not help on the sabbath (14:1 – 6). As the anointed one, Jesus had as his mission the bringing of the gospel to the poor, the proclaiming of liberty to captives, the recovery of the sight of the blind and the sending forth of the oppressed into freedom (see 4:18 – 19 and 7:22), thus fulfilling the prophecy of Isaiah (Isaiah 61:1 – 2; 58:6).

Those who must be invited to the dinner are those for whom Jesus was anointed with the Spirit, namely all those for whom the gospel was intended. At the banquet in the house of Levi, we learned that everyone is a sinner. The Pharisees, who thought themselves righteous and protested the presence of sinners, excluded themselves from the dinner. At this sabbath meal at the house of a Pharisee, we now learn that everyone is poor, crippled, lame and blind. Those who think themselves well, represented in Jesus' parable by those who would normally be invited to a dinner, also exclude themselves from the dinner.

Such a dinner is a sign that Jesus was truly the Messiah, the one who was to come. As Jesus told John's disciples, there was no need to look for any other (7:19 – 23). The church must be a source of hope for all, even the least of human beings, and the eucharist must be a visible expression and a proclamation of that hope.

**Jesus and One of the Guests**   One of those at table with Jesus answers with an extraordinary beatitude (14:15):

> One of his fellow guests
> on hearing this said to him,
> "Blessed is the one who will dine in the kingdom of God."

For his fellow guest, Jesus was describing a meal in the kingdom of God, the messianic banquet in which every human kingdom and all human beings would recognize God's sovereignty. At this meal no one would be excluded and everyone would appreciate the value of all the others present. Even the poorest and the most helpless would have an honored place at table in the kingdom of God.

The guest's beatitude raises an important issue, that of the relationship between the eucharist and the kingdom of God. The issue is taken up again at the Last Supper, where Jesus looks ahead to eating and drinking in the fulfillment of the kingdom of God (22:16, 18). The eschatological banquet to which Jesus referred would begin after his passion-resurrection in the Lord's Supper.

A eucharist that reflects what Jesus taught the Pharisees, the scholars of the law, the invited guests and the host reveals the kingdom of God in our midst (17:20 – 21), modest mustard seed though it be (13:18 – 19). Like a leaven, the presence of the kingdom eventually leavens the whole dough (13:20 – 21).

Jesus responded to the beatitude with a parable about a man who gave a great dinner to which those first invited did not come (14:16 – 24):

> He replied to him,
> "A man gave a great dinner to which he invited many.
> When the time for the dinner came,
> he dispatched his servant to say to those invited,
> 'Come, everything is now ready.'
> But one by one, they all began to excuse themselves.
> The first said to him,
> 'I have purchased a field
> and must go to examine it;
> I ask you, consider me excused.'
> And another said,
> 'I have purchased five yoke of oxen
> and am on my way to evaluate them;
> I ask you, consider me excused.'
> And another said,

'I have just married a woman,
and therefore I cannot come.'
The servant went and reported this to his master.
Then the master of the house in a rage
   commanded his servant,
'Go out quickly into the streets and alleys of the town
and bring in here the poor and the crippled,
   the blind and the lame.'
The servant reported,
'Sir, your orders have been carried out
and still there is room.'
The master then ordered the servant,
'Go out to the highways and hedgerows
   and make people come in
that my home may be filled.
For, I tell you,
none of those men who were invited will taste my dinner.' "

Those who were first invited did not accept the master's invitation to the dinner. Their excuses recall the excuses and conditions made by those invited to follow Jesus: "Let me go first and bury my father" (9:59); "I will follow you, Lord, but first let me say farewell to my family at home." (9:61) Accepting the invitation to dinner is accepting the invitation to follow Christ in the community of the church. Refusing the invitation is refusing to follow Christ in the church.

When those first invited excused themselves from coming, the master invited the poor and the crippled, the lame and the blind, the dispossessed among the Jewish people. Then because there was yet room, he opened what had been a Jewish table to the Gentiles. The noon meal at the home of a Pharisee (11:37–54) showed how those who participated in the eucharistic meal had to reach out to those who were poor and helpless. This Sabbath dinner shows how the poor and the helpless must be invited and welcomed at the eucharist itself. In its eucharist, the church reveals its catholicity as it extends hospitality to all.

## Hospitality at the House of Zacchaeus (Luke 19:1 – 10) [25]

Each of the three previous meals on the journey to Jerusalem in some way or other mentions the meal explicitly. The story of Martha and Mary refers to the meal indirectly with the vocabulary of table service *(diakonia, diakonein)*. The two meals taken at the homes of Pharisees refer directly either to eating a noon meal *(aristao)* or to eating bread *(esthio-phagein-arton)*. This fourth meal, taken at the house of Zacchaeus (19:1 – 10), does not refer to a meal explicitly, directly or indirectly, but the meal is clearly implicit.

*"Zacchaeus, come down quickly, for today I must stay at your house."*

(Luke 19:5)

The story of Zacchaeus is a story of hospitality. In the ancient world, as in so much of the world today, hospitality involved offering the guest something to eat. Not to offer someone something to eat meant denying that person hospitality. Not to accept what was offered to eat meant rejecting hospitality. The story of Zacchaeus is consequently best understood as the fourth in the series of meals on the journey to Jerusalem with Jesus the prophet.

Like the other stories, it tells much about eucharist. In particular, it associates eucharistic hospitality with justice, concern for the poor and salvation. The story's message of eucharistic salvation is integrated into the story's very structure. Like Luke's other stories, the story of hospitality at the house of Zacchaeus has an introduction, a body and a conclusion. The introduction includes verses 19:1 – 5, ending with Jesus' statement, "Zacchaeus, come down quickly, for today I must stay at your house." The conclusion opens with this same theme, "Today salvation has come to this house." (19:9 – 10) This type of structure, known as an inclusion, reveals the story's basic theme: having Jesus as one's guest means being host to one's salvation. The same structure is

> **Table VII: Setting for the hospitality at the house of Zacchaeus**
>
> 17:11—19:48  Continuing to Jerusalem
>
>    Gratitude, preparedness   17:11–37
>    Prayer, being like a child, inheriting eternal life, wealth
>       18:1–30
>    Announcement of the passion and resurrection   18:31–34
>    The blind beggar of Jericho   18:35–43
>    Hospitality at the house of Zacchaeus   **19:1–10**
>       **19:1–4**   Zacchaeus wants to see Jesus
>       **19:5**      Jesus must stay at Zacchaeus's house
>       **19:6–8**   Crowd grumbles, Zacchaeus responds
>       **19:9–10** Salvation has come to Zacchaeus's house
>    Parable showing the Kingdom is not about to appear 19:11–27
>    Entry into Jerusalem and cleansing of the Temple   19:28–48

used to great effect in the story of the disciples of Emmaus (24:13 – 35), where the basic theme is the recognition of the risen Lord (see 24:16, 31).

**Context and Tradition**   The story of the sabbath meal at the home of a Pharisee (14:1 – 24) comes quite early in the second part of the journey to Jerusalem (13:22 — 17:10). The story of hospitality at the home of Zacchaeus (19:1 – 10) comes near the end of the next section (17:11 — 19:27), as Jesus was about to begin the final ascent to the Mount of Olives, Jerusalem and the temple (19:27– 45).[26]

The story of Zacchaeus follows and is closely related to the story of Jesus' healing of a blind beggar while approaching

Jericho (18:35 – 43).[27] Indeed, the two stories together respond to the question raised a bit earlier, "Then who can be saved?" (18:26) Jesus had just said, "How hard it is for those who have wealth to enter the kingdom of God! For it is easier for a camel to pass through the eye of a needle than for a rich person to enter the kingdom of God." (18:24 – 25)

The first story shows how the blind man tried to approach Jesus but was prevented by the crowd until Jesus asked that he be brought to him. It then tells how the blind man pleaded with Jesus "Lord, please let me see" (18:41) and how Jesus gave him sight, "Have sight; your faith has saved you." (18:42)

The story of hospitality at Zacchaeus's house is very similar. Like the blind man, Zacchaeus wanted to approach Jesus but was prevented by the crowd. That is why he ran ahead and climbed the sycamore tree. Like the blind man, Zacchaeus wanted to see. More specifically, he wanted to see Jesus.[28] Hosting Jesus, he revealed keen moral vision, showing that he was a true descendant of Abraham. Both stories are about blindness or the inability to see, the gift of sight, and the salvation brought by Jesus.

Like the other meal stories in the journey narrative, the story of hospitality at Zacchaeus's house is a Lukan composition inspired by various traditional elements. The most important of these traditions is the story of Bartimaeus, the blind man of Jericho, as told by Mark in 10:46 – 52.

In Mark, the story of the blind Bartimaeus unfolds as Jesus is leaving Jericho on the way up to Jerusalem. Because Jesus was already leaving Jericho, the story leaves no room for another event there. In Luke, as in Mark, the blind man was sitting by the roadside, crying out to Jesus, "Son of David," while people rebuked him, until Jesus asked that he be brought to him. In all of these and in other details, Luke's closeness to Mark leaves no doubt that Mark was his source.

Luke's story, however, differs from Mark's in three significant details. In Luke, the event does not take place as Jesus was leaving Jericho but as he was approaching it. By modifying Mark's setting, Luke made room for a second story which he patterned on the first. In the second story — that of Zacchaeus, a chief tax collector in Jericho — Jesus had already entered Jericho and was passing through it.

The second detail concerns the names of the personages involved. By dropping Bartimaeus's name — the blind man in Luke remains nameless — and by introducing the name Zacchaeus in the second Jericho story, Luke gave the chief tax collector who could not see Jesus more prominence than the blind man of Jericho. Not being able to see Jesus was far more serious than not being able to see!

The third detail concerns the theme of salvation, an important but somewhat secondary theme in the cure of the blind man, but an absolutely central theme in the story of Zacchaeus, where it is explicitly presented as integral to Jesus' mission.

Taken together, these three modifications suggest that Luke patterned the story of Zacchaeus on key elements from the traditional story of Bartimaeus. It also suggests that in Luke, the story of the unnamed blind man at the entrance to Jericho — Mark's Bartimaeus — was meant as an introduction for the story of Zacchaeus, the little man who overcame every obstacle to see Jesus and welcome Jesus and salvation into his home.

The story of Zacchaeus also is related to the complaint of the Pharisees (15:1 – 2) and Jesus' response to them (15:3 – 32), and it may have been inspired by traditions underlying these as well as by the story of Bartimaeus. When the Pharisees accused Jesus of welcoming sinners and eating with them, Jesus answered with the three parables of the lost and the found (15:3 – 7, 8 – 10, 11 – 32). The story of Zacchaeus is especially evocative of the father's words as he pleads with his older son: "But now we must celebrate and rejoice, because your brother was dead and has come to life again; he was lost and has been found" (15:32). Jesus' last words to Zacchaeus were, "For the Son of Man has come to seek and to save what was lost" (19:10).

**Setting: Jesus and the Chief Tax Collector**  The story begins by indicating the setting, introducing the personages and describing the situation. Told in great detail, the introduction takes up approximately half of the story. The climax comes when Jesus addresses Zacchaeus, who has climbed a sycamore tree to be able to see him. The words of Jesus to Zacchaeus function as a kind of literary hinge that both brings the introduction to a climax and opens the body of the story (19:1 – 5):

> He came to Jericho
> and intended to pass through the town.
> Now a man there named Zacchaeus,
> who was a chief tax collector and also a wealthy man,
> was seeking to see who Jesus was;
> but he could not see him because of the crowd,
> for he was short in stature.
> So he ran ahead and climbed a sycamore tree
> in order to see Jesus,
> who was about to pass that way.
> When he reached the place,
> Jesus looked up and said to him,
> "Zacchaeus,
> come down quickly,
> for today I must stay at your house."

The setting is even more complex than usual for Luke, and it shows a great deal of imagination. First there is the way through Jericho and a sycamore tree close by the way. Then there is the house (19:5, 9) of a man named Zacchaeus. Emphasis is on the home rather than on the dining room, but this is not so unusual because the dining room was the home's main reception room. Besides, for a large dinner the guests easily overflowed from the dining room into the adjacent rooms. This is the case in the parable of the great feast, where the master wanted to fill his whole house with people (14:23).

The Greek word for "home" *(oikos),* which appears in 19:5 and 19:9, can mean "house" — a physical structure; "home" — a place where people dwell; "household" — the people dwelling in a home, including the family and others; and by metonymy "family" — including ancestors and descendants, as in the expression, "the house of David."

In 19:1 – 10, *oikos* refers to Zacchaeus's household, the people dwelling in the home, including the family and others, such as domestics — servants or slaves — and any houseguests. When Jesus declares that today he must stay at Zacchaeus's house he means he must come and stay as a houseguest.

Zacchaeus's family home was situated in Jericho, where the ascent to Jerusalem begins (see 19:11, 28). In Jesus' time, Jericho was a great city with an important Herodian residence. Luke expects everyone to know about Jericho. Had he not had such an expectation he would have introduced the city into the narrative with a more expansive expression, such as "Now as he approached a city named Jericho" or "He came to a city named Jericho," as he did when introducing Nazareth in 1:26 and Bethlehem in 2:4. Instead, he referred to the city quite directly, "Now as he approached Jericho" (18:35) and "He came to Jericho." (19:1)

The participants in the story include Jesus. As in the previous meal (14:1 – 24), Jesus is referred to by name (19:3, 5, 9) but also as Lord (19:8; see 10:38 – 42). In his final statement to Zacchaeus, he refers to himself as the Son of Man. Besides Jesus, there is also the crowd, which prevents Zacchaeus from approaching Jesus (19:3) and which later tries to prevent Jesus from approaching Zacchaeus (19:7).

Then, of course, there is Zacchaeus, the principal personage in the story. Luke does not expect readers to know about Zacchaeus, hence the introduction, "a man there named Zacchaeus" (19:2). Zacchaeus was a chief tax collector. This is the second and last meal story involving a tax collector. The first, which told of the meal in the house of Levi, who was not a chief tax collector or customs officer *(architelones)* but an ordinary one *(telones)*, was the first in the series of meals with Jesus the prophet. This meal in the home of a chief tax collector *(architelones)* is the seventh and last in that series.

In relation to the feast in the home of Levi the tax collector (5:27 – 39), the hospitality meal in the home of Zacchaeus represents a climax. Jesus has gone from the home of an ordinary tax collector to that of a chief tax collector, just as he had gone from two ordinary symposia (7:36 – 50; 11:37 – 54) in the home of an ordinary Pharisee to a sabbath symposium in the home of a leading Pharisee (14:1 – 24).

Zacchaeus was also a rich man. This seems to have been the case with Levi as well, but because his wealth did not figure as an important element in the story, it was not mentioned. Zacchaeus's wealth is central to his story. Because he refers to extortion (19:8), some of the wealth, if not a good part of it, may have been gained through his position as a chief tax collector.

Finally, Zacchaeus was short in stature. The reference to his physical height is significant because it is what prevented him from seeing Jesus through the crowd that surrounded him. In Luke's literary context, the expression "short in stature" may also suggest his being short in moral stature.

Jesus' opening statement to Zacchaeus introduces the main theme of the story. Jesus announced that it was necessary *(dei)* for him to stay *(meinai)* at Zacchaeus's house that day. Luke did not expect the readers to know of Zacchaeus (see 19:2), but he presents him as well-known to Jesus and to the crowd. Jesus called Zacchaeus by name. Had they not known Zacchaeus, the crowd would not have protested Jesus' staying at his home.

**Jesus at Zacchaeus's House**   Jesus' opening words to Zacchaeus bring the introduction to a high point. The story contains Zacchaeus's response, seemingly in the midst of a grumbling crowd. The body of the story concludes with Jesus taking up his opening statement and developing it much further (19:6 – 9):

> And he came down quickly
> and received him with joy.
> When they all saw this,

they began to grumble, saying,
"He has gone to stay at the house of a sinner."
But Zacchaeus stood there and said to the Lord,
"Behold, half of my possessions, Lord,
I shall give to the poor,
and if I have extorted anything from anyone
I shall repay it four times over."
And Jesus said to him,
"Today salvation has come to this house
because this man too is a descendant of Abraham."

The main issue was raised by Jesus when he announced he had to stay at Zacchaeus's house that day (19:5). The Greek verb for "stay," *meno*, means "abide." Jesus would make his home at Zacchaeus's home that day. We already know who Zacchaeus was. The crowd obviously knew him as well and they carried the issue even further: "He has gone to stay *(katalusai)* at the house of a sinner." (19:7) Jesus' relationship to sinners had come up already, indeed several times: in the story of the woman who wept at Jesus' feet (7:36–50), and in Jesus' accepting to dine with sinners in the story of the banquet at Levi's house (5:27–39; see also 15:1–32).

The verb *katalusai*, here translated "to stay," is associated with hospitality—the giving, accepting, refusing and rejecting of hospitality (see 9:12). The noun derived from the verb *kataluo* is *kataluma*, which was prominent in Jesus' birth story. There was no place for Mary and Joseph in the *kataluma* (hospitality) of the city of David (2:7). It reappears at the Last Supper of Jesus with his disciples, which would be taken in a Passover *kataluma* (22:7; see Mark 14:14).

Going to the house of a sinner indicated Jesus' solidarity with a sinner. It was necessary that Jesus join in solidarity with Zacchaeus for him to be saved. The Greek verb "must" *(dei)* in "I must stay at your house" is a very important one in Luke. Literally it means "it is necessary." The verb is used only in connection with Jesus' mission and the great events of salvation. We find it, for example, in Jesus' prophetic announcement of the passion in 9:22. It reappears at the Last Supper, which would be taken on the day it was necessary *(edei)* to sacrifice the Passover lamb (22:7). In the story of Zacchaeus it presents Jesus coming to the house of Zacchaeus as the fulfillment of his mission of bringing salvation to sinners.

After Jesus addressed Zacchaeus, "he came down quickly and received him with joy," that is, he joyfully welcomed him to his home. It was then that the crowds began to grumble, not when Jesus declared his intention to go to Zacchaeus's home, not when Zacchaeus came down to him from the sycamore tree, but after Zacchaeus welcomed Jesus to his home. The situation is very similar to the story of Levi the tax collector, where the Pharisees and their scribes were themselves present at the banquet when they complained that Jesus' disciples were eating and drinking with tax collectors and sinners (5:29 – 30). Those who grumbled that Jesus had gone to stay, that is, accept hospitality, at the house of a sinner were consequently present at the same meal.

The story, however, remains ambivalent about the setting. When Zacchaeus's response to the crowd is introduced, the narrator says that "Zacchaeus stood there and said to the Lord. . . ." It is as though the event were still back at the sycamore tree with Zacchaeus standing before Jesus surrounded by a large crowd. In a sense the crowd is not at the house of Zacchaeus, but from another point of view it is. As in the story of Levi, Luke evokes an early context in the ministry of Jesus but transposes it into a Christian community setting of table hospitality. We are never allowed to lose track of the earlier setting, but neither are we allowed to lose sight of its contemporary and eucharistic relevance.

The post-Easter life of the community is also implied in the use of the title "Lord," first by the storyteller — "But Zacchaeus stood there and said to the Lord" — and then by Zacchaeus, "Behold, half of my possessions, Lord." This is the title Simon Peter used in the story of his call after the extraordinary catch of fish, "Depart from me, Lord, for I am a sinful man." (5:8) Like

Zacchaeus, Simon Peter had been a sinner and was unworthy of the Lord's presence, but this did not deter Jesus, the Lord, from calling him to be a fisher of human beings (5:10). The same title was used both by the narrator and by Martha when she hosted Jesus at her home.

By addressing Jesus as Lord, a Christian title, Zacchaeus gave proof of his conversion. He was a sinner.[29] As a tax collector, he had extorted money from people, but in the measure he did this he fulfilled the law and repaid what he extorted four times over.[30] He demonstrated inner purity and showed concern for justice and love for God by giving alms to the poor, as Jesus had demanded of the Pharisees in an earlier meal (see 11:41 – 42). All this Zacchaeus was already doing. The story thus presents him as a Christian who hosted the assembly and the Lord Jesus at his home.

To indicate what Zacchaeus was already doing, namely, giving alms to the poor and repaying four times what he may have extorted, the present tense is used. Referring to the earlier context at the moment of Zacchaeus's conversion, the present tense can be read as implying the future. In that case it indicates what Zacchaeus intended to do in the future in order to become interiorly pure and to right the wrong for which he has been responsible.

Interpreters often try to resolve this tension between what Zacchaeus intended to do and what he was already doing by opting for one or the other. Because both can be defended, it seems best to let the tension stand as a mark of literary creativity, enabling Luke to evoke an earlier setting in the ministry of Jesus while transposing it into the setting of the early church.

In his answer to Zacchaeus and those murmuring at the fact that he came to Zacchaeus's home, Jesus equated his coming there with the coming of salvation (19:10; see 19:5). For Jesus to come as a guest is for salvation to come as a guest. To be host to Jesus is to be host to salvation.

Zacchaeus was a descendant of Abraham, to whom God in his mercy promised salvation — to him and to his descendants forever (see 1:47, 54 – 55). Zacchaeus was one of those descendants. Indeed, anyone with the right dispositions could be a descendant of Abraham. As John the Baptist told the crowds, there was no point in claiming they had Abraham for a father because "God can raise up children to Abraham from these stones" (3:8). In coming to the home of Zacchaeus and being welcomed there at his table, Jesus was fulfilling the promise of salvation made to Abraham.

The hospitality meal at the home of Zacchaeus was a salvific event, answering the question, "Then who can be saved?" (18:26), or who can "enter the kingdom of God" (18:25)? As a salvific event, the meal in the house of Zacchaeus was equal to dining in the kingdom of God. All who give up everything and follow Jesus "for the sake of the kingdom of God . . . receive an overabundant return in this present age and eternal life in the age to come" (18:28 – 30). In the eucharist they dine in the kingdom that already is in their midst, and in the heavenly banquet they will dine in the fullness of the kingdom.

**Concluding Saying**    Jesus ends his response with a statement (19:10):

> For the Son of Man has come
> to seek and to save what was lost.

Jesus' concluding statement recalls the parables of the lost sheep, the lost coin and the lost son (15:3 – 31), which he addressed to the Pharisees and the scribes when they complained about his welcoming sinners and eating with them (15:1 – 2). It was Jesus' mission to seek and save what was lost. He continues to fulfill his mission in the eucharist, challenging all who murmur, grumble and protest that Jesus joins at table with sinners who have accepted and are accepting his call to repentance.

In the house of Levi, Jesus prophetically challenged those who protested that his disciples were eating and drinking with tax collectors and sinners. To join Jesus at table was to accept his call to *metanoia*. The disciples had no reason to avoid the company of those committed to *metanoia* in Jesus' following.

In the house of Simon the Pharisee, Simon objected that Jesus allowed a sinful but repentant woman to touch him, bathe his feet with tears and dry them with her hair. Seated at the feet of Jesus, the woman was a disciple. Simon needed to be reconciled with one who had repented and been forgiven.

In the house of Zacchaeus, Jesus challenged those who protested his presence as a guest in a tax collector's house. But Zacchaeus repented, and when Jesus accepted his hospitality, salvation came to that house. Jesus' very mission was at stake! No one could stand in the way of Jesus' coming and of his presence there. It was necessary *(edei)* that Jesus come to the house of Zacchaeus. Salvation came of divine necessity.

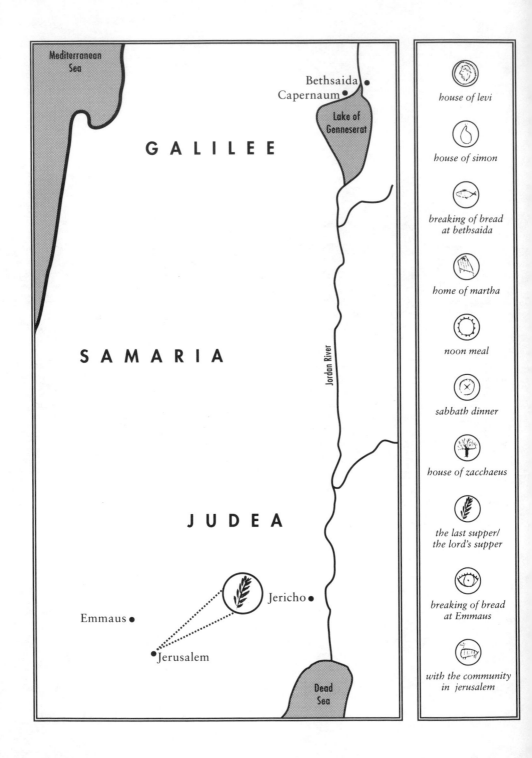

Mediterranean
Sea

GALILEE

Bethsaida
Capernaum

Lake of
Genneserat

SAMARIA

Jordan River

JUDEA

Emmaus

Jericho

Jerusalem

Dead
Sea

*house of levi*

*house of simon*

*breaking of bread
at bethsaida*

*home of martha*

*noon meal*

*sabbath dinner*

*house of zacchaeus*

*the last supper/
the lord's supper*

*breaking of bread
at Emmaus*

*with the community
in jerusalem*

# At Table with Jesus the Christ: The Last Supper

We now come to the Last Supper, the most important meal in Luke's story of the origins of eucharist (22:14 – 38).[1] Jesus referred to the Last Supper's importance while at table with his disciples: "I have eagerly desired to eat this Passover with you before I suffer, for, I tell you, I shall not eat it again until there is fulfillment in the kingdom of God." (22:15 – 16) The Last Supper brings Luke's story of meals to a great climax, recapitulating the basic themes of the seven previous meals, holding them to the light of the passion-resurrection and presenting them in a new Christian synthesis.

In Luke, the story of the Last Supper comes at the beginning of the passion-resurrection narrative, as it does in Mark and Matthew. The story is presented in two sections: Jesus' instructions for preparing the Passover (22:7 – 13) and the supper itself (22:14 – 38). The preparations are intimately linked to the very beginning of the passion and to the plot to have Jesus put to death.

After a brief introduction (22:14), the supper can be divided into three closely related units, beginning with a statement of the supper's nature and meaning (22:15 – 20), and continuing with the implications of Judas's betrayal (22:14 – 30) and Peter's denial (22:31 – 38) for life in the Christian community.

The Last Supper is to the previous meals with Jesus what the passion-resurrection is to his life and ministry. In those earlier meals, as in the rest of his ministry, Jesus challenged everyone to be true to their identity as disciples and followers. In doing this he fulfilled his mission as a prophet "mighty in deed and word before God and all the people" (24:19). But Jesus was more than a prophet. The question of his identity kept coming up at every turn, especially during the Galilean ministry (4:14 – 9:50),[2] until finally Peter declared him the Christ of God (9:20).

The Last Supper was a meal with Jesus the Christ. As presented in Luke 22:14 – 38, it both announces and anticipates the Lord's Supper. It shows how the eucharist is both the memorial of the definitive event of Jesus' life — the passion-resurrection — and the Lord's Supper — a meal shared at the table of the Lord. As such, the Last Supper is far more than the last meal Jesus shared with disciples in the course of his ministry. It draws its meaning from Jesus' mission, fulfilled in the passion-resurrection, and develops the implications of the passion-resurrection for the mission of the church as it continues its earthly journey.

**Context and Tradition**  Jesus' Last Supper and the eucharist are completely bound up with the events of the passion-resurrection, where Jesus the prophet is manifested as the Christ. Peter announced Jesus as "the Messiah [*Christos*] of God" (9:20), and Jesus responded: "The Son of Man must suffer greatly and be rejected by the elders, the chief priests, and the scribes, and be killed and on the third day be raised." (9:22; see 9:44 – 45; 18:31 – 32) Later, when the disciples of Emmaus still thought of Jesus as a prophet, albeit "mighty in deed and word," Jesus responded: "Was it not necessary that the Messiah *[Christos]* should suffer these things and enter his glory?" (24:26)

The Last Supper recapitulates all the previous meals in Luke's story of the eucharist. Like those in the Galilean ministry, it calls the disciples to repentance *(metanoia)* in the following of Christ (5:27 – 39) and to reconciliation in the community of the Twelve (7:36 – 50). It also sends them on mission (9:10 – 17). Like the meals on the journey to Jerusalem, the Last Supper takes up some of the most vital concerns for the life of the community, beginning with discipleship and service (10:38 – 42) and including inner purification (11:37 – 54), attitudes and relationships in the community (14:1 – 24), and some basic ethical implications of solidarity with Jesus the prophet (19:1 – 10).

Theologically, the major difference between the Last Supper and the previous meals is its relationship to Christ's death and resurrection. The Last Supper holds up to the light of Christ's passion-resurrection the many themes already presented, and develops these in relation to the Christian's own dying and rising. At the Last Supper, all of these are presented in relation to the dying and rising of Christ. The result is a dramatically new kind of meal, from both a theological and a literary point of view.

No other meal was given such elaborate preparations (22:7 – 13), and the story of the preparations is critical for understanding the eucharist as a sacrificial meal. As at the breaking of the bread at Bethsaida (9:10 – 17), Jesus is the host at the Last Supper, but while the meal at Bethsaida evoked only a few expressions from the early Christian liturgy of eucharist, the Last Supper includes an entire liturgical narrative, spelling out the nature and meaning of the event as eucharist. The liturgical narrative in Luke's account of the Last Supper is most closely related to the one Paul presented in 1 Corinthians 11:23 – 25, and it appears to reflect that same tradition at a later stage of its development in the church of Antioch.

Following Mark for the meal's setting (see Mark 14:12 – 16), Luke presented the eucharist as a Passover meal, a sacred meal in which the participants share in the great events of salvation, but he arranged the account quite differently and incorporated elements of tradition that are found elsewhere in Mark's gospel. These will require special attention as we examine each of the literary units contributing to Luke's account.

The Israelite Passover was a sacred meal taken in family groups at which Jews remembered the key events in their history that freed them from servitude and made them into a people. Through this annual celebration, Jews became part of a story reaching back to Moses and his experience of the God of Abraham, Isaac and Jacob. In doing so, they claimed their tradition and passed it on to their children. No other feast was so intimately related to their Jewish identity as the people of God.

The Christian Passover also is a sacred meal, taken not in family groups but in Christian communities, remembering the defining event in their history, liberating them from evil and making them a people open to all human beings. Unlike the Israelite Passover, the Christian Passover is celebrated once a week on the first day of the week, and even daily, besides its solemn celebration in the Paschal Triduum. Like the dynamics at work in the Israelite Passover, the dynamics of the Christian Passover enable its participants to situate themselves in their history, one which reaches back to the climax of Jesus' life in the passion-resurrection, and through it to the history that included Moses, Jacob, Isaac, Abraham, and even Adam.

As the first human being, Adam represents the climax of original creation (Genesis 1:1 — 2:4a). As the new Adam, Jesus represents the climax, the first-born, of the new creation (Colossians 1:15), recapitulating and interpreting the experience of the entire human race. In their Passover, Christians claim the story of humanity and pass it on to their children, now neither Jew nor Greek (see Galatians 3:26 – 29). The eucharist is thus a proclamation of the gospel in symbol and deed as well as in sign and word. No other celebration in the life of Christians is more intimately related to their identity.

Like the meal at Levi's house (5:27 – 39) and the three at the homes of Pharisees (7:36 – 50; 11:37 – 54; 14:1 – 14), the Last

Supper reflects the carefully planned format of a Hellenistic symposium. But like the breaking of bread at Bethsaida (9:10 – 17), the meal at the house of Martha (10:38 – 42) and the hospitality extended by Zacchaeus (19:1 – 10), it also reflects the most basic element of a hospitality meal, which was to welcome people on a journey.

As the last meal of Jesus' historical life, the Last Supper is presented as Jesus' farewell discourse or testament.[3] And this is precisely its most basic literary form. The literary elements in the story showing how the farewell discourse is related to the sacred Passover meal, to the Hellenistic symposium and to traditional meals of hospitality are extremely significant, but secondary.

Like all farewell discourses, Jesus' is written to address future audiences, in this case future generations of Christians. Luke's literary presentation of the Last Supper is similar to that in the Gospel of John, where a farewell discourse by Jesus also is found. Of the two, however, Luke is the only one to include an early liturgical narrative of eucharist in Jesus' farewell discourse, showing how the eucharist we celebrate not only recalls a past event but also speaks to the future.

Finally, the story of Jesus' farewell discourse, standing at the head of Luke's account of the passion, resurrection and ascension interprets these historically and theologically and shows how Christians enter into their mystery. The Last Supper is Luke's special prologue for the story of the passion-resurrection.[4] In this respect it is like the infancy narrative, which tells the story of the entire gospel — indeed of the whole of Luke-Acts — in miniature.[5] In the same way, the story of the Last Supper tells Luke's entire story of the passion-resurrection in miniature.

In the earlier meals, we saw how the eucharist unites us in solidarity with Jesus' ongoing ministry as a prophet. In the two post-resurrection meals, we shall see how the eucharist unites us in solidarity with Jesus the Lord. But now, in the Last Supper, we see how the eucharist unites us with Jesus the Christ at the climax of salvation history in the historic event of his dying and rising. Together with the passion-resurrection, and as its memorial, the Last Supper is the epitome of Jesus' life and mission.

## Preparing the Passover (Luke 22:7 – 13)[6]

*"Go and make preparations for us to eat the Passover."*

(Luke 22:8)

"Now the feast of Unleavened Bread, called the Passover, was drawing near, and the chief priests and the scribes were seeking a way to put him to death, for they were afraid of the people." (22:1 – 2) The chief priests and the scribes had their own way of preparing for Passover. Their preparations would succeed, thanks to the complicity of Judas, one who was counted among the Twelve[7] but whom Satan had entered (22:3 – 6).

Jesus too was preparing for Passover, the definitive Passover. "When the day of the Feast of Unleavened Bread arrived, the day for sacrificing [literally, the day it was necessary to sacrifice] the Passover Lamb, he sent Peter and John" into the city to make preparations for Jesus and the apostles to eat the Passover. The two did as instructed (22:7 – 13).

The annual celebration of the Israelite Passover was a memorial of Israel's liberation from slavery in Egypt. By presenting Jesus' Last Supper as an Israelite Passover, the early Christians associated it with Israel's liberation from Egypt. But they also related it to Jesus' death and resurrection, extending the ancient liberation to the entire human race.

The eucharist, which is anticipated in the Last Supper, fulfills the Israelite Passover by extending liberation to all human beings. The Christian Passover retains the Israelite Passover in its background and assumes its meaning and values, but transforms the ancient Passover into a Passover for both Jew and Gentile.

At first, the early Christians who maintained their association with the temple and the synagogue continued to celebrate the Israelite Passover (Acts 20:6), as they did the Israelite feast of Pentecost (Acts 20:16). But little by little, as more and more Christians came from Gentile family backgrounds, the eucharist, a weekly memorial, took the place of the annual memorial of Passover, which was absorbed into the annual Easter Triduum.

The setting for Jesus' Last Supper — and for the passion-resurrection — was the Feast of Unleavened Bread,[8] an annual pilgrimage festival that drew large crowds to Jerusalem. As Luke tells us, the name of the feast was Passover (22:1). The day of the Feast of

Unleavened Bread was when the Passover Lamb was sacrificed in preparation for the Passover meal, which would be taken that night after sundown (22:7 – 8).

Jesus had been teaching in Jerusalem for some time with all the people "hanging on his words" (19:48), even getting up "early each morning to listen to him in the temple area" (21:38). The chief priests and the scribes had been looking for a way to put Jesus to death (19:47), but they had been unsuccessful because of all the people flocking to hear him.

As the feast approached, the crowds became greater and the chief priests and the scribes feared what the people might do. It became even more urgent that Jesus be put to death (22:1 – 2). It was then that Satan entered Judas, one counted among the Twelve, who offered to hand Jesus over in the absence of the crowd (22:3 – 6). Conspiring with the chief priests and the scribes, Judas too was unwittingly preparing the new and definitive Christian Passover, fulfilling the old feast in a Christian Feast of Unleavened Bread (22:1 – 6).

When the day arrived, Jesus sent Peter and John,[9] two of the Twelve,[10] with instructions (22:7 – 13):

When the day of the feast of Unleavened Bread arrived,
the day for sacrificing the Passover lamb,
he sent out Peter and John, instructing them,
"Go and make preparations for us to eat the Passover."
They asked him,
"Where do you want us to make the preparations?"
And he answered them,
"When you go into the city, a man will meet you
carrying a jar of water.
Follow him into the house that he enters
and say to the master of the house,
'The teacher says to you,
"Where is the guest room
where I may eat the Passover with my disciples?"'"

He will show you a large upper room that is furnished.
Make the preparations there."
Then they went off
and found everything exactly as he had told them,
and there they prepared the Passover.

**The Christian Passover**  There is much discussion about whether
Jesus' Last Supper was historically an Israelite Passover meal.
Good reasons have been given both for and against this position.[11]
What is clear is that in Luke, as in the other synoptic gospels, the
Last Supper is *theologically* a Christian Passover meal, and that
would remain true even if it had been taken at a completely dif-
ferent time with no relationship to the Israelite Passover.

The fact that Luke, like Mark and Matthew, introduced an
early Christian liturgical text into the story of the Last Supper
enhances the picture but blurs it at the same time. It enhances it
from a theological point of view, showing how Jesus' Last Supper
was related to the Lord's Supper of the Christian community. It
blurs it from a historical point of view, making it difficult to distinguish between what Jesus actually did and said on the eve of
his death[12] and how the early Christians presented what he did
and said in their story of the Lord's Supper.[13]

In Luke, Jesus' Last Supper is both a historical event and a liturgical event, a pastoral reflection on the the passion-resurrection
and a celebration of Christian faith. Luke's literary synthesis of
the Last Supper — a singular pre-passion event — and the
Lord's Supper — a renewable post-resurrection event — transforms the Jewish feast of Passover and Unleavened Bread into a
Christian event.

As told in the gospels, the Last Supper is both a religious meal
emphasizing God's loving presence among the participants, and a
sacred meal emphasizing God's awesome holiness and transcen-
dance. It consequently is related theologically to the Jewish
Passover, a religious, non-sacrificial meal developed after the
destruction of the temple in the year 70 CE, and to the Israelite

Passover, a sacred, sacrificial meal still practiced in the time of Jesus before the temple's destruction. Celebrating the eucharist as a purely non-sacrifical *seder*[14] (as the Jewish Passover meal has been called from early rabbinical times) falls short of the Christian Passover presented in Luke and the other gospels.

**Someone Carrying a Water Jar**  The preparations for Passover and the Last Supper focus especially on the setting. Jesus sent Peter and John into the city where someone carrying a jar of water would meet them. The Greek text speaks of a "man" *(anthropos)* carrying a water jar. It is often noted that this was most unusual because carrying water was the work of a woman. A man carrying a water jar would have indicated either Jesus' prophetic knowledge of events to come or a prearranged signal.

Luke's use of the generic term *anthropos,* however, requires that we seek another interpretation. In itself the word *anthropos* refers not so much to a male as to a person.[15] In this case, the one carrying the water jar could be either a man or a woman.[16] Even in cases where the distinction is made, as when Lukes gives an example of each, use of the word *anthropos* as the counterpart for *gune* (woman) tones down the distinction.[17] In order to highlight the distinction, another word for "man," namely *aner* would have been used.

Luke respected but did not emphasize the distinction between men and women.[18] We see this very clearly in the story of Peter's denial. In Mark, Peter was approached twice by a maid *(paidiske)* and then by the bystanders (Mark 14:66 – 72). In Luke he was approached first by a maid *(paidiske)*, then by another *(heteros)*, and then by still another *(allos)*. Responding, Peter addressed the maid as *gune* (in the vocative case, *gunai)* and the other two as *anthropos* (in the vocative case, *anthrope)*. The second and third persons coming up to Peter were men, as indicated by the masculine pronouns *heteros* and *allos*. But in relation to the maid, each was simply "another" person.

If *anthropos* could refer to a woman as well as to a man, what are we to make of Jesus' instructions regarding the person carrying the water jar? The key may lie in the literary parallel between the preparations for the Passover and those for Jesus' entry into Jerusalem (19:28 – 34). On entering the village, the disciples would find a tethered colt on which no one had ever sat (19:30). Because there was no way of verifying whether anyone had sat on the colt or not, Jesus' instructions were neither based on a prearranged sign nor intended as authentication of his prophetic knowledge. The purpose of the instructions was literary and theological, showing how Jesus, knowing exactly what was happening, remained in full control of his life and mission while fulfilling his Father's will.

The same is true of the instructions for the Passover supper. There were indeed plots against Jesus' life, but Jesus was not a blind victim of plots and betrayal. Luke shows him fully aware of the course of events and consciously preparing to fulfill the Israelite Passover with the sacrifice of his own life. Jesus was aware of everything, to the most insignificant detail, even how someone carrying a water jar would meet them on entering the city.

**The Guest Room**   The two disciples were to follow the person carrying a water jar into a house and ask where the "guest room" was situated where Jesus might eat the Passover with his disciples. The word often translated as "guest room" is *kataluma,* a term that is actually much broader than "guest room" and that is commonly used in the Septuagint to indicate a place of hospitality for people on a journey. It is the term found in the story of Jesus' birth, where it is usually translated as "inn" (Luke 2:7). The verb form from which *kataluma* is derived, *kataluo,* appears in two of the earlier meal stories (9:12; 19:7), where hospitality was a main issue.

The *kataluma* for Christ's Passover with his disciples (22:11 – 12) would be a large, furnished upper room. Houses in Jerusalem often had a room built as a second story above one of the rooms of the ground floor. Access to the upper room *(anagaion)* was from stairs in the inner courtyard. It is there in the *kataluma,* the upper room *(anagaion)* of a house in the city, that Jesus would take his place at table with the disciples (22:14).

**Sacrificing the Pasch**   The preparations were done on the day of Unleavened Bread, when it was necessary to sacrifice the Pasch (22:7). Many have noted that, contrary to Mark's indication in 14:12, the "first" day of Unleavened Bread was not the day for sacrificing the Passover lamb. The sacrifice was performed on the previous day. The criticism would apply if Mark had followed the Jewish way of reckoning the day from sundown to sundown. But as he did for the day of Jesus' death (15:33)[19] Mark very likely followed the Roman way, in which the day began not at sundown but at dawn or 6 AM. Luke did the same (23:44).[20] Both Mark and Luke were consequently quite correct in stating that "the first day" (Mark) or "the day" (Luke) of Unleavened Bread was the day for sacrificing the Passover lamb.

More important is Luke's reference to that day as the day it was necessary *(edei)* to sacrifice the Pasch. Mark did not mention this note of necessity. Luke introduced it as he so often did,[21] with reference to extremely important events connected with Jesus' mission and the history of salvation.[22] Divine necessity is what moves history from promise to fulfillment. When the hour *(hora)* came, Jesus took his place at table with the apostles. This was the hour for the Passover meal. Using the term *edei* in connection with sacrificing the Pasch, Luke suggested that the sacrifice would be in the person of Jesus and that his personal sacrifice would be shared with the apostles. The hour of the meal was consequently the hour of Christ's personal sacrifice.[23]

**With His Disciples**   Each gospel presented the Last Supper of Jesus as the Lord's Supper of the church, something that is already anticipated in the Supper preparations. In Mark, the two disciples asked Jesus, "Where do you want us to go and prepare *for you* to eat the Passover?" (Mark 14:12) In his instructions, Jesus told them to ask the master of the house, "Where is the guest room where I may eat the Passover *with my disciples?*" (Mark 14:14) Jesus told them to "Make the preparations *for us* there." (Mark 14:15) The disciples had inquired about preparing the Passover *for Jesus,* as though this would not be their Passover as well. Jesus' response made it very plain that this Passover was theirs as well as his (Mark 14:15).

In Luke, Jesus took the initiative from the beginning, telling Peter and John, "Go and make preparations *for us* to eat the Passover." (22:8) We find the same insistence in the message Jesus gave them for the master of the house, "Where is the guest room where I may eat the Passover *with my disciples?*" (22:11) This ecclesial dimension of Jesus' Passover as the Passover of the church is one of the hallmarks of Luke's presentation of the Last Supper.[24]

The preparations for the Passover showed Jesus not as the blind victim of a plot to destroy him but as one whose eyes were open to what was truly happening. He would extend hospitality to others even as it was denied him. Those aiming to take away his life were in fact enabling him to give his life. Jesus himself, the Lamb of God, would be the Passover of the church. And the church, here represented by the Twelve, would join him in his personal sacrifice and fulfill its apostolic mission.

## The Passover (Luke 22:14–38)

*"I have eagerly desired to eat this Passover with you before I suffer."*

*(Luke 22:15)*

Peter and John followed Jesus' instructions, found everything as he had said and prepared the Passover (22:13). When the hour came, everything was ready for Jesus' Passover with his disciples (22:11). The story begins with a brief introduction (22:14):

When the hour came,
he took his place at table
with the apostles.

As earlier with the explicit reference to the day *(he hemera,* 22:1), mentioning that the hour *(he hora)* has arrived calls attention to the moment's importance. When the day of the Unleavened Bread came, when it was necessary to sacrifice the Passover lamb, Jesus sent Peter and John to prepare for them to eat the Passover (22:7). Now on that same day the hour of sacrifice had come, and Jesus reclined at table and the apostles with him (22:14).

There had been meals with tax collectors (5:27–39; 19:1–10), with Pharisees (7:36–50; 11:37–54; 14:1–24), with women (10:38–42) and with a large crowd (9:10–17). This would be a meal with his apostles.

The apostles — the Twelve — also had been with him at Bethsaida when Jesus hosted the 5,000, and had assisted him by serving (9:10–17). On that occasion, he challenged and taught the Twelve (9:12; see 9:1) about their apostolic role (9:10) as hosts with him for the breaking of the bread.

At the Last Supper, Jesus would again be the host, but this time the apostles themselves would be the guests. The Last Supper would be a meal not for the crowds and all those to whom the apostles were sent on mission, but for the apostles themselves. They would be associated with Jesus' deepest intentions as he fulfilled his life mission and as he prepared them for their mission as apostles.

In the preparations for the Passover, the Twelve were referred to as disciples (22:11), highlighting their relationship to Jesus the teacher. And he certainly would teach them in this meal. But now as the Passover meal begins, the Twelve are referred to as the apostles, emphasizing their relationship to Jesus the Christ. It is as apostles that Jesus taught the disciples at the Last Supper.

When the meal is viewed as the Last Supper, the apostles (the Twelve) are seen primarily as disciples — the term most often used to describe Jesus' followers in the gospel, but never in Acts.[25] But when the meal is viewed as the Lord's Supper, the disciples (the Twelve) are presented as as the apostles — a term used a few times in the gospel, but very frequently in Acts.[26] Literarily, the

Last Supper provides a transition from the community of disciples, who followed the Lord Jesus until his passion and death, to the community of apostles, those sent by Christ the Lord after his resurrection.

**The Supper**   We now come to the supper itself, which is dominated by the first part of Jesus' farewell discourse (22:15 – 20). Luke tells Jesus' message in two parts,[27] one presenting the Last Supper and the other the Lord's Supper. As the Last Supper, the meal is related to Jesus' historical life with the community of disciples (22:15 – 18). As the Lord's Supper, the meal is related to Jesus' risen life with the apostolic community (22:19 – 20).

*Last Supper*   Luke's emphasis on this supper as the Last Supper is unique in our gospel literature. In Mark and Matthew, we *sense* that this is to be the Last Supper. We sense this from the context and from Jesus' announcement at the start of the meal that one of those eating with him was about to betray him (Mark 14:17 – 21; Matthew 26:20 – 25). But it is only after citing the liturgical or eucharistic text (Mark 14:22 – 24; Matthew 26:26 – 28) that Jesus refers to this meal as the "last": "Amen, I say to you, I shall not drink again the fruit of the vine until the day when I drink it new in the kingdom of God." (Mark 14:25; see Matthew 26:29)[28]

In Luke, the order in Mark and Matthew is reversed. Jesus speaks of the betrayal (22:21 – 23) after the meal and after citing the eucharistic text (22:15 – 20). He announces at the start of the meal, before giving the eucharistic text, that this meal is to be the Last Supper. The announcement comes in two parallel statements (22:15 – 16, 17 – 18).[29]

The first statement refers to Jesus eating the Passover of suffering with the apostles (22:15 – 16):

> He said to them,
> "I have eagerly desired to eat this Passover

with you
before I suffer
for, I tell you,
I shall not eat it [again]
until there is fulfillment in the kingdom of God."

The second statement refers to Jesus drinking the cup of thanksgiving with the apostles (22:17 – 18):

Then he took a cup,
gave thanks,
and said,
"Take this and share it among yourselves;
for I tell you [that]
from this time on
I shall not drink of the fruit of the vine
until the kingdom of God comes."[30]

Speaking first of eating the Passover, Jesus placed the meal in the context of his historical life when he spoke of his eager desire.[31] It was not that he desired to eat the Passover as such. Jesus had done that many times before, as Luke indicated in the story of Jesus and his parents in the temple: "Each year his parents went to Jerusalem for the feast of Passover, and when he was twelve years old, they went up according to the festival custom." (2:41 – 42) What Jesus desired was "to eat *this* Passover," a Passover defined by his imminent suffering *(pathein)*,[32] and he desired to eat it *"with you."*

In the same statement, Jesus also oriented the meal toward the future, when he would again eat the Passover with his apostles, in fulfillment of the kingdom of God. This supper Jesus was now sharing with the apostles was surely the Last Supper of Jesus' historical life, but in it Jesus looked forward to that supper's fulfillment after his resurrection in the kingdom of God.

In the second statement, concerning drinking the cup, Jesus also placed the meal in the context of his historical life, but obliquely. Jesus' desire to eat this Passover was now being ful-filled, and so he gave thanks. The cup Jesus drank was the cup of suffering from which he prayed to be spared but which he accepted should it be his Father's will (22:42). Jesus asked his apostles to share his cup of thanksgiving even as they shared in the Passover. As a community they were to join him in drinking from the cup of suffering.

In the same statement Jesus oriented the cup to the future, when he would drink again of the fruit of the vine in the king-dom of God. This was surely the last time Jesus would drink the cup during his historical life, but he would drink it again after the resurrection with the coming of God's kingdom in the life of the church.[33]

Eating the Passover and drinking the cup, Jesus looked for-ward to fulfillment in the kingdom of God, to that day when someone would be able to say not just "Blessed is the one who will dine in the kingdom of God" (14:15), but "Blessed is the one who now dines in the kingdom of God."

Fulfillment in the kingdom of God began with the life of the apostolic church but it did not come all at once. Perfect fulfill-ment lies on the horizon of history, where its vision defines the mission of the church. For this the church prayed and continues to pray: "Thy kingdom come" (11:2). For this, the church cele-brates the eucharist.

*Lord's Supper*  After presenting the Last Supper in two parallel units packed with theological meaning, Jesus' discourse moves on to the Lord's Supper. Like the Last Supper, it is told in two units rich in theology. Luke's statements about Jesus' last Passover and about the cup of the Last Supper are very significant in them-selves, situating the Last Supper both in historical and in eschato-logical perspective. As major statements concerning the most basic intentions of Jesus, they deserve close study and reflection. But significant as they are in the context of the Last Supper, they are but an introduction for the Lord's Supper.

To bring out the uniqueness of Passover, the youngest child at the Jewish *seder* asks, "Why is this night different from all other nights?" To bring out the uniqueness of Jesus' last Passover, we need to ask, "Why was this Passover like no other Passover?" The answer is clear: "Because this is the Passover in which Christ offered himself to save all of us from death."

At the first Passover, God saved his people from death. In its celebration, the Jewish people commemorate this great act of salvation. At his last Passover, Jesus saved the whole world from death. In its celebration, Christians commemorate his act of universal salvation. They do this in the Lord's Supper, fulfilling Jesus' last Passover together with the promise inherent in the first Israelite Passover. The first Passover led to the covenant at Sinai and the creation of the Israelite people. The Lord's Supper celebrates the new covenant and the creation of the Christian people.

The Lord's Supper recapitulates the Last Supper in a memorial of Christ's death and resurrection and as a celebration of his risen life. Like Luke's two-part presentation of the Last Supper, the Lord's Supper's is also told in two parts: one presenting the bread-body of Christ, the other the cup-covenant in Christ's blood. Both parts are from a liturgical formula well known to Luke's readers from their weekly celebration of the eucharist, as it had been in an older and slightly different version in the Christian communities who received it from St. Paul (1 Corinthians 11:23–25).

The first part of the liturgical formula presents what Jesus did and said in relation to the bread (22:19):

> Then he took the bread,
> gave thanks,
> broke it,
> and gave it to them,
> saying,
> "This is my body,
> which will be given for you;
> do this in memory of me."[34]

The second part of the liturgical formula presents what Jesus did and said in relation to the cup (22:20):

> And likewise the cup
> after they had eaten,
> saying,
> "This cup is the new covenant in my blood,
> which will be shed for you."

Each of the two parts opens with the conjunction "and *[kai],*" presenting them literarily as a continuation of the Last Supper and connecting the two parts with one another. Luke introduced the verb "which will be given *[didomenon],*" which is absent in the formula given in 1 Corinthians 11:24, "This is my body that is for you." Luke's reading, "which will be given for you," historicizes the eucharistic text, connecting Christ's giving of his body *(soma)* with the passion. The same is true regarding the cup, "which will be shed for you." The Lord's Supper, a liturgical event in which Jesus asks that those present "do this in memory of" him, is thus solidly anchored in the historical event of the Last Supper and the passion.

The first part of the liturgical formula focuses on the bread and presents the Lord's Supper as an act of thanksgiving to God and as an act of personal sharing. Both aspects, Christ's thanksgiving and Christ's sharing, constitute Christ's body. Commanded by Christ to do this in his memory, the participants are asked to renew Christ's thanksgiving to God as well as Christ's sharing among themselves. The two, thanksgiving and sharing, are inseparable. There is no genuine thanksgiving without sharing, and no real sharing without thanking God.

The tendency today is to interpret the proclamation "This is my body" from the experience of the liturgy, in which the presider holds the bread in his hands while saying, "This is my body." In that context, "this" refers directly to the bread and indirectly to what the bread symbolizes. In the literary text of Luke 22:19, as in the other New Testament texts for the Lord's

Supper, the word "this" refers to "he took bread, gave thanks, broke it, and gave it to them." In this context, "this" refers directly to Christ's *action,* to what he did, and indirectly to the whole event. When Christ tells the apostles to do this in memory of him, he commands them to do what he has done. When they do this in the Lord's Supper, fulfilling his command, he becomes present, thanking God and offering himself in and through their thanksgiving and self-offering.

The liturgical proclamation, "This is my body, which will be given for you," recalls the words of Christ offering himself, and speaks the words of the church associating itself with Christ's offering and making his offering present sacramentally. The body given is that of Christ. It is also that of the church, the sacrament of the body of Christ.

The eucharist is the Passover of Christ and the Passover of the church. It is the Passover of Christ in, with and through the temporal sacrifice of the church. It is also the Passover of the church through, with and in the eternal sacrifice of Christ.

The second part of the liturgical text focuses on the cup: "and likewise the cup after they had eaten" (22:20a). In Mark and Matthew, the cup formula parallels the bread formula: "Then he took a cup, gave thanks and gave it to them (Mark 14:23; Matthew 26:27). In Luke, as in Paul (1 Corinthians 11:25), this part of the formula is in summary form. Luke refers to the cup action by comparing it to the bread action: "and likewise the cup." He does not spell it out. In Luke, as in Paul, the emphasis is not so much on the action as on its meaning, as proclaimed by Christ: "This cup is the new covenant in my blood, which will be shed for you." (22:20b)

The first part of the formula, "This cup is the new covenant in my blood," is quite different from its parallel for the bread, "This is my body." The formula for the bread does not mention bread, while the formula for the cup does mention the cup, "this cup." However, the term "cup" does not refer to a physical object, as one might conclude from the experience of the liturgy, where the presider holds the cup while speaking the words, "Take this, all of you, and drink from it: This is the cup of my blood, the blood of the new and everlasting covenant. It will be shed for you and for all so that sins may be forgiven. Do this in memory of me." In Luke the "cup" refers to an *event,* to Christ taking the cup, giving thanks and giving it to the apostles. That *event* is the new covenant in Christ's blood, establishing a new set of relationships among the participants in the life of Christ.

The term "covenant" refers to the historic event at Mount Sinai when the tribes of Israel were formed into one people (Exodus 24:1 – 11). That covenant was in blood, the blood of animals that were offered in sacrifice. For Israelites and other ancient peoples, blood was the symbol of life. Sprinkling the blood of the sacrificial animals on the altar and on the people symbolized the union of God and people, now sharing in the one life that was offered to God. So it is that the covenant at Sinai formed the people of Israel into a people of God.

The cup of the Lord's Supper was not just a renewal of the Sinai covenant. It was "the new covenant," a reference to Jeremiah 31:31 – 34, which announced "a new covenant" with the law inscribed not on tablets of stone but on people's hearts and with God forgiving the people's sins. The "new covenant" established by Christ would not be in the blood of animals, but in his own blood, "which would be shed for you." It would be established in the sacrificial blood of Christ, the Passover Lamb (see 22:7).

When at the Lord's Supper Christians do what Christ did — namely, take the cup, give thanks and give it to one another — they join Christ in offering their own blood for others. They renew the new covenant in Christ's blood. They forgive one another, extend peace to one another and strengthen the covenant relationship that makes them one people of God.

Christ's taking the cup after they had eaten corresponds to the form followed in a symposium, where the cups were given to the participants and wine was poured once the table had been cleared after the meal. The cup formula in Luke thus provides an excellent transition to the remainder of the discourse. There was no need to repeat the command, "Do this in memory of me," as we find in Paul. In the rest of the discourse, all of which is part of the post-prandial cup, Jesus would spell out very concretely what it meant to "do this in memory of me."[35]

The second part of the discourse (22:21 – 30) takes up the matter of betrayal. Like the supper, it is divided into two parts, the first referring to the Last Supper (22:21 – 23), and the second referring to the Lord's Supper (22:24 – 30).

**Betrayal at the Last Supper**   After presenting the Lord's Supper (22:19 – 20), Jesus returns to the Last Supper, where one of the Twelve, one of those at table with him, was about to betray him. This segment of the discourse, which is quite short, begins with Christ announcing the betrayal and concludes with the reaction of those at table (22:21 – 23):

> And yet behold,
> the hand of the one who is to betray me
> is with me on the table;
> for the Son of Man indeed goes
> as it has been determined;
> but woe to that man by whom he is betrayed."
> And they began to debate among themselves
> who among them would do such a deed.

The difference between Luke's account and the one in Mark 14:18 – 21 is very striking. In Mark, Christ began by announcing the betrayal, "Amen, I say to you, one of you will betray me, one who is eating with me." The apostles, who had just learned of the betrayal and that the betrayer was actually eating with Christ, then began to be distressed and to ask, "Surely it is not I?" Jesus further announced that the betrayer, who was eating with him, was now dipping with him into the dish, thereby identifying the betrayer. Jesus then commented on the event, focusing on the fate of the betrayer and the enormity of the crime.

In Luke, Christ presumes the apostles know about the coming betrayal and announces that the hand of the betrayer is with him on the table, an indication almost as vague as Mark's reference to "one who is eating with me."[36] Unlike Mark, however, Luke makes no effort to dispel the vagueness. In Luke, Christ comments on the evil of the betrayal but without specifying who the betrayer might be. Hence the apostles' reaction. Knowing that there was a betrayer in their midst, but not knowing who it was, they "began to debate among themselves who among them would do such a deed."

By comparison with Mark, Luke deemphasizes the role of the betrayal and of the betrayer at the Last Supper. Just as the Last Supper (22:15 – 18) introduced the Lord's Supper (22:19 – 20), the betrayal at the Last Supper (22:21 – 23) points ahead to the betrayal at the Lord's Supper (22:24 – 30).

**Betrayal at the Lord's Supper**   The betrayal at the Last Supper ended with the disciples debating among themselves who could possibly do such a thing. As the betrayal at the Lord's Supper opens, the apostles are continuing the debate (22:24):

> Then an argument broke out among them
> about which of them
> should be regarded as the greatest.

The statement echoes a nearly identical statement in 9:46: "An argument arose among the disciples about which of them was the greatest."[37] Here in Christ's discourse, the argument responds to the previous debate (22:23) over which of them could possibly betray Christ. The debate at the Last Supper is resolved at the Lord's Supper: The one who betrays Christ is the one who seeks to be regarded as the greatest.

Christ then addresses this new betrayal in the life of the church. First he speaks to the apostles about the exercise of authority and about the quality of service in the community (22:25 – 27):

He said to them,
"The kings of the Gentiles
lord it over them
and those in authority over them
are addressed as 'Benefactors';
but among you
it shall not be so.
Rather,
let the greatest among you
be as the youngest,
and the leader as the servant.
For who is greater:
the one seated at table
or the one who serves?
Is it not the one who is seated at table?
I am among you as the one who serves."

Christ begins by evoking the figure of people in the world who seek to be regarded as the greatest, namely the kings of the Gentiles and others in authority.[38] He then warns the apostles and the church that their way of ruling and exercising authority is not consistent with life in the body of Christ (see 22:19) and in the new covenant in his blood (see 22:20). In the apostolic community, the greatest must consider themselves the least, like the little child in 9:47–48, and the leaders must have the attitude of the servant *(ho diakonon)*. Jesus dealt with this attitude earlier in a parable on the place of servants who ought not to seek gratitude merely for fulfilling their duty.[39]

As in Jesus' parable on the attitude of the servant (17:7–10), Christ now brings up a rhetorical question about the one who is greater. Is it the one who is seated at table or the one who serves? The expected response is that it is the one who is seated at table. Christ emphasizes the expected answer, "Is it not the one seated at table?" But that is not the real answer. Life in the body of

Christ, in the new covenant, indeed in the kingdom of God, reverses many expectations.

Jesus presents himself as having the attitude of a servant: "I am among you as [the] one who serves *[ho diakonon]*." At the Last Supper, Jesus was among the apostles as the one who serves. At the Lord's Supper, the proper apostolic attitude was that of servant. Otherwise, those at the Lord's Supper would not be doing what Christ did in memory of him.

Christ then addresses the apostles on their place and role in the kingdom (22:28–30):

> It is you who have stood by me in my trials;
>
> And I confer a kingdom on you,
>
> just as my Father has conferred one on me,
>
> that you may eat and drink at my table in my kingdom;
>
> and you will sit on thrones
>
> judging the twelve tribes of Israel.

The Twelve have not broken solidarity with Christ. They have remained with him in his trials, in the great tests *(peirasmoi)*[40] with which his historical life ended and through which his risen life began. From the perspective of the Lord's Supper, Christ looks back to the events of the passion. In Mark, all of the disciples abandoned Christ when Judas came with an armed crowd to seize him (Mark 14:50; see also Matthew 26:56). In Luke, the apostles never abandon Christ. Judas, who was counted among the Twelve, did more than abandon him, but the Twelve—that is, the church in its apostolic foundations—stood with him.

Christ remained faithful to his Father to the end, and so the Father conferred the kingdom on him. Because the apostles remained faithful to Christ in the test, Christ conferred the kingdom on them. Passover was fulfilled in the kingdom of God, and Christ again was eating it at the table of the new Passover and drinking of the fruit of the vine (see 22:15–18). It is because the apostles remained faithful to Christ that he conferred the kingdom on them, that they might eat and drink at the table in Christ's kingdom (see 14:15).

It is because they remained faithful to Christ that the apostles would judge "the twelve tribes of Israel," now fulfilled and transformed into the church, whose story is told in Luke's second volume, the Acts of the Apostles. In fulfilling the twelve tribes of Israel, the church would include Christians of Gentile origin as well as Christians of Jewish origin. But in judging, the apostles would not act like the kings of the Gentiles, lording it over others (22:25), but like Christ, the one who serves (2:26–27).

The third part of Christ's farewell discourse (22:31–38) takes up the denial of Christ. Like the first part on the supper itself and the second on the betrayal, it is divided into two parts, the first referring to the Last Supper (22:31–34), and the second referring to the Lord's Supper (22:35–38).

**Denial at the Last Supper**  In Mark, Christ announced Peter's denial after the supper at the Mount of Olives (Mark 14:26, 27–31; see also Matthew 26:30, 31–35). Luke made the announcement part of Christ's discourse at the Last Supper. After addressing the matter of betrayal at the Lord's Supper (22:24–30), Christ returned to the Last Supper and announced that Simon, whom he named Peter (6:14), was about to deny so much as knowing him (22:31–34):

"Simon, Simon,
behold Satan has demanded to sift all of you like wheat,
but I have prayed
that your faith may not fail;
and once you have turned back,
you must strengthen your brothers."
He said to him,
"Lord,
I am prepared to go to prison
and to die with you."
But he replied,

"I tell you, Peter,
before the cock crows this day,
you will deny three times
that you know me."

The discourse gives Simon Peter's denial more prominence than it did Judas' betrayal, which it rather downplayed. Recall that Judas was not named or identified and that the passage ended with the apostles debating who among them would do such a deed. For the denial, Simon is addressed directly by Christ, signalling an important announcement and indicating special concern by repeating the name, "Simon, Simon."[41]

"Satan has demanded to sift all of you [plural] like wheat but I have prayed that your [singular] faith may not fail." (22:31–32) Peter would turn away, but he would turn back. Thanks to Christ's prayer, Peter's faith would not fail, and thanks to Christ's special commission that he strengthen the apostolic community, its faith would not fail either.

The denial announcement looks to the future in the life of the church, as did the betrayal announcement. The greater prominence given the denial stems from Simon Peter's future role among the apostles.

Peter protested with a prayer of commitment and solidarity: "Lord, I am prepared to go to prison and to die with you." (22:33)[42] But Christ assured him that before the cock crowed that day, Peter would have denied knowing him not once, but three times.[43]

**Denial at the Lord's Supper**   The Lukan communities were facing difficult times, in which they too would be tempted to deny Christ. After addressing the denial at the Last Supper (22:31–34), Christ addressed the denial at the Lord's Supper, the ongoing denial in the life of the church (22:35–38):

He said to them,
"When I sent you forth

without a money bag or a sack or sandals,
were you in need of anything?"
"No, nothing,"
they replied.
He said to them,
"But now one who has a money bag should take it,
and likewise a sack,
and one who does not have a sword
should sell his cloak and buy one.
For I tell you
that this scripture must be fulfilled in me,
namely, 'He was counted among the wicked';
and indeed what is written about me
is coming to fulfillment."
Then they said,
"Lord, look,
there are two swords here."
But he replied, "It is enough!"

Christ began by recalling how in the past he sent them out as the seventy[-two], asking them to carry no money bag, no sack, no sandals (10:4). That had been a change from the early apostolic days when he sent them out as the Twelve: "Take nothing for the journey, neither walking stick, nor sack, nor food, nor money, and let no one take a second tunic (9:3).[44] The instructions for the seventy[-two] said nothing about the walking stick or food.

By Luke's time, the earlier adaptations were not enough. In the future, "one who has a money bag should take it and likewise a sack." But there was an even bigger change: "One who does not have a sword should sell his cloak and buy one." (22:36) Earlier, when they followed Christ's instructions as the seventy[-two], they had been in need of nothing. They should therefore have confidence that it would be the same with Christ's new instructions.

The Lukan communities were moving into times of persecution. Christ "was counted among the wicked" in fulfillment of the scriptures (see Isaiah 53:12), and they who joined him in the new Passover, offering their lives with him, needed to stand firm under persecution. That also is how they would do what Christ did in memory of him. Failure to stand firm with him would be to deny him.

More particularly, denial would come by misconstruing the instructions Christ gave to purchase a sword. Jesus' sword was symbolic, like the sword of the Lord in Ezekiel 21. A sword is an instrument of slaughter. In Ezekiel, the sword of the Lord is a symbol of divine judgment and punishment.

Christ asked those who were to "sit on thrones judging the twelve tribes of Israel" (22:30) to purchase a sword in view of the kingdom conferred upon them (22:29). That sword was the word of God (see Ephesians 6:17), like the two-edged sword of discernment (Hebrews 4:12), and the two-edged sword coming from the mouth of the Son of Man (Revelation 1:16; 1:12, 16), and that of the King of kings and Lord of lords (Revelation 19:15).

To fulfill their mission as servants and judges in the new covenant, the apostles had the sword of the word of God. By rejecting Christ's symbolic sword and turning instead to a physical instrument of violence and death, the church would deny Christ and fail in its mission of the word of God.

When the apostles responded, "Lord, look, there are two swords here," Christ brought the discourse to a close: "It is enough." Christ had already said what was needed, and there was no point in continuing.

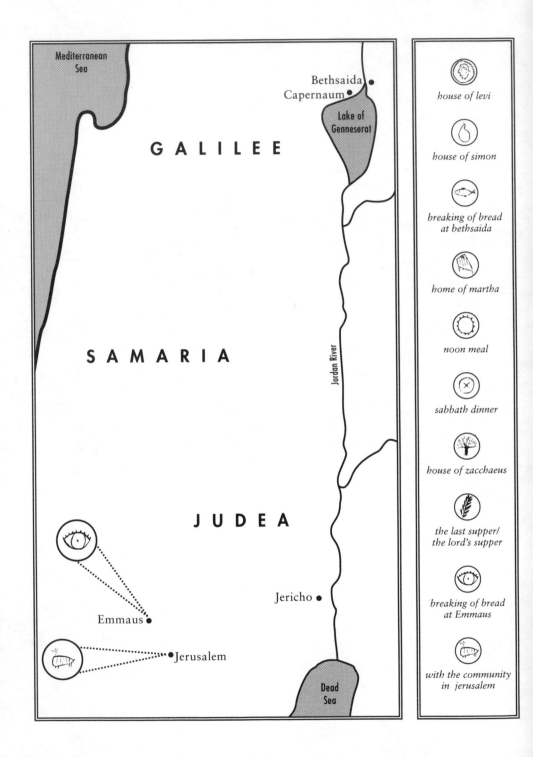

*Chapter V*

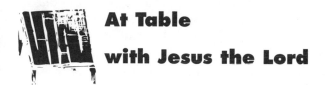

# At Table
# with Jesus the Lord

$T$he Last Supper was the last and greatest of Jesus' prophetic meals, recapitulating the seven meals with Jesus the prophet and bringing Luke's story of the origins of eucharist to a great climax. The story presented the Last Supper as a meal with Jesus the Christ, a title associated with Jesus' historic mission and its fulfillment in the passion-resurrection. The Last Supper related the eucharist to an event, Christ's passion-resurrection. It showed how the eucharist, as the memorial of that event, makes the event present whenever Christians do what Christ commanded them in memory of him (Luke 22:19).

While recapitulating Christ's life with his disciples and the Twelve, the Last Supper also pointed to the Lord's presence with them after the resurrection. As the Lord, Jesus would be present in the apostolic church. Luke showed this by presenting the Last Supper also as the Lord's Supper, a meal with the Twelve, his apostles and disciples (22:16, 18), on whom he conferred the kingdom of God (22:29–30).

The story of the Last Supper placed great emphasis on how the supper was really the last in Christ's historical life. It also looked beyond the events of his passion-resurrection to the fulfillment of his mission in the kingdom of God. It did this by giving the liturgical text from the Lord's Supper as celebrated at Antioch and in the many communities sprung from its missionary activity throughout much of the eastern Mediterranean.

Viewed as the Last Supper, Christ's Passover with his disciples marked the end of an era whose covenant was sealed in the blood of animal victims. Viewed as the Lord's Supper, it announced the beginning of a new era with a new covenant in Christ's blood.

Luke's story of the origins of the eucharist concludes with two additional meals, one taken at Emmaus with two disciples Jesus met on the way (24:13–35) and the other in Jerusalem with the whole community gathered with the Eleven (24:36–53).[1] What distinguishes these two meals from all the others is Jesus' presence as risen Lord. The Last Supper presented the eucharist in relation to the historic event of Christ's passion-resurrection. As such, the eucharist is the memorial of Christ's passion-resurrection. The two post-resurrection meals present the eucharist in relation to Jesus' ongoing state as risen Lord. As such, the eucharist is the Lord's Supper.

The two stories dwell on the Lord's presence with the apostles and disciples and on the implications of his presence as risen Lord. Because the risen Lord is Lord of all (Acts 10:36), the eucharist is intimately related to the church's universal mission and the welcome it must extend to all, irrespective of race, sex, ethnicity, nationality or social class. Because the risen Lord transcends mortal existence and its historical limitations, he is present to the church in symbol or sacrament in a meal taken in solidarity with him.

These stories also stress the community's need to break bread together as Jesus broke bread with the Twelve. They present the eucharist as "the Breaking of the Bread," a name emphasizing the sharing aspect of the eucharist. The name first appears in Luke 24:35, in the summary-conclusion of the Emmaus story, but it recalls the breaking of bread in 9:10–17 and the Last Supper (22:19), and points toward the life of the church in the Acts of the Apostles (see Acts 2:42–47; 20:7–12; 27:33–38).

## The Breaking of the Bread at Emmaus (Luke 24:13–35)²

Luke's story of the origins of the eucharist would not be complete without speaking to the fulfillment of the eucharist in the kingdom of God. And so, after the seven meals with Jesus the prophet and the Last Supper with Jesus the Christ, Luke tells the story of two meals with Jesus the Lord. The first is the incomparable story of the disciples of Emmaus. The story is about two disciples who left Jerusalem discouraged and met Jesus, now risen, but were unable to recognize him. It tells how Jesus opened their minds to understand the scriptures, and opened their eyes to recognize him in the breaking of the bread.

*"Was it not necessary that the Messiah should suffer these things and enter into his glory?"*

(Luke 24:26)

As in the previous meal stories, the setting in time and place and the various personages are integral elements. We shall consequently pay close attention to these and the way they are presented as the story unfolds.

The story is about "two of them" (24:1), two of the community of disciples referred to in the story of the women who visited the tomb (24:9). That there were two is significant, recalling how Jesus sent out the seventy[-two] "ahead of him in pairs to every town and place he intended to visit" (10:1). Besides the two, there is Jesus the Nazarene, "a prophet mighty in deed and word" (24:19), the Messiah (24:26) and the Lord (24:34), as well as "the eleven and those with them" (24:33).

The event took place "on that same day" (24:13), that is, "on the first day of the week" (24:1), the day the women went to the tomb, failed to find the body of the Lord Jesus and received the message of the resurrection (24:1–11). After hearing the women, some did not believe their story, but Peter went to the tomb, and seeing the burial cloths alone he "went home amazed at what had happened" (24:12).

The story is situated on a journey from Jerusalem to Emmaus, at Emmaus itself and then back in Jerusalem with the community. On the way to Emmaus, a village 60 *stadia* — about seven miles — from Jerusalem, the two disciples engaged in dialogue with Jesus, but without recognizing him (24:16–27). It was only at Emmaus, after Jesus agreed to stay with them, that they recognized him in the breaking of the bread (24:28–31). Back in Jerusalem, the two disciples rejoined the Eleven and the others to be greeted with the announcement that the Lord was risen and had appeared to Simon (24:32–35).

**Context and Tradition**  The story of the disciples of Emmaus is one of three stories in Luke's resurrection narrative (24:1–53). The first tells of two visits to the tomb, one by a group of women followers (24:1–11) and one by Peter (24:12). The second story is that of the disciples of Emmaus (24:13–35). The third tells of an appearance to the community in Jerusalem (24:36–49). Each story is quite distinct from the others, but the three are very closely related regarding time, place and personages. All three take place on the same day, in or near Jerusalem, and all involve personages from the same community of disciples.

The immediate context for the story of Emmaus is that of the visits to the tomb (24:1–12). At early dawn, "on the first day of the week," Mary Magdalene, Joanna, Mary the mother of James, and some others (24:11)[3] went to the tomb and found the stone rolled away, but when they entered "they did not find the body *[soma]* of the Lord *[Kurios]* Jesus" (24:1–3). Many of the expressions used in the story evoke the resurrection.

"The first day of the week," literally "day one of the week," recalls day one of creation in Genesis 1:1–5, as it does elsewhere in the New Testament. The events in Luke 24:1–53, from the women's visit to the tomb to the ascension, tell the beginning of the new creation.

The word "body" (in Greek *soma)* normally refers to a living person, not to a corpse (for which the Greek word would be *ptoma)*. Even when it does refer to a dead body, as when Joseph of Arimathea took "the body" of Jesus down from the cross and the women saw where Jesus' "body" was laid, the word "body" connotes the living person of Jesus. Luke 24:3 leaves no room for hesitation about this because "the body" is that "of the Lord Jesus." For one who is alert to the meaning of these expressions, a question immediately comes to mind: What led the women to seek the body of the risen Lord in the tomb? They might have expected to find the corpse of Jesus of Nazareth, but not the body of the Lord Jesus!

The reader's reaction is soon confirmed by two men in dazzling garments who appeared to the women when they entered the tomb: "Why do you seek the living one among the dead?" (24:5) This first question brings up another: If the body of the Lord, the living one, is not to be found in the tomb among the dead, where is he to be found? The answer to this second question is in the story of Emmaus.

The above observations on the women's visit to the tomb show that Luke changed the purpose of the story as told by Mark. In Mark, the visit to the tomb formed the conclusion of the gospel. Luke transformed it into an introduction for the story of Emmaus and the rest of his gospel. Other elements in the story indicate the same. For example, the two men in the tomb recall Jesus' prophetic announcement of the handing over and crucifixion of the Son of Man and his rising on the third day (24:7). Their announcement introduces the disciples' contrasting review of the same events in their dialogue with Jesus on the way to Emmaus. At the tomb, the words brought the women understanding and hope. In the Emmaus story, the same words expressed the disciples' lack of understanding and discouragement (24:19–21).

The disciples of Emmaus even told Jesus of the women's visit to the tomb and how others also had gone (24:24; see 24:12). Understandably, they omitted that the Eleven and the others thought the women's story was nonsense (24:11). The disciples of Emmaus were among those who did not believe the women.

In its present form, the story is a Lukan composition, integrating various elements from kerygmatic, liturgical, catechetical and credal tradition into a journey narrative. Very likely, however, the place name Emmaus and the personal name Cleopas preserve a historical reminiscence. A story, similar in some respects to the present one but impossible to reconstitute, may have been associated with an early Christian named Cleopas, whose home was at Emmaus.

As in the breaking of the bread at Bethsaida (9:10–17), and the meals at the homes of Martha (10:38–42) and Zacchaeus (19:1–10), the breaking of the bread at Emmaus is an informal meal of hospitality, which we have distinguished from the formal meal known as the symposium. The presence of both types of meals in Luke's gospel suggests that the origins of eucharist should be sought both in the symposium and in the domestic family meal.

**The Setting: On the Way to Emmaus**   The story of Emmaus opens with a well-defined introduction, something for which Luke is noted.[4] The introduction situates the event in time and place, introduces the two disciples and Jesus, who joined them as they were discussing on their way to Emmaus, and raises the story's principal issue, namely, that something prevented the disciples from recognizing Jesus (24:13–16):

> Now that very day
> two of them
> were going to a village seven miles from Jerusalem
> named Emmaus,
> and they were conversing about all the things
> that had occurred.
> And it happened that while they were conversing
> and debating,
> Jesus himself drew near and walked with them,
> but their eyes were prevented from recognizing him.

The story opens by situating the event in time: "Now that very day," that is, "the first day of the week" (24:1), the first day of the new creation,[5] a day full of promise, in sharp contrast with the disciples' discouragement. Leaving Jerusalem, the disciples were abandoning the way (see 9:51)[6] on the very day the promise of Jesus' entire life was being fulfilled (24:50–53).

The two disciples call to mind the seventy[-two] whom Jesus sent out in pairs (10:1). These 70 further recall the 70 elders — in the Septuagint, *presbuteroi* — of Israel who participated in the ratification of the covenant at Sinai (Exodus 24:1–2, 9–11) and whom Moses selected to lead the people with him on the journey through the desert (Numbers 11:16–25). To these 70, two others were later added, Eldad and Medad (Numbers 11:26–30). This association with the seventy[-two] in Exodus and Numbers strongly suggests that the two disciples of Emmaus were elders, *presbuteroi*, presbyters of the new covenant, not unlike those appointed by Barnabas and Paul to lead churches toward the end of their first mission from Antioch (Acts 14:23). Presbyters, in this early context, does not refer to those we now call priests. These presbyters, of course, must not be confused with those that would later be called priests. In Luke-Acts, the term presbyter was used much more broadly.

Like the two who greeted the women in the tomb (24:4–7), these elders were meant to be prophetic teachers. Like the two in the tomb, they were to remind the community of what Jesus did and said while he was still among them. They would thus help the community understand events that even now were being fulfilled in their midst. However, before they could take up their roles as elders in the community, the disciples of Emmaus themselves needed to be reminded of events that happened in the days previous and taught of their meaning

The story of Emmaus, therefore, is not about two ordinary disciples but about two presbyters, prophetic teachers, who were abandoning the way. Still, they were not going very far. Luke goes out of his way to say that Emmaus was only 60 *stadia*,[7] seven miles, from Jerusalem. Actually, there was no village named Emmaus 60 *stadia* from Jerusalem. But no matter. It was more important to show that the disciples were not going very far and would be able to return. Luke could have known the geography of the area, but may have been willing to bend geographical precision so that the disciples might return to Jerusalem later that same day.[8]

In the course of the disciples' conversation, Jesus joined them on the way, but their eyes were not able to recognize him. With this, Luke has given to readers a knowledge the disciples did not have and thereby has made them privy to Jesus' identity. As a result, readers hear the disciples telling Jesus about his death and about their loss of hope, while the readers know all the while that the disciples are telling these things to Jesus himself.

With that, a series of three questions comes to mind. Why were the disciples unable to recognize Jesus? What was preventing their eyes from doing so? And how did they eventually come to recognize him? There is no way of answering these questions without first examining what it means to recognize.

It is common enough not to recognize someone we have not seen for a few years. It may be we last saw the person as a child or as a young adult. People may have changed a great deal and no longer resemble the image we have of them. When we eventually do recognize the person, it is due to closer observation and because we have found some similarities with the person we remember. The resemblance may be in the person's eyes, for example, or it may be a mannerism or a speech pattern.

It is with such an experience in mind that we tend to ask why the disciples of Emmaus did not recognize Jesus on the way. We then conclude they did not recognize him because his appearance as risen Lord was very different from what it had been as a historical figure. In other words, Jesus had become unrecognizable until somehow it was given to someone to recognize him. This approach, however, does not account for the statement that "their eyes *were prevented* from recognizing him." As Luke tells it, the inability to recognize Jesus had something to do with the eyes of the disciples, not with a change in Jesus' form or appearance. Such a change could also have been a factor, but in Luke's story of the disciples of Emmaus it remains very secondary.[9]

The Greek verb translated as "to recognize" is *epiginosko*. Luke first used the verb in the gospel's preface while presenting the purpose of his "narrative of the events that have been fulfilled among us" (1:1), namely, "so that you may realize *[epignos]* the certainty of the teachings you have received" (1:4). "That you may realize" could also be translated as "that you may really know," or "that you may have secure knowledge." In Luke's preface, this knowledge bears on the words, the message, with which Theophilus[10] was catechized *(katechethes)*.

The verb *epiginosko* is again used in the prologue when Zechariah came out of the sanctuary unable to speak, and people realized *(epignosan)* that he had seen a vision (1:22). In this case the knowledge bears on something that happened, an event realized as fact. The verb also is used in the story of Jesus and the paralytic, where Jesus knew *(epignous)* the thoughts of the scribes and Pharisees when he forgave the paralytic his sins (5:22). In this third case, the knowledge is the penetrating kind that grasps people's unexpressed thoughts.

In the story of Emmaus, "to recognize" *(epiginosko)* has a similar meaning, but the full, secure and penetrating knowledge is not of a message but of a person. Knowing a person is very different from knowing the truth of a message, the reality of an event or the secret of people's thoughts. Knowing a person presupposes a personal relationship with the person. It is based not on someone's exterior appearance but on mutual disclosure and inner attunement. To say that the eyes of the disciples were prevented from recognizing Jesus is to say that something prevented the disciples from really knowing Jesus in the first place. And this is the reason they could not recognize him now as the risen Lord. The dialogue in the first part of the story goes on to show what it was that prevented them from recognizing him.

The inability of the two disciples to recognize Jesus is related to the disciples' lack of understanding after Jesus' first and second announcement of the passion. When Jesus told them the Son of Man was to be handed over (9:44), "they did not understand this saying; its meaning was hidden from them so that they should not understand it" (9:45). Preoccupied with which of them was the greatest (9:46), they were unprepared to deal with the implications of the passion for them, and so could not and indeed should not understand it. At this point in their discipleship it was still too much for them to grasp and accept.

Even when Jesus announced the passion for the third time (18:31 – 33), "the word remained hidden from them and they failed to comprehend what he said" (18:34). There would be no comprehending what Jesus said until they could personally face the passion with him and enter into its mystery. As the story of the disciples of Emmaus opens, they have not yet come to this.

The statement that the eyes of the disciples were prevented from recognizing Jesus (24:16) serves as a literary hinge or transition, both concluding the introduction and introducing the body or main part of the story. Later, the statement that their eyes were opened and they recognized him (24:31) serves in the same way, both concluding the body of the story and introducing the conclusion.

The structure of the story is therefore quite simple, with an introduction leading up to the pivotal statement that the disciples' eyes were prevented from recognizing Jesus (24:13 – 16) and a conclusion beginning with the statement that their eyes were opened and they recognized him (24:31). This concluding statement resolves the tension sustained since 24:16 and introduces the story's denouement (24:31 – 35). The body or main part of the story (24:16 – 31) shows how the disciples went from the non-recognition to the recognition of the risen Lord.[11]

This structure parallels that of the story of Zacchaeus, where the introduction (19:1– 5) ends with Jesus' statement, "Today I must stay at your house" (19:5), and the conclusion (19:9 – 10) begins with a parallel statement by Jesus, "Today salvation has come to this house." (19:9) Zacchaeus's story shows how the coming of Jesus as a guest in one's home is the coming of salvation (see 19:5 – 9).

**Opening Dialogue**  The story opens with a dialogue between Jesus and the disciples. It begins with a brief exchange in which Jesus takes the initiative and the disciples show astonishment that Jesus does not know what has taken place (24:17–19a):

> He asked them,
> "What are you discussing as you walk along?"
> They stopped, looking downcast.
> One of them, named Cleopas, said to him in reply,
> "Are you the only visitor to Jerusalem who does not know
> of the things that have taken place there in these days?"
> And he replied to them,
> "What sort of things?"

At the start of the dialogue, Jesus acts as a total stranger to the disciples, knowing nothing of their preoccupations. His questions presuppose that their journey ("as you walk along") and discussion were significant, but make no allusion to the journey's destination. What mattered was not where they were going but that they were going *away* from Jerusalem and the community of Jesus' disciples.

The disciple who responded was named Cleopas. This is the first and only time Cleopas is mentioned in the gospel or anywhere in the New Testament. Outside of this story, we know nothing about him. It is normal enough to want to identify Cleopas's companion,[12] but the temptation should be resisted. It suffices that the other disciple is simply Cleopas's companion on the journey and a presbyter. This allows every reader to identify with the unnamed disciple and join Cleopas on the way to Emmaus.

Cleopas's response to Jesus is noteworthy from two points of view. First, he was amazed that Jesus did not know what had just transpired. He had assumed that everyone must surely have known and that Jesus must be the only one who did not. His response refers to Jesus as a "visitor" *(paroikeis)*, a sojourner, someone who interrupted his journey and stayed in Jerusalem for a while before resuming, as pilgrims did for Passover. Second, Cleopas assumed that unlike Jesus but like everyone else, he and his companion really knew what happened in Jerusalem. As would soon be apparent, the disciples had seen what happened but did not really *know* what happened. Like Luke's readers (see 1:4), they lacked genuine knowledge.

Jesus, of course, knew what happened but did not tell them that he knew — at least not immediately. Instead he asked the disciples to tell him what happened. As we hear their story, it becomes quite plain that they knew the sequence of events but did not understand. Hence their discouragement. The disciples' response is cast in the language of faith and hope, the language of the good news, but in their report it has become the language of blind discouragement and disillusionment, the language of bad news.

**The Disciples' Response**    The disciples began by evoking the figure of Jesus and summarizing his career from his emergence as a prophet to his death (24:19b–20):

> They said to him,
> "The things that happened to Jesus the Nazarene,
> who was a prophet
> mighty in deed and word before God and all the people,
> how our chief priests and rulers
> both handed him over to a sentence of death
> and crucified him."

Recalling the good old days, the disciples spoke of Jesus of Nazareth as one whom all recognized as a great prophet.[13] Their description of Jesus as "a prophet mighty in deed and word" evokes the figure of Moses, as described by Stephen in a Christian review of biblical history that led to his martyrdom: "Moses was educated [in] all the wisdom of the Egyptians and was powerful in his words and deeds." (Acts 7:22) However, the disciples' expectations regarding Jesus as a new Moses did not allow for Jesus' passion and death. Their blind reference to the chief priests and rulers recalled not only the passion (22:1—23:56) but also, ironically, Jesus' own announcements of his passion and death at the end of the Galilean ministry (9:22, 43–45) and on the journey to Jerusalem (18:31–34).

Memory and remembering were very important for the early Christian community. Memory brought up the past, applied it to the present and oriented it in the future. We have a good example of this creative process of remembering in the story of the women's visit to the tomb. The two men who greeted the women asked them to remember what Jesus said to them while still in Galilee and his announcement "that the Son of Man must be handed over to sinners and be crucified, and rise on the third day." The women remembered (24:6–8) and went to announce these things to the Eleven and the others.

The disciples of Emmaus also recalled the passion, but for them memory was not creative remembering, which illumines the present, but nostalgic reminiscence, which clings to the past. But there is no escaping the present. Hence the discouragement of the two disciples.

The disciples continued by telling of the hope that they once entertained but which had turned out to be groundless (24:21):

> But we were hoping
> that he would be the one to redeem Israel;
> and besides all this, it is now the third day
> since this took place.

Again the disciples' response evokes Stephen's discourse telling how redeeming Israel was also the mission of Moses: "This Moses, whom they had rejected with the words, 'Who appointed you ruler and judge?' God sent as [both] ruler and deliverer." (Acts 7:35; see 7:27) The Greek verb used for "redeeming" is *lutroomai,* meaning "setting free" or "liberating." The word Stephen used to describe Moses as "deliverer" was the corresponding noun *lutrotes,* meaning "redeemer" or "liberator." Moses had been rejected. Even so, God made him ruler and deliverer.

Stephen even referred to Moses' farewell discourse in Deuteronomy: "It was this Moses who said to the Israelites, 'God will raise up for you, from among your own kinsfolk, a prophet like me.'" (Acts 7:37; see Deuteronomy 18:15) The verb for "raising up" is *anistemi,* the same that was used for the raising of Jesus from the dead (see Luke 18:33 and 24:7).

For the storyteller and the reader, the parallel between Jesus and Moses is obvious. Both were rejected, and both did indeed redeem or deliver Israel. But this parallel was lost on the disciples. All the elements for understanding were there, but they still did not understand. The difference between the position of the story-teller and that of the disciples makes for great storytelling and very effective irony, drawing the reader ever deeper into the story.

The irony in the disciples' words comes to a climax when they refer to this being "the third day," an expression used in the New Testament to present Jesus' resurrection as salvific or liberating.[14] In Luke 18:33 and 24:7, the expression was explicitly associated with Jesus' rising *(anistemi).*

For the disciples, "the third day" indicated how absolutely hopeless matters had become. For the storyteller and Christian readers, it speaks of how hopeful things truly were, in spite of appearances.

The disciples concluded by telling how some people had visited the tomb of Jesus that morning (24:22–24):

> Some women from our group, however,
> have astounded us:
> they were at the tomb early in the morning
> and did not find his body;
> they came back and reported
> that they had indeed seen a vision of angels
> who announced that he was alive.
> Then some of those with us
> went to the tomb
> and found things just as the women had described,
> but him they did not see.

The disciples have summarized the whole of Jesus' life up to and including what happened that very day (see 24:1–12). There seemed to be hope in the women's report of angels announcing that Jesus was alive. Without realizing it, the disciples gave the grounds for this hope in their use of the word "body" *(soma)*, a term ordinarily associated with someone who is alive (see also 24:3). But the disciples were among those who considered the women's report nonsense and did not believe them (see 24:11).

For the disciples, believing had to come from seeing, not hearing. They ended their brief discourse by saying that some of their number actually went to the tomb and verified that it was indeed open and empty. The body of Jesus was not there — "but him they did not see." Like those who went to the tomb, the disciples needed to see Jesus alive in order to believe. The irony in their statement is that they were now telling this to Jesus. Seeing Jesus was one thing, recognizing him quite another.

**Jesus' Response**   The disciples had completed their review of the bad news about Jesus, and Jesus responded succinctly and to the point (24:25–26):

> And he said to them,
> "Oh, how foolish you are!
> How slow of heart to believe all that the prophets spoke!
> Was it not necessary
> that the Messiah should suffer these things
> and enter into his glory?"

Jesus brought the disciples back to the message of the prophets — all of them — and chided them for not believing "all that the prophets spoke." The Greek term here rendered as "foolish" is *anoetoi,* literally "unknowing" or "lacking in understanding." The disciples had not believed the women who returned from the tomb, nor had they believed *all* that the prophets spoke, especially regarding the Messiah's suffering and entering into glory. The passion of Jesus consequently remained meaningless to them, leaving them blind to Jesus in his suffering, dying and rising.

The disciples' relationship to Jesus had stopped at the threshold of the passion, when they still viewed him as "a prophet mighty in deed and word before God and all the people" (24:19). The passion demanded that they relate to Jesus as the Christ, as one who suffered, died and rose from the dead. Because the disciples were unable to relate to Jesus as the Christ dying and rising, they were unable to recognize him as Lord. It was their inability to accept the passion that prevented their eyes from recognizing Jesus.

Jesus taught them about the necessity of the passion for the Christ to enter into the glory of God. The verb to express this necessity, *dei,* here used in the imperfect, *edei,* is an important theological term for Luke, always referring to the divine order of salvation and Christ's integral part in it. Ultimately the necessity of salvation sprang from a loving and merciful God, who freely wills the salvation of all human beings. However, that necessity was expressed in and through ordinary historical contingencies. The historical necessity that Christ suffer was thus grounded in the divine salvific will.[15]

Jesus used the same term in the story of Zacchaeus, "Today, I must *[dei]* stay at your house." (19:5) For Jesus to stay at the house of Zacchaeus was for salvation to come to his house (19:9). The verb was used again in the preparations for the Last Supper, which would take place on the day it was necessary *(edei)* to sacrifice the Passover lamb (22:7). The Passover lamb was thus symbolically associated with the person of Christ, the lamb of the Christian Passover.

The dialogue closes with a summary of Jesus' teaching, interpreting everything in all the scriptures that had to do with himself, beginning with Moses and the Law, and continuing with the prophets (24:27):

> Then beginning with Moses and all the prophets
> he interpreted to them
> what referred to him in all the scriptures.

From the very start, Jesus stressed the importance of believing *all* that the prophets had spoken. Now he interpreted for them, not only *all* the prophets but *all* the scriptures. Until now, the disciples' hope in Jesus was based on only some of the prophets and scriptures, presenting him as a Mosaic prophet, but stopping short of Moses' rejection. They needed to reflect on all of the scriptures, especially the prophets, to understand that as the Christ he had to suffer the passion and enter into his glory (24:26). Only then would they be able to recognize who the "prophet mighty in deed and word before God and all the people" (24:19) truly was. Only then would they see the sense of the crucifixion (24:20), grasp the signficance of "the third day" as the day of divine deliverance (24:21) and believe the announcement that Jesus was alive (24:22–24). Taught by the Lord Jesus what it meant for him to be prophet and Christ, the disciples were now prepared to know and recognize him in the breaking of the bread.

**At Home in Emmaus**   As the dialogue ended, Jesus and the disciples were arriving at Emmaus. When Jesus made as if to go on, the disciples invited him to stay with them, as it was getting late. Jesus accepted their invitation (24:28–29):

> As they approached the village to which they were going,
> he gave the impression that he was going on farther.
> But they urged him,
> "Stay with us,
> for it is nearly evening
> and the day is almost over."
> So he went in to stay with them.

Resorting to an awkward circumlocution, "as they approached the village to which they were going," the story avoids mentioning Emmaus a second time. It is clear, however, that the disciples had arrived home. As followers of Jesus, they had left home (see 9:57–62) as Levi had (5:28), and Simon Peter before him, and

others including James and John (5:11). But now they were abandoning the way and were returning home. Jesus, however, had
not abandoned them. Like the shepherd in the parable, he had
come in search of them (15:4–7). Still, when they arrived at
Emmaus, Jesus made as if he were going on. Just as we were told
earlier in the story that the figure they did not recognize was
actually Jesus, Luke now alerts us to the fact that Jesus had no
intention of going on but was merely giving the impression of
doing so.

Jesus' maneuver drew the two disciples to offer him hospitality. As in the story of the breaking of the bread at Bethsaida
(9:12), it was nearly evening and the day was almost over, but
unlike the apostles who wanted to send the crowds away, they
invited Jesus to stay with them. From their point of view the day
was almost over. But from the gospel's point of view, this was still
"the first day of the week," and it was far from over!

"Stay with us," they said, and Jesus went in to stay with them.
The Greek verb "to stay" *(meno)* has a rich background in
Luke's gospel, beginning with Mary going to stay with her
kinswoman Elizabeth (1:56). It means "to dwell," as when we
learn that the Gerasene demoniac did not dwell in a house (8:27),
and it is most frequently associated with the hospitality that was
offered the disciples and apostles and was accepted by them on
their missionary journey (9:4; 10:7). It is what Jesus did when he
came to stay at the house of Zacchaeus (19:5) and is an important part of the mission of Peter (Acts 9:43) and Paul (Acts
16:15; 18:3, 20; 21:7, 8; 28:16). In all these cases, it refers to
making one's home with others and dwelling with them.

For Luke, the church is a place of hospitality, a welcoming
home, and Christians are people who make their home in and
with one another. John's gospel applied this interpersonal aspect
of mission to the meaning of Jesus' life. The Father dwells in
Jesus (John 14:10). Indeed, the Father and Jesus dwell in one
another (John 15:4). Using the image of the vine and the
branches (John 15:1–16), Jesus also asked the disciples to stay or
dwell in him as he dwelled in them. As the disciples of Emmaus

invite Jesus to stay with them and he accepts, the Johannine imagery immediately comes to mind.

**The Breaking of the Bread**    The disciples offered Jesus hospitality. Still taking him for a stranger who had been visiting in Jerusalem, but one with whom they had been speaking along the way, they invited him to stay at their home. And Jesus went in to stay with them. The story has now reached its climax — the breaking of the bread (24:30–31):

> And it happened that,
> while he was with them at table,
> he took bread,
> said the blessing,
> broke it,
> and gave it to them.
> With that their eyes were opened,
> and they recognized him,
> but he vanished from their sight.

Of its very nature, offering hospitality includes sharing a meal together. There is no sharing one's home without sharing a meal. And so it is quite normal that we would soon find Jesus and the two disciples at table. But this does not turn out to be an ordinary meal.

It is Jesus, not the disciples, who "took bread, said the blessing, broke it." It is Jesus who gave bread to them, not they who gave it to him. The disciples invited Jesus to be their guest, but the roles were instantly reversed as Jesus assumed the position of the host. The meal Jesus hosted was rather formal for such short notice. Jesus and the disciples were not simply sitting at table but *reclining* at table, as was done for a formal meal or a symposium.

When he was the principal guest at a symposium, Jesus had an honored position. As a prophet, he always went beyond what was expected of him as guest of honor, frequently challenging his host and the other guests on various points of hospitality (see 7:36–50; 14:1–24) and basic ethical issues (11:37–54). On other occasions Jesus was actually the host (9:10–17; 22:14–38), and he exceeded what was expected of the host. But this is the first time that as a guest Jesus actually took the position of the host. This alone, along with the meal's solemnity as a reclining banquet,[16] suggests that the breaking of the bread at Emmaus must be viewed as a eucharistic meal, one taken at the table of the Lord.

Any hesitation about this is dispelled by what Jesus did while reclining with them at table. Taking the bread, blessing, breaking and giving it to the disciples refers to the breaking of bread, the eucharist, just as it did when Jesus hosted the 5,000 at Bethsaida and the Twelve at the Last Supper. Liturgically, the entire formula is needed for the Lord's Supper, but literarily, a few key expressions —in particular the opening words—suffice to evoke it clearly. As at Bethsaida, the opening words of the liturgical formula serve as a title, bringing the whole formula to mind.

At Emmaus, the liturgical statement is more refined literarily than it was at Bethsaida and at the Last Supper. At Bethsaida, all the elements were there—taking, blessing, breaking and giving —but were adapted to the needs of the story with its five loaves and two fish, as in Mark 6:41. At the Last Supper, roughly the same elements remained very close to the liturgical text in use at Antioch, with two participles—"taking" and "giving thanks"— followed by two verbs in the indicative—"broke" and "gave." Liturgically this is fine because of its relation to the rite, but literarily it is somewhat clumsy: "and taking bread, having given thanks, he broke and gave to them" (22:19). At Emmaus we have two parallel clauses, each with a participle and a verb in the indicative: "taking the bread, he blessed, and breaking, he gave to them," showing how well Luke could retain the liturgical flavor of a text while using it in a story.

In the breaking of the bread, the disciples' eyes were opened and they recognized Jesus. When Jesus first joined them, they thought of him merely as a prophet from Nazareth, albeit "powerful in deed and word before God and all the people," and this prevented them from recognizing him as the Christ who had to suffer and enter into his glory. After the dialogue on the way, thanks to Jesus' lesson in biblical hermeneutics, they understood that Jesus was the Christ and they were moved to invite the still unrecognized stranger into their home. But it is only when he shared his person with them and they reciprocated, opening their person to him in the breaking of the bread, that their eyes were finally opened and they recognized him as Lord.

In the story, the figure of Jesus was presented as a historical personage, a stranger to the disciples, a sojourner visiting Jerusalem for the Feast of Passover. When the disciples recognized the Lord Jesus in the breaking of the bread, the stranger disappeared. Jesus is not present in the eucharist as the historical figure, the prophet from Nazareth, but as the risen Lord.

The story of Emmaus shows that the presence of Jesus the risen Lord is a sacramental presence. In the breaking of the bread at Emmaus, the whole event, including the participants, their expectations and the way they shared their person with one another constituted the sacrament. The critical factor in making the sacrament meaningful was the person of the stranger who joined the disciples in their life journey. Distinctions further specifying where and how the Lord Jesus is present in the eucharist would come much later in church history, usually in the heat of controversy.

**Back to Jerusalem**　The disciples' recognition of Jesus in the breaking of the bread brings the body of the story to an end and introduces the conclusion (24:31–35). As Jesus vanished from their sight, the disciples resumed the conversation they were having before Jesus joined them (24:14), but the intervening events — the dialogue with Jesus on the way and the breaking of bread with him at their home in Emmaus — had made an enormous difference. In their conversation, the disciples could now see the relationship between what happened on the way and their meal with Jesus (24:32). In addition, they were moved to return to Jerusalem, to the community where they were greeted with the good news of the resurrection and Jesus' appearance to Simon. The story ends with a brief word from the narrator, summarizing the whole event (24:32–35):

> Then they said to each other,
> "Were not our hearts burning [within us]
> while he spoke to us on the way
> and opened the scriptures to us?"
> So they set out at once and returned to Jerusalem
> where they found gathered together the eleven
> and those with them
> who were saying,
> "The Lord has truly been raised
> and has appeared to Simon!"
> Then the two recounted what had taken place on the way
> and how he was made known to them
> in the breaking of the bread.

The dialogue with Jesus had a profound effect on the disciples. It moved them to invite the stranger to stay with them. Ultimately it prepared their hearts to recognize him in the breaking of the bread, even though at the time they were unaware of its influence. It was only later when they actually recognized Jesus that they became aware that their hearts had been afire all along.

In the dialogue, Jesus opened *(dienoigen)* the scriptures to them, giving them new understanding of what happened to him in Jerusalem, weaning them from reminiscence, activating their memories and transforming their despair into hope. In the breaking of the bread, their eyes were opened *(dienoichthesan)* and they recognized him.

The relationship between the dialogue and the breaking of the bread invites reflection on the relationship between the liturgy of the word and the eucharistic liturgy.[17] Like the dialogue, which prepared the disciples for recognizing Christ in the breaking of the bread, the liturgy of the word prepares the assembly for experiencing Christ in the eucharistic liturgy. Like the breaking of the bread, which enabled the disciples to understand their experience of Christ opening the scriptures to them, the eucharistic liturgy enables the assembly to grasp the liturgy of the word.

With a new understanding of the passion, and having recognized the risen Lord in the breaking of the bread, the disciples immediately returned to Jerusalem. The story opened with the disciples despondently abandoning the community. It ends with them returning in haste to the Eleven and those with them. But before they had a chance to tell their experience, they were greeted with the proclamation: "The Lord has truly been raised and has appeared to Simon." (24:34) Returning with good news, they were greeted with good news.

At the Last Supper, Simon was given the mission to strengthen his brothers and sisters (22:32). When the women returned from the tomb with the message of the resurrection, Simon went to the tomb, looked inside and saw the burial cloths alone, leaving him in awe *(thaumazon)* at what happened (24:12). Now the Lord had appeared[18] to him, enabling him to fulfill the special mission given him at the Last Supper.

The story ends with the narrator summarizing the disciples' report of "what had taken place on the way and how he was made known to them in the breaking of the bread" (24:35). Until now, the experience of recognition was associated with the disciples' eyes, which at first were prevented from recognizing him (24:16) but then were opened to recognize him (24:31). This association presents the experience in relation to the sense of sight and makes it very concrete, but for many it may also have distracted from the nature of the experience as a form of knowing, the form involved in knowing a person. Such knowledge always comes in the form of a free gift, *a fortiori,* when the person known is the God or the Lord Jesus Christ.[19]

The story of the disciples of Emmaus moved Luke's presentation of the origins of the eucharist a major step forward. Earlier

Luke showed how the Last Supper, with its emphasis on the passion of Christ, had to be related to the Lord's Supper and Christ's resurrection, or else an essential dimension of the eucharist would be lacking. In the story of Emmaus he showed how the table of the Lord had to be related to the passion of Christ, or else again one of its essential elements would be lacking.

The story also showed how the eucharist, while referring to the past, is an event of the present. The eucharist is not only the memorial of the passion-resurrection of Christ. It is the Lord's Supper. The risen Lord, living gloriously in the kingdom, is present at the table of the Lord. However, in order to recognize him, to really know him, we must be open to his word, making sense of the passion in our lives. Like the disciples of Emmaus, we must offer hospitality to the stranger on the way. With that the church continues to recognize the risen Lord in the breaking of the bread.

The eucharist is an event in which we welcome the stranger to our community. It is an event from which we are sent out on mission. The story of Emmaus showed the Lord revealing himself in the experience of eucharist. The next story shows the Lord, present at eucharist, sending the community to all nations. If the church is community by its very nature, it is also missionary by its very nature.

## With the Community in Jerusalem (24:36 – 53) [20]

We have now come to the tenth and last meal in Luke's story of the origins of eucharist, the second of those taken with Jesus the Lord. At the Last Supper Jesus declared that he would not eat again and drink of the fruit of the vine until there was fulfillment in the kingdom of God (22:15 – 18). With the passion and resurrection, that fulfillment arrived.

The Emmaus story focused on the recognition of the risen Lord in the breaking of the bread. It showed Jesus gradually revealing himself in a discussion on the way and in a meal at the home of two disciples. It also showed the community sharing the message of the resurrection among themselves. Community faith sharing, an integral aspect of Christian *koinonia,* is absolutely basic for the life of the church.[21]

The second meal with Jesus the Lord took place in Jerusalem, where the disciples of Emmaus rejoined "the eleven and those with them" (24:33). It was Jesus' first meal with the full assembly of the church, one to which Peter would refer in his discourse to the household of Cornelius: "This man God raised [on] the third day and granted that he be visible, not to all the people, but to us, the witnesses chosen by God in advance, who ate and drank with him after he rose from the dead." (Acts 10:40–42)

The meal with the full assembly in Jerusalem focuses on the mission that flows from table solidarity with "Jesus Christ, who is Lord of all" (Acts 10:36). Because the risen Jesus is Lord of all, those who dine with him accept responsibility for bringing the gospel to all.

The Emmaus story showed how the eucharist is a welcoming event. Because the risen Lord is Lord of all, the eucharistic assembly must be open to everyone, including the stranger. The final meal in Jerusalem shows how the eucharist is a missioning event. Because the risen Lord is Lord of all, the eucharistic assembly must reach out to everyone, Jew and Gentile, proclaiming the forgiveness of sins.

The meal at Emmaus showed the church universal in its eucharistic welcome. The meal at Jerusalem shows the church universal in its eucharistic outreach.

> *"Thus it is written that the Messiah would suffer and rise from the dead on the third day and that repentance, for the forgiveness of sins, would be preached in his name to all the nations, beginning from Jerusalem."*
> (Luke 24:46–47)

**Context and Tradition**   The tenth meal in Luke's story of the origins of eucharist forms the conclusion of the gospel, the last event in the journey begun in 9:51, where Luke announced this would be a journey to the ascension. Seven of the meals with Jesus took place along that journey, the four with Jesus the prophet on the way to Jerusalem (10:38–42; 11:37–54; 14:1–24; 19:1–10), the Passover, which was to be Christ's Last Supper (22:7–13, 14–38), and the two Easter meals with Jesus the Lord (24:13 –35; 24:36–53).

The story follows immediately that of the two disciples on route to Emmaus and is very closely related to it, taking up some of the same themes and developing them from a different point of view. As Luke introduces it — "While they [the disciples who returned from Emmaus, the Eleven and those with them] were still speaking about this"—the story is the continuation of the story of Emmaus. But now that the disciples have returned to the community, they no longer figure explicitly. This last story is of an event involving the whole community assembled. A fuller description of the community gathered in Jerusalem can be found in Acts 1:13–14. Those who were with the apostles (Acts 1:13) included "some women, and Mary the mother of Jesus, and his brothers" (Acts 1:14).

Like the story of Emmaus, that of the supper in Jerusalem has no New Testament parallel that might be considered a source. The story is referred to in Mark's "Longer Ending" (Mark 16:14–18), written around the year 125 CE, but as with the Markan report of the Emmaus disciples (Mark 16:12–13), its focus is quite different from that of Luke.

As in the case of other stories, notably the dinner at the home of Simon the Pharisee (7:36–50) and the hospitality extended at the home of Martha (10:38–42), Luke seems to have been inspired by traditions also taken up in John's gospel. The parallels between Luke 24 and John 20 are too many to be accidental.

Like the Johannine account of the resurrection, the Lukan account has two visits to the tomb, the first involving Mary of Magdala (John 20:1–2; Luke 24:1–11) and the second involving Peter (John 20:3–10; Luke 24:12). In both gospels, the two visits to the tomb are followed by a story in which one or more disciples fail to recognize the risen Lord until he reveals himself to them. In John, the disciple is Mary of Magdala, who thought she was speaking to the gardener until Jesus called her by name (John 20:11–18). In Luke, the disciples of Emmaus thought they were speaking to a stranger visiting in Jerusalem until Jesus made himself known to them in the breaking of the bread (24:13–35).

Then comes Luke's story of the meal with the whole community in Jerusalem (24:36–53), where Jesus stood in their midst and greeted them: "Peace be with you." (24:36) The story's counterpart in John 20:19–23 also has Jesus coming and standing in their midst and greeting them: "Peace be with you." (John 20:19; see also 20:21, 26) Both stories insist on the reality of Jesus' risen body. In Luke, the disciples think they are seeing a spirit, and Jesus shows them his hands and his feet (24:37–40). In John, Jesus shows them his hands and his side (John 20:20), and the theme of doubting is more extensively developed in the story of Thomas (John 20:24–29). In Luke, the mission given the disciples is to preach "repentance for the forgiveness of sins" (24:47), and the gift of the Spirit, "the promise of my Father" (24:49) is announced. John refers to the disciples' mission of forgiving sins and shows Jesus giving them the Holy Spirit (20:21–23).

Within this traditional framework, Luke has integrated the meal (24:41–43) and Jesus' presentation of the basic preaching of the apostolic church (24:44–48).[22] He also provided the story with a solemn conclusion in which Jesus blesses the assembled community as he ascends into heaven (24:50–52). The story and the whole gospel ends with a summary of the disciples "continually in the temple praising God" (24:53).

The story is a tightly knit unit told in three closely related parts. In the first part, after a transitional link with the story of Emmaus (24:36a), Jesus appears to the community, greets them, assures them he is real and not just a spirit, requests something to eat and eats the fish they offer him (24:36b–43). This first part provides the basis for the second, in which Jesus gives a brief final discourse, connecting what he taught them while he was still among them with their mission to all nations, and announces that he is about to send them the promise of his Father (24:44–49). In the third part, Jesus bestows on them the promise of his Father, solemnly blessing them as he ascends into heaven (24:50–53).

Like the story of Emmaus, this second meal story with Jesus the Lord may reflect the early Christian liturgy beginning to take shape. It begins with a greeting of peace (24:36) and some reassurance, includes both a meal (24:41–43) and a discourse (24:44–49), and ends with a parting blessing for the worshiping community (24:50–52).

**The Setting: Greeting and Reassurance**   The disciples of Emmaus, the Eleven and those with them were still speaking about the Lord's resurrection, his appearance to Simon and the experience of the disciples of Emmaus when Jesus stood in their midst and greeted them (24:36):

> While they were still speaking about this,
> he stood in their midst and said to them,
> "Peace be with you."

The assembly began with a greeting: "Peace be with you." (24:36) Peace is a major theme in Luke. At Jesus' birth, angels sang of peace: "Glory to God in the highest and on earth peace to those on whom his favor rests." (2:14) At Jesus' entry into Jerusalem, the people proclaimed peace: "Blessed is the king who comes in the name of the Lord. Peace in heaven and glory in the highest." (19:38) As risen Lord, Jesus now greets the assembled community with peace. Peter referred to the event in his discourse at the household of Cornelius: "You know the word [that God] sent to the Israelites as he proclaimed peace through Jesus Christ, who is Lord of all." (Acts 10:36)

In his instructions for the mission of the seventy[-two], Jesus told them to say on entering a house, "Peace to this household." (Luke 10:5) If a person of peace lived there, peace would rest on him or her. The missionaries were then to stay[23] and eat and drink what was offered to them (10:6–7).

Peace is the characteristic greeting of the risen Lord in the midst of the community (see John 20:19, 21, 26), of the community on mission, and of the community gathered at the Lord's table, where the greeting could have various forms. Paul drew on such liturgical greetings for the greetings at the beginning of each of his letters.[24] In the Pauline greetings, peace is always associated with grace, God's gift in the new covenant. Peace is the effect of grace. Peace also was used as a farewell greeting or dismissal, as we saw at the meal in the house of Simon the Pharisee, where Jesus' final words to the woman were "go in peace" (7:50).[25]

The community's initial reaction to the greeting does not reflect the peace offered them. First they had to be reassured of the reality of the presence of the Lord Jesus among them (24:37–40):

> But they were startled and terrified
> and thought that they were seeing a ghost.
> Then he said to them,
> "Why are you troubled?
> And why do questions arise in your hearts?
> Look at my hands and my feet,
> that it is I myself.
> Touch me and see,
> because a ghost does not have flesh and bones
> as you can see I have."
> And as he said this,
> he showed them his hands and his feet.

The story of Emmaus showed how the disciples recognized the risen Lord in the breaking of the bread. In the story of the Jerusalem assembly, Jesus shows the community that the person they recognized was real. At first, the disciples thought they were seeing a spirit[26] and "were startled and terrified," as the women were when two men in dazzling garments appeared to them in the tomb (24:4). Their reaction shows none of the community's faith excitement at the end of the story of Emmaus. For Luke this is thematically a new story with special issues of its own.

Jesus asked the assembly why they were terrified and why such questions arose in their hearts. He then invited them to look at his hands and his feet. As a robed figure, Jesus thus sought to demonstrate the reality of his bodily presence. In John, when Jesus showed the community his hands and his side he was showing them his wounds, but there is no question of this in Luke. It is only in John that we learn that Jesus was nailed to the cross (John 20:25) and that his side was pierced (John 19:34). From the other gospels, including Luke, we learn that Jesus was crucified but are not told *how* he was attached to the cross.

Jesus then invited the community to touch him and see that unlike a purely spiritual being he was a person of flesh and bones. As he said this, he showed them his hands and his feet that they might touch him and really see. At this point, we need to ask not so much who the risen Lord really was but how he was really present to them. In the story of Emmaus, the risen Lord was really present in and through a stranger on the church's journey. The presence was real, but in symbol or sacrament, to use today's terminology. The same can be said of the present story. The risen Lord is really present among the community. He is present in the assembly of a community of real flesh and blood.[27]

**The Meal**   We now come to the meal, in which Jesus continues to reassure the community of the reality of his personal presence. The meal was much simpler than the one in the Emmaus story, but this does not make it any less rich theologically (24:41–43):

> While they were still incredulous for joy
> and were amazed,
> he asked them,
> "Have you anything here to eat?"
> They gave him a piece of baked fish;
> he took it and ate it in front of them.

When Jesus showed the assembly that his personal presence among them was real, their initial fright disappeared. They were still incredulous for joy and full of amazement when Jesus asked if they had anything to eat. Under ordinary circumstances, Jesus should not have had to ask. They should have spontaneously offered food to him.

At the Last Supper, Jesus was in the midst of the disciples as one who serves (22:27). He now stood in their midst asking to be served:[28] "Have you anything here to eat?" and "they gave him a piece of baked fish" (24:41–42). Jesus, the risen Lord, was following the instructions he had given the seventy[-two] for the mission, and was acting as model for the future mission. After greeting them with peace (see 10:5), Jesus accepted what they offered him (see 10:7–8), a piece of baked or broiled[29] fish, and he ate it in their presence.

The fish calls to mind the breaking of the bread at Bethsaida, where the meal consisted of bread and fish (9:10–17), and the extraordinary catch of fish when Jesus told Simon Peter and his companions James and John that henceforth they would be catching people (5:1–11). The marvelous catch of fish was symbolic of the Christian mission and the great numbers that would hear and accept the gospel (see also John 21:1–14).

**A Final Discourse** The meal in 24:41–43 provides an excellent foundation for Jesus' final discourse on the mission to all the nations (24:44–49). In the story of Emmaus, the dialogue prepared the disciples to recognize Jesus in the meal. In Jerusalem, the meal prepares them for understanding Jesus' discourse.

Jesus began by situating what he was about to say in relation to what he taught them in his earthly ministry. They would finally understand what he meant when he announced his passion-resurrection (24:44):

> He said to them,
> "These are my words that I spoke to you
> while I was still with you,
> that everything written about me

in the law of Moses and in the prophets and psalms
must be fulfilled."

In the first part of the story (24:36–43) Jesus insisted on the
reality of his presence among them. That does not mean his presence was the same as before. If it did, Jesus would not have had
to insist that what they saw and recognized was truly himself.
Jesus' presence as risen Lord was very different from his presence
as a historical figure. Jesus implied this difference at the very
beginning of the discourse when he referred to the words he
spoke to them while he was still with them. He certainly was
with them now, as he had just insisted and actually demonstrated. But he no longer was with them as he had been. Before
he was with them as a historical figure. Now he was with them in
sign and symbol, that is, as sacrament.

Jesus also responded to everything written about him in the
scriptures, more specifically in the law of Moses, the prophets
and the psalms. In this, Jesus spelled out the threefold division of
the Old Testament in the order of the Hebrew Bible, the Torah
(Law), the Neviim (Prophets), and the Qetubim (Writings), or at
least part of the Qetubim, namely the Psalms.[30] All the things
about him in the Scriptures stood as promise in relation to fulfillment.[31] They were now fulfilled, as he himself announced when
he was still with them.

Indeed, it was necessary *(dei)* that these scriptures be fulfilled.
God's salvific plan could not be aborted. In Luke's resurrection
narrative, the same necessity *(dei)* governed the handing over, the
crucifixion and the resurrection of the Son of Man on the third
day (24:7). In the story of Emmaus, it referred to the Christ who
had to suffer and enter into his glory (24:26). Now it refers
directly to the fulfillment of the scriptures, as it did at the Last
Supper for a particular passage of scripture, namely, "He was
counted among the wicked." (22:37; see Isaiah 53:12)

He then gave the assembly what he had already taught them
concerning the passion-resurrection, as he had done for the disciples of Emmaus (24:26) and as the two men in the tomb had

done for the women (24:7). But Jesus now extended the message
to include the nature, objectives and scope of the mission that
flowed from his passion-resurrection (24:45–47):

> Then he opened their minds
> to understand the scriptures.
> And he said to them,
> "Thus it is written
> that the Messiah would suffer
> and rise from the dead on the third day
> and that repentance,
> for the forgiveness of sins,
> would be preached in his name
> to all the nations,
> beginning with Jerusalem."

Jesus had told the disciples what was written in three
prophetic statements of the passion-resurrection (9:22; 9:44;
18:31–33), which he adapted from Mark 8:31; 9:31; 10:32–34.
Until now their minds were closed to understanding Jesus' teaching. After Jesus announced his passion-resurrection for the second
time, Luke noted: "But they did not understand this saying; its
meaning was hidden from them so that they should not understand it." (9:45) And even after the third and more detailed
announcement, Luke noted: "But they understood nothing of
this; the word remained hidden from them and they failed to
comprehend what he said." (18:34) Like the disciples of Emmaus
at the start of their encounter with Jesus, they still did not understand. Their minds had yet to be opened to understanding Jesus'
teaching on the scriptures in his regard, just as the eyes of the
Emmaus disciples had to be opened to recognize him in the
breaking of the bread.

Jesus' passion-resurrection brought salvation to all peoples.
Those in solidarity with Jesus—who rose from the dead on the
third day, the day God saves his people—must preach repentance
_(metanoia)_ for the forgiveness _(aphesis)_ of sins, that all might be

saved. The theme of *metanoia* was introduced in the first of
Luke's stories of meals with Jesus, the feast at the home of Levi
the tax collector (5:32). On that occasion Jesus referred to tax
collectors and others deemed to be sinners.

After his passion-resurrection, now that Jesus was Lord of all,
the same message had to be preached to all the nations, beginning with Jerusalem. Jesus' passion-resurrection transformed the
table of Jesus the prophet into that of Jesus Christ the Lord and
made it the springboard for the church's universal mission. Jesus'
message at this point in his final discourse looks directly to the
story of the church on mission in the Acts of the Apostles.

Jesus ends the discourse by declaring the disciples witnesses,
announcing that he would send the promise of his Father upon
them, in anticipation of Pentecost, for which they must stay in
Jerusalem (24:48–49):

> You are witnesses of these things.
> And [behold] I am sending
> the promise of my Father upon you;
> but stay in the city
> until you are clothed with power from on high.

The apostles and those with them were certainly eyewitnesses
*(autoptai,* 1:2) to everything to which Jesus referred, but more
than that, they were witnesses *(martures)* of these things. As
eyewitnesses, they enjoyed firsthand knowledge of everything.
As witnesses, they were charged with transmitting that knowledge to others. One might be an eyewitness by accident, but to be
a witness one had to be called. Matthias, for example, was an
eyewitness, but he was not a witness until he was called to be a
witness to the resurrection (Acts 1:23).

Jesus was sending "the promise of his Father"[32] on them, making them heirs to the promises God made to Abraham (1:55, 73),
that through his progeny all the families of the earth would be
blessed (see Genesis 12:2–3; 18:18; 22:18; 26:4). They were to
remain in Jerusalem until they were clothed with power from on

high, that is, until they received the Holy Spirit. It is through the power of the Holy Spirit that they would pursue their mission as the Lord's "witnesses in Jerusalem, throughout Judea and Samaria, and to the ends of the earth" (Acts 1–8).

**Blessing and Departure**    Luke's tenth and final meal story reaches its conclusion in a dramatic gesture of blessing and ascension (25:50–53):

> Then he led them [out] as far as Bethany,
> raised his hands,
> and blessed them.
> As he blessed them
> he parted from them
> and was taken up to heaven.
> They did him homage
> and then returned to Jerusalem with great joy,
> and they were continually in the temple praising God.

When the eyes of the disciples of Emmaus were opened and they recognized him, Jesus vanished from their sight (24:31). Now, after completing his final discourse, Jesus ascended into heaven, bringing the appearance to an end.

The ascension was first announced at the end of the prologue, when Jesus told his parents it was necessary *(dei)* for him to be with his Father (2:49). It was again referred to by Moses and Elijah at the transfiguration when they spoke of the *exodos* Jesus had to fulfill in Jerusalem (9:31). It was also the objective of Jesus' journey to Jerusalem, when the days of his ascension were fulfilled (9:51).

The key to the necessity of Jesus' ascension is in the blessing. Returning to his Father, Jesus had completed his mission. The promises made to Abraham were fulfilled, that through his progeny all the families of the earth would be blessed. Jesus' blessing of the community symbolically expressed the blessing promised to Abraham.[33]

The community responded by worshiping Jesus risen and now ascended into heaven and by following his instruction to stay in the city. They returned to Jerusalem with great joy. The gospel of great joy announced by the angel to the shepherds at Jesus' birth was fulfilled. In Jesus they had a savior who was Christ and Lord (2:10–11).

The story and the gospel end with a brief summary of the community continually in the temple praising God.[34] Jesus had entered into the glory of his Father's heavenly dwelling, while the Christian community continued to praise God in God's earthly dwelling. The story began with Jesus greeting the assembly with peace. It ends with Jesus blessing the assembly and with the assembly doing homage to Jesus and giving praise to God.

# Dining in the Kingdom of God

*I*t was over 50 years since Jesus took his place at table with the apostles for the Last Supper. At the time, Tiberius was emperor at Rome, Pontius Pilate the governor of Judea and Herod the tetrarch of Galilee (Luke 3:1). Annas and Caiaphas were the high priests (3:2). Later that night, in the courtyard of their house, Peter denied so much as knowing Jesus (22:54–62). The following morning, the opportunity to hear Jesus brought Pilate and Herod together. Weakness and contempt became friends that day (23:12).

The world had changed since then. Tiberius, Pilate, Herod, Annas, Caiaphas, the apostles and even Peter, were long gone. Jerusalem lay in ruins, smashed to the ground (see 19:41–44) and trampled underfoot (see 21:20–24). Even the temple was destroyed—with not one stone left upon another (see 21:5–6)—as was the house of the high priest along with the dwellings of the very rich overlooking the temple area from the western hill.

But throughout the world of Paul, in what are now Syria, Turkey, Greece and Cyprus, Christians (Acts 11:26) assembled to do what Jesus did the night of his Last Supper. They took bread, gave thanks, broke it and gave it to one another, saying, "This is my body, which will be given for you." They also took the cup after eating, pronouncing it the "cup of the new covenant in my blood, which will be shed for you." They did this in memory of Jesus the Christ, who died and rose that all might live (22:19–20; see also 9:16; 24:30).

The Lord's Supper and the words, "This is my body that is for you. . . . This cup is the new covenant in my blood" (1 Corinthians 11:24–25) were part of the tradition they had received from Paul and which, like Paul, they handed on to others. The word "body" referred to the person or self of Christ and to their own personal self as a community in Christ. The word "blood" referred to the life of Christ and to their own life in Christ. In the eucharist, Christians offered themselves and their whole life with, in and through Christ, and continued Christ's life and mission to all peoples.

The old world of the Pauline missions (46–62 CE) had grown much larger by the ninth decade, when Luke wrote his gospel and the Acts of the Apostles. It had expanded into the world of Luke, reaching throughout the Roman Empire and well beyond, its map revealed by the list of those present at Jerusalem for Pentecost: "Parthians, Medes, and Elamites, inhabitants of Mesopotamia, Judea and Cappadocia, Pontus and Asia, Phrygia and Pamphylia, Egypt and the districts of Libya near Cyrene, as well as travelers from Rome, both Jews and converts to Judaism, Cretans and Arabs" (Acts 2:9–11). Throughout that world, Christians took bread, gave thanks and broke it in memory of Jesus the Christ.

Luke's readers assembled on the first day of the week (24:1, 13, 36; Acts 20:7) for the breaking of the bread (24:35; Acts 2:42; 20:7, 11), celebrating the Christian Passover as a weekly event, heralding the new creation and announcing the kingdom of God. In the breaking of the bread, they celebrated the Lord's Supper, deepening their knowledge of Jesus as prophet, Christ and Lord, recognizing him in the breaking of the bread (24:13–35)

and witnessing to his death and resurrection from the dead
(24:36–53).

They assembled in the home of a leading member of the community to share their faith and come to a better understanding of
what it meant to be Christians. Together they reflected on the
endless swirl of events threatening to engulf them in a passion of
their own (24:19b–25). In the process, the bonds uniting them in
a new covenant in Christ's blood were strengthened.

**The Shape of the Lord's Supper**  Luke did not describe in detail what
they did in the assembly for the Lord's Supper and the breaking
of the bread. But indirectly we learn much from his accounts of
meals with Jesus. They began, as others did, by greeting one
another, but with a very special greeting of peace, giving voice to
the risen Lord in their midst, "Peace be with you." (24:36) They
also dealt with questions that may have arisen in their hearts
(24:38), and they renewed what Christ did at the Last Supper,
remembering his passion-resurrection, giving thanks, breaking
bread and saying, "This is my body which will be given for you"
(22:19) and "This cup is the new covenant in my blood, which
will be shed for you." (22:20)

They spoke of the events fulfilled in their midst (1:1): Christ's
life, death and resurrection. They also reflected on what these
events demanded of them (24:47).

They prayed that the Father's kingdom come (11:2) and
embrace the ends of the earth (Acts 1:8). Already they knew the
kingdom present in their midst (22:15–18; 9:11; 14:15). Indeed,
in their assembly for the Lord's Supper and their breaking of the
bread in memory of the Lord, they dined in the kingdom of God.
Their very assembly was a prayer for the kingdom, renewing
Christ's act of thanksgiving in deed and word (22:19). Already
sharing in the kingdom of the Father who gave them bread for
sharing with others on their Christian journey to God (11:3),
they prayed that the kingdom come not only in them but through
them to the ends of the earth.

They also gave homage to the Lord Jesus, remembering how he sent the promise of the Father upon them and blessed them, making all of them children of Abraham (see 3:8; 19:9). And they blessed one another, that through their witness (24:47–48) all the families of the earth, indeed all nations, would in truth be blessed (24:50–53).

**An Inclusive Assembly**  Sometimes the Lord's Supper was quite formal (22:7–13, 14–38), patterned on the Hellenistic symposium (see 5:27–39; 7:36–50; 11:37-54; 14:1–24). Sometimes it was quite informal (24:13–35; 24:36–53; Acts 20:7–11), more like a family meal at which hospitality was extended to someone on a journey (see 9:10–17; 10:38–42; 19:1–10; see also 11:5–8).

The Hellenistic symposium did not include women and children. Nor did it include slaves. Domestic meals and meals extending domestic hospitality did include women and children; normally, however, slaves ate apart. The fact that Christians gathered in their homes both for formal, symposium-like meals and for ordinary, domestic meals may have provided the experience and the precedent for breaking out of the social and cultural strictures of the Hellenistic world.

The fact that Christians thought of themselves as a family must also have been a factor. All "those who hear the word of God and act on it" were mother and brother and sister to Jesus. They were Jesus' family (8:19–21; see Acts 1:14). Women and children were part of the family and shared in the family meal.

The breaking of the bread as a domestic family, including the women and the children, may have challenged the more formal practices associated with the symposium, which excluded them. In Luke's story of meals, the two kinds of meals mutually influence one another.

Elements of the symposium can be found in the less formal hospitality meals, where terms associated with the symposium are used (see 9:10–17) and where one finds a discourse after the meal, following the common practice for a symposium (see

24:36–53). And elements of the less formal meals can be found in those patterned on the symposium, where Jesus regularly challenged the tendency to be exclusive (see 5:27–39; 7:36–50; 14:1–24).

From the inclusion of women and children, who in Roman law were not free persons, it was a rather simple step to include slaves who, of course, were also not free. Christian solidarity with Jesus, risen from the dead and Lord of all, demanded that all be welcomed at the Lord's Supper. The very composition of the assembly was an integral element in the community's eucharistic witness (see 24:48).

**Mission and Sacrament**  In the eucharist, the Lukan communities exercised their mission, which was based on the mission of Jesus the Anointed, that is, the Christ. Jesus first presented that mission in the synagogue at Nazareth, applying Isaiah's prophetic message to himself (4:18–19; see Isaiah 61:1–2; 58:6):

> "The Spirit of the Lord is upon me,
> because he has anointed me
> to bring glad tidings to the poor.
> He has sent me to proclaim liberty to captives
> and recovery of sight to the blind,
> to let the oppressed go free,
> and to proclaim a year acceptable to the Lord."

Such was the essence of Jesus' mission and the gospel according to the scriptures.

Later, when John sent his disciples to inquire whether Jesus was indeed the one who was to come, Jesus responded (7:22):

> "Go and tell John what you have seen and heard:
> the blind regain their sight,
> the lame walk,
> lepers are cleansed,

the deaf hear,

the dead are raised,

the poor have the good news proclaimed to them."

That mission, summarized in the proclamation, "The kingdom of God is at hand for you," was given the Twelve (9:1–2, 6) and the Seventy[-two] (10:9). The same mission was to find concrete expression in the Christian assembly. Such was the instruction Jesus gave the Pharisee who hosted him at a sabbath meal (14:12–14):

"When you hold a lunch or a dinner,

do not invite your friends or your brothers

or your relatives or your wealthy neighbors,

in case they may invite you back

and you have repayment.

Rather, when you hold a banquet,

invite the poor, the crippled, the lame, the blind;

blessed indeed will you be

because of their inability to repay you.

For you will be repaid at the resurrection of the righteous."

The instruction led one of Jesus' fellow guests to exclaim, "Blessed is the one who will dine in the kingdom of God."

When the Christians followed Jesus' injunction their mission also became a sacrament. Welcoming the stranger, as the disciples of Emmaus did, they recognized the risen Lord in the breaking of the bread (24:13–35). By welcoming all those who repented and whose sins were forgiven — people of every nation beginning with Jerusalem — their assembly became a living witness to the resurrection of the Lord Jesus (Acts 4:33) and a sacrament of the kingdom of God (24:36–53).

**Ideals and Realities**   From Luke's story of the origins of the eucharist, we see what the early Christians did and what it meant when they assembled on the first day of the week for the Lord's Supper and the breaking of the bread; at least we see what they were meant to do. They had heard the gospel, and the kingdom was in their midst (17:21). Already they were dining in the kingdom of God (22:15–18), but not fully. The kingdom was still coming (17:20), a basic intention of prayer (11:2–4). Their dining in the kingdom of God was real but still lacking in many ways, sometimes quite sadly.

Even so, Luke could evoke the eucharist they experienced as he told the gospel story of meals with Jesus, addressing the most basic issues confronting them. By presenting the story of the origins of the eucharist in a series of ten meals, Luke showed how Jesus continued to challenge the communities with the attitudes and behavior necessary for dining fully in the kingdom of God.

Luke's story of the origins of the eucharist in meals with Jesus the prophet (5:27–39; 7:36–50; 9:10–17; 10:38–42; 11:37–54; 14:1–24; 19:1–10), with Jesus the Christ (22:7–13, 24–38) and with Jesus the Lord (24:13–15; 24:36–53) continues to challenge us. The issues that were important in the Christian world of Luke remain just as important today. Like the whole of Luke's gospel, these stories are classic, transcending time and place to address Christians of every time and place. There will be no genuine renewal of the eucharistic liturgy without heeding their message.

**At Table with Jesus the Prophet**  In the eucharist, Christians dine with Jesus the prophet. And so they must be open to his prophetic challenge and ready to join him in challenging others. Such are the demands of table solidarity. To escape those demands, one must withdraw from the table.

The first and most basic challenge is that of conversion *(metanoia)*, a lifetime process for everyone. It is the challenge of the great feast in the house of Levi (5:27–39). Those who dine with Jesus the prophet must be willing to be transformed by his presence. We must become like him as he became like us. No one is excluded from the challenge of *metanoia*. No one is righteous. All are in need of repentance for the forgiveness of sins.

The second challenge is that of reconciliation. It is the challenge of the great dinner at the house of Simon the Pharisee (7:36–50). Those who dine with Jesus the prophet must willingly reach out in loving reconciliation to those who repent and are forgiven. Reconciliation is a constant process.

The third basic challenge is that of mission, always full of surprises. It is the challenge of the breaking of the bread in the city of Bethsaida (10:10–17). Those who dine with Jesus the prophet must be willing to welcome and nourish those who come to hear him preach and teach about the kingdom of God. They must be ready for the unexpected, knowing that no one need be overwhelmed. The eucharistic table does not demand they be the great benefactors, but that they lead all in sharing the bread of the Christian exodus.

The fourth challenge involves the conditions for genuinely Christian service or ministry. It is the challenge of hospitality at the house of Martha (10:38–42). All tend to become anxious and worried about many things, neglecting the one thing necessary, that is, listening attentively to the word of the Lord. Without this one thing, everything loses its Christian value.

The fifth challenge has to do with external, ritual cleanness while neglecting interior purification and cleanness. It is the challenge of the noon meal at the home of a Pharisee (11:37–54). Those who dine with Jesus the prophet must attend to interior cleanness, lest they become a source of scandal, preventing others from acquiring the attitudes and the faith knowledge appropriate for dining in the kingdom of God.

The sixth challenge involves seeking honor, privilege and personal gain, either as a guest seeking the best place at table, or as the host inviting only those who are apt to bring honor and reward for oneself. It is the challenge of the sabbath dinner at the house of a leading Pharisee (14:1–24). To dine in the kingdom of God, guests must seek the lowest place, and the host must invite the poor and helpless.

The seventh challenge has to do with justice and generosity toward the poor. It is the challenge of hospitality at the house of Zacchaeus (19:1–10). Jesus must fulfill his mission, personally bringing salvation to sinners. Welcoming Jesus at one's home demands that Christians act justly, make up for any injustice, give alms, and ensure both interior and exterior cleanness for oneself (see 11:41).

**At Table with Jesus the Christ**   There is no greater challenge than that of the Last Supper (22:7–13, 14–38), in which Christ lovingly offered his very person in sacrifice for those assembled, for all those who would assemble in the future, and even for all who would be called but would decline the invitation to dine in the kingdom of God. Meal solidarity with Jesus the Christ requires that the participants join Christ in his sacrifice, doing what he did in memory of him, offering their own lives that all might live, and making his sacrifice an active force in the world (22:14–20).

The challenge of the Last Supper was also about betrayal and denial, and so is its fulfillment in the Lord's Supper. Betrayal at the Last Supper meant handing Jesus over to those who plotted his death (22:21–23). Betrayal for Christians assembled at the Lord's Supper means lording it over one's brother and sister Christians and demanding to be recognized as "benefactors." Among those who join at the table of Jesus the Christ, the greatest has to be as the youngest, the leader as the servant (22:24–30).

Denial for those who assembled at the Last Supper meant refusing to acknowledge any relationship with Jesus (22:31–34). Denial for those assembled at the Lord's Supper means taking up the warrior's sword against persecution. Those joining Christ at his table must rather take up the sword of the Holy Spirit, which is the word of God (22:35–38).

**At Table with Jesus the Lord**   The challenges of the table of Jesus the Lord are also great, as is shown in the breaking of the bread at

Emmaus (24:13 – 35) and with the community in Jerusalem (24:36 – 53). The challenges of the table of the Lord have to do with understanding the passion and death of Christ and recognizing the risen Lord in the breaking of the bread. They also have to do with the witness to be given by those who share the Lord's table.

To recognize the risen Lord one must face the ongoing passion and death in each Christian and in the life of the church. It requires that the assembly be ready to break bread with the stranger on the journey, whoever that stranger may be. Only when their table reflects the universality of Jesus' lordship will they recognize him in the breaking of the bread (24:13 – 35).

To give witness to the resurrection of the Lord, those who share at the Lord's table must not only welcome all but actually bring the message of conversion for the forgiveness of sins to all, whether Jew or Gentile. They must not only recognize the risen Lord in the stranger but see him really present in the flesh and bones of their own assembly, most especially in those calling on them for witness to the resurrection of the Lord (24:36 – 53).

**A Gospel Event**   The eucharist is nothing less than a living compendium of the gospel in deed and word. For Christians in the Lukan communities, the eucharist was a gospel event displaying the full range of gospel experience and demanding fully as much as the gospel itself. To know and live eucharist, indeed to *be* eucharist, was to know, live and be the gospel of Jesus Christ, our Lord and Lord of all. So it must be for communities in the church today.

In many ways, the Lukan communities did not live up to the demands of the eucharist. Neither do we. Doing so would mean fully entering into the kingdom of God, dining in the kingdom of God — no longer in the swirl of earthly challenges but in the heavenly banquet.

In a series of ten meals with Jesus the prophet, Christ and Lord, Luke set out the demands of eucharist. These demands may appear overwhelming, but no more so than the gospel presentation of the ideal of Christian life. Impossible as it may seem, that ideal must never be lowered. It is a beacon beckoning all of us toward the humanly impossible and the kingdom of God.

Responding to the gospel call of eucharist, we do well to read one story at a time, holding our celebration of eucharist to its light, attending to one issue after the other, beginning with the most basic.

The gospel is about the kingdom of God, and eucharist is the heart of the gospel. Blessed is the one who dines in the kingdom of God!

# Endnotes

## Preface

[1] Father Chrysogonus Waddell, OCSO, "A Local Project for Refectory Prayers," *Liturgy* 2 (October 1967): 32.

[2] Ibid.

## Chapter I

[1] For a good general study of the eucharist in the New Testament, see Xavier Leon-Dufour, *Sharing the Eucharistic Bread: The Witness of the New Testament,* trans. Matthew J. O'Connell (New York: Paulist Press, 1987). For shorter studies, see J. Delorme et al., *The Eucharist in the the New Testament: A Symposium,* trans. E. M. Stewart (Bethlehem: Helicon Press, 1965); and Jerome Kodell, *The Eucharist in the New Testament,* Zacchaeus Studies: New Testament (Collegeville: The Liturgical Press, 1991).

[2] For two recent works written from similar concerns and with analogous points of view, see Alexander Schmemann, *The Eucharist, Sacrament of the Kingdom* (Crestwood NY: St. Vladimir's Seminary Press, 1988); and David N. Power, *The Eucharistic Mystery, Revitalizing the Tradition* (New York: Crossroad Publishing Company, 1992).

[3] *First Apology,* 66; see Maurice Jourjon, "Justin," in Willy Rordorf, *The Eucharist of the Early Christians,* trans. Matthew J. O'Connell (New York: Pueblo Publishing Company, 1978), 72.

[4] *Dialogue with Trypho,* 41. Ibid., p. 77: "The offering of fine flour that was prescribed for those cleansed of leprosy was a prefiguration of the bread of the eucharist which our Lord Jesus Christ commanded us to offer in memory of the passion he underwent for the sake of those whose souls are cleansed of all evil."

[5] *Commentary on John's Gospel (In Ioh. Tract)* cxx. 19. 2 (PL 35, 1953) and *The City of God (De Civ. Dei)* 15, 26 (PL 41, 472): "*sacramenta*

. . . *quibus credentes initiantur."* For a reveiw of the Patristic interpretation of John 19:34, see S. Tromp, SJ, *"De Nativitate Ecclesiae Corde Iesu in Crucis,"* in *Gregorianum* 13 (1932): 524.

6 The text is in Leo's Sermon 58, the seventh on the passion, chapter 3: "But Jesus, sure in his resolve and determined to fulfill his Father's plan, brought the old dispensation to an end *[vetus testamentum consummabat]* and founded the new Pasch *[et novum Pascha condebat]*. While his disciples were reclining at table with him to eat the mystical supper, and while in Caiaphas' courtyard people were discussing how Christ could be killed, he himself was establishing the sacrament of his body and blood *[ille corporis et sanguinis sui ordinans sacramentum]."* P.L. 54, c. 333; *Leon le Grand* III, *traduction et notes de Dom Rene Dolle, Sources Chretiennes* 74 (Paris: Cerf, 1961), 51.

7 See *Dictionnaire de Theologie Catholique,* 1924 ed., s.v. *"Eucharistie, d'apres les Peres,"* by G. Bareille.

8 These controversies were over a real versus a symbolic understanding of the presence of Christ in the eucharistic bread and wine. The major figures in the ninth-century controversies were Paschasius Radbertus and Ratramnus. The major figure in the eleventh century was Berengarius of Tours. See *Dictionnaire de Theologie Catholique,* 1924 ed., s.v. *"Eucharistie du IXe a la fin du XIe siecle,"* by F. Vernet.

9 See *Summa Theologica* III, q. 73, a. 5., which deals with "Whether the Institution of This Sacrament was Appropriate." Thomas answers that "This sacrament was appropriately instituted *[convenienter hoc sacramentum institutum fuit]* at the supper, when Christ conversed with His disciples for the last time."

10 The Council of Trent refers to the institution of the eucharist in Session XIII, "Decree Concerning the Most Holy Sacrament of the Eucharist," Chapter II, "The Reason for the Institution of This Most Holy Sacrament."

11 *Sacramentum Mundi,* 1968 ed., s.v. "Eucharist: B. 'Institution of the Eucharist by the Historical Jesus,' " by J. Betz.

12 Ibid., 258.

[13] The Christian usage of the term "gospel" first referred to the person and saving mission of Jesus Christ. When the term was applied to the Christian message concerning these, it referred to the gospel's communication through the spoken word. Application to the written word and to the works that came to be called "gospels" came late For the term's background outside the New Testament, usage in the New Testament and application to New Testament books, see *Theological Dictionary of the New Testament,* ed. G. Kittel, 1964 ed., s.v., *"euaggelion,"* by Friedrich.

[14] The similarity of the four gospels is great enough to indicate a special gospel genre. For the literary genre of the gospels, see David E. Aune, *The New Testament in Its Literary Environment* (Philadelphia: The Westminster Press, 1987), 17–45.

[15] For the various introductory questions concerning the historical background of Luke's gospel and a sketch of Lukan theology, see Joseph A. Fitzmyer, *The Gospel according to Luke I-IX,* The Anchor Bible, 28A (Garden City: Doubleday & Company, Inc., 1981), 3-283. For a brief survey of recent studies, see Eugene LaVerdiere, "The Gospel of Luke: What the exegetes are saying about Luke's Gospel today," *The Bible Today* 18 (July 1980): 226–35.

[16] For the literary structure of Luke's gospel and the place of journeys in that structure, see Eugene LaVerdiere, *Luke,* New Testament Message # 5 (Collegeville: Michael Glazier/The Liturgical Press, 1980). See also Hans Conzelmann, *The Theology of St. Luke* (New York: Harper & Brothers, 1960), 60–73.

[17] Although Bethlehem was associated with King David's origins, it was not known as "the city of David." The expression actually referred to Jerusalem, which was "the city of David." By applying this term to Bethlehem, Luke meant to associate Bethlehem with Jerusalem and the rejection of Jesus when he came there at the end of his life. We do something similar when we apply the expression "the windy city" to a city other than Chicago. The expression, which originated in a reference to Chicago politicians, associates another city with Chicago in this respect and becomes descriptive of that other city, while everyone knows that Chicago is "the windy city."

[18] For an introduction to the meals in Luke's gospel, and more specifically to the motif of food, see Robert J. Karris, *Luke: Artist and*

*Theologian* (New York: Paulist Press, 1985), 47–78. For an anthropological study, see Jerome H. Neyrey, "Ceremonies in Luke-Acts: The Case of Meals and Table Fellowship," *The Social World of Luke-Acts,* ed. Jerome H. Neyrey (Peabody MA: Hendrickson Publishers, 1991), 361–87. For the banquet theme in Lukan theology, see John Navone, *Themes of St. Luke* (Rome: Gregorian University Press, 1970), 11:37. A very recent book on the theme of meals in Luke which appeared as this book was in production is Arthur A. Just, Jr., *The Ongoing Feast: Table Fellowship and Eschatology at Emmaus* (Collegeville: Pueblo/The Liturgical Press, 1993).

[19] For the significance and symbolism of the manger in Luke 2:7, 12, 16, see C. Homer Giblin, "Reflections on the Sign of the Manger," *Catholic Biblical Quarterly* 29 (1967): 87-101; Raymond Brown, *The Birth of the Messiah* (Garden City: Doubleday and Company, Inc., 1977), 418–20: "Jesus is born in the city of David, not in lodgings like an alien, but in a manger where God sustains His people" (p. 420); and Robert Karris, *Luke: Artist and Theologian,* for whom, "Jesus in the manger is food for the world" (p. 49).

[20] See Fitzmyer, *The Gospel Acording to Luke I-IX,* 510–11; and Karris, *Luke: Artist and Theologian,* 52-53.

[21] See Fitzmyer, *The Gospel According to Luke I-IX,* 548–51 and 695–98.

[22] For a brief description of the symposium in Greco-Roman antiquity "both as a social custom and a loosely structured literary form," see David E. Aune, *The New Testament,* 122; see also *The Oxford Classical Dictionary,* ed. N. G. L. Hammond and H. H. Scullard, 2d ed., s.v. "Symposium"; and Dennis E. Smith, "Table Fellowship as a Literary Motif in the Gospel of Luke," *Journal of Biblical Literature* 106 (1987): 614–17.

[23] For a brief description of the literature based on the Hellenistic symposium, see the entry in *The Oxford Classical Dictionary,* s.v. "Symposium Literature," which presents this literature as "a loosely defined literary genre" consisting of "descriptions of the conversations at symposia." The point of departure for all modern study of this genre and still the most important work is that of Josef Martin, *Symposion: die Geschichte einer literarischen Form* (Paderborn: Verlag Ferdinand Schoeningh, 1931).

[24] All do not include the meal at the home of Levi among those reflecting the Hellenistic symposium, but see J. Delobel, *"L'onction par la pecheresse," Ephemerides Theologicae Lovanienses* 42 (1966): 415 – 75, especially p. 461.

[25] See J. Delobel, 458 – 75. Delobel found that the symposium genre provides an important compositional principle that can account for many of the redactional changes Luke made while drawing on oral tradition and his Markan source.

[26] See E. Springs Steele, "Luke 11:37 – 54 — A Modified Hellenistic Symposium?" *Journal of Biblical Literature* 103 (1984): 379 – 94.

[27] See X. de Meeus, *"Composition de Lc., XIV et genre symposiaque," Ephemerides Theologicae Lovanienses* 37 (1961): 847 – 70. This is the seminal article for later work on the influence of the symposium and symposium literature on meals in Luke.

[28] See William S. Kurz, "Luke 22:14 – 38 and Greco-Roman and Biblical Farewell Addresses," *Journal of Biblical Literature* 104 (1985): 251 – 68, especially p. 253 and note 8 on that page.

[29] See *The Interpreter's Dictionary of the Bible*, 1962 ed., s.v. "Hospitality," by V. H. Kooy; D.W. Riddle, "Early Christian Hospitality," *Journal of Biblical Literature* 57 (1938): 141 – 54; *The Interpreter's Dictionary of the Bible*, 1962 ed., s.v. "Meals," by J. F. Ross.

[30] Concerning slaves in the the social setting of the New Testament, see Carolyn Osiek, "Slavery in the Second Testament World," *Biblical Theology Bulletin* 22 (1993): 174 – 79.

[31] For Jesus' role and title as prophet, see Fitzmyer, *The Gospel According to Luke I-IX*, 213 – 15. For the literary role of prophecy in Luke-Acts and the two-volume work's prophetic structure, see Luke Timothy Johnson, *The Gospel of Luke*, in the *Sacra Pagina* series (Collegeville: The Liturgical Press, 1991), 15 – 21.

[32] For Jesus' role and title as the Christ or as Christ, see Fitzmyer, *The Gospel According to Luke I-IX*, 197 – 200.

[33] For Jesus' role and title as Lord, see Fitzmyer, *The Gospel According to Luke I-IX*, 200 – 204; I. De la Potterie, *"Le titre kurios applique a*

*Jesus dans l'evangile de Luc,"* in Albert Descamps and R. P. Andre de Halleux, eds., *Melanges Beda Rigaux* (Gembloux: Editions J. Duculot, 1970), 117–46.

## Chapter II

[1] For a historical critical study of Luke 5:27–32 and 5:33–39, see Fitzmyer, *The Gospel According to Luke I-IX,* 587–93; for a literary theological approach, in which Luke 5:27–39 is seen as one unit, see LaVerdiere, *Luke,* 83–87.

[2] For the New Testament use of the term, see the *Theological Dictionary of the New Testament,* ed. G. Kittel, 1967 ed., s.v. *"metanoeo, metanoia,"* by Johannes Behm.

[3] For the role of tax collectors and their place in the gospels, see, *The Anchor Bible Dictionary,* 1992 ed., s.v. "Tax Collector," by John R. Donahue.

[4] Matthew told the same call story as that of Matthew instead of Levi (9:9-13). Later he also identified the apostle Matthew (Mark 3:18; Luke 6:15) as Matthew the tax collector (Matthew 10:3). In the second controversy (Matthew 9:14–17), those who approached Jesus were not an anonymous "they" (Mark) or the Pharisees and their scribes (Luke) but the disciples of John, who asked, "Why do we and the Pharisees fast [much] but your disciples do not fast?" (Matthew 9:14).

[5] Such a minisymposium would be a subordinate literary form within the genre defined by Luke's gospel as "a narrative of the events that have been fulfilled among us" (1:1).

[6] Grammatically, the house appears to be that of Jesus, but the context suggests it was the house of Levi. In Mark's gospel, the house or home is quite symbolic. When Jesus enters someone's home (see Mark 1:29–31), it then becomes the home of Jesus (see Mark 2:1). Being with Jesus in the home means being in solidarity with Jesus (see Mark 3:20); staying outside while Jesus is inside is a rejection of solidarity (see Mark 3:31–35).

[7] In this we have a good indication of how, in this part of the gospel, Luke transformed older stories with a basic Christological focus into stories with a basic ecclesiological focus while grounded in Christology.

[8] See A. H. Mead, "Old and New Wine, St. Luke 5:39," *The Expository Times* 99 (May 1988): 234–35.

[9] For a historical critical analysis of the passage see Fitzmyer, *The Gospel According to Luke I-IX*, 683–94. For a literary and theological approach, see LaVerdiere, *Luke*, 107–10. For a detailed analysis of Luke's compositional techniques in creating 7:36–50, and the story's relationship to the Hellenistic syposium, see J. Delobel, *Ephemerides Theologicae Lovanienses* 42 (1966): 415–75.

[10] The New Testament distinguishes among the terms "repentance" *(metanoia)*, "forgiveness" *(aphesis)* and "reconciliation" *(katallage)*. The term reconciliation is not used very frequently in the New Testament (see Romans 5:11; 11:15; 2 Corinthians 5:18, 19). The related verb, "to reconcile" *(katallasso)*, appears in Romans 5:10; 1 Corinthians 7:11 and 2 Corinthians 5:18, 19, 20. Both play an important role in Paul's theology of Christ's mission. *Metanoia* is a condition or prerequisite for forgiveness and reconciliation. *Aphesis* is the divine response to *metanoia*, and *katallage* is its goal. The distinctions among the three are obviously significant, but they are often blurred in pastoral life today and need to be addressed in catechesis. Although the terms themselves are not used outside of Paul, the notion is certainly present in many gospel stories. Consider, for example, Jesus' parable of the prodigal son, where the younger son and the father are reconciled but the older brother refuses to be reconciled to his younger brother (Luke 15:11–32).

[11] Jesus did something similar in an exchange with a scholar of the law (10:25–37). When the scholar asked who his neighbor was, Jesus told him a story about a good Samaritan, one whom he would not normally have considered his neighbor (10:30–35), and told him to do as the Samaritan did (10:36–38).

[12] The designation "the Twelve" represents more than a list of twelve particular disciples or apostles. It is a theological statement about the church, recalling Israel's nature as a covenant of twelve tribes but transforming that nature and redefining it. For Israel and the old covenant, the twelve tribes formed a particular people. For the church

and the new covenant, the Twelve represents a people open to all. The community of the Twelve refers to the universal church.

[13] The meaning of the expression, being "at the feet" of someone, is clearest in Paul's apologia before the Jews at Jerusalem: "I am a Jew, born in Tarsus in Cilicia, but brought up in this city. *At the feet of Gamaliel I was educated strictly in our ancestral law and was zealous for God, just as you are today." (Acts 22:3) By declaring himself at the feet of Gamaliel, Paul recognized and acknowledged that he was a disciple of Gamaliel. To be at another's feet means recognizing one's own position as a disciple and the position of the other as teacher.

[14] In Simon's name, we have another link with Mark's story of a woman anointing Jesus at a dinner in the home of Simon the leper (Mark 14:3).

[15] See Eugene LaVerdiere, *When We Pray* (Notre Dame: Ave Maria Press, 1983), 131–35.

[16] For a historical critical commentary, see Fitzmyer, *The Gospel According to Luke I-IX,* 761–69; and "The Composition of Luke, Chapter 9," *Perspectives on Luke-Acts,* ed. C. H. Talbert (Danville VA: Association of Baptist Professors of Religion, 1978), 139–52. For a brief literary and theological commentary, see LaVerdiere, *Luke,* 128–29. See also E. E. Ellis, "The Composition of Luke 9 and the Source of Its Christology," *Current Issues in Biblical and Patristic Interpretation. Studies in Honor of Merrill C. Tenney* (Grand Rapids: Wm. B. Eerdmans, 1975), 120–27.

[17] For the location and history of Bethsaida, see *The Anchor Bible Dictionary,* 1992 ed., s.v. "Beth-Saida," by James F. Strange.

[18] Jesus would do the same at the Last Supper, where he hosted a dinner for the Twelve in a "guest room" *(kataluma),* a place where he could extend hospitality, which was provided for him (22:11).

[19] For the theme of hospitality in Luke-Acts, see John Koenig, *New Testament Hospitality* (Philadelphia: Fortress Press, 1985), 85–123.

[20] On the unity and structure of Luke 9:1–50, see Robert F. O'Toole, "Luke's Message in Luke 9:1–50," *Catholic Biblical Quarterly* 49 (1987): 74–89.

[21] The relationship between Luke 9:1–50 and 9:51—19:44 is an important element in David Moessner's study of the literary and theological meaning of the Lukan travel narrative. See Moessner, *Lord of the Banquet* (Minneapolis: Fortress Press, 1989), 45–79.

[22] In drawing from Mark, Luke did not include any of the sections where Mark tells the story of the mission to the Gentiles. Mark's second story of the breaking of the bread (Mark 8:1–9) is situated on the other side of the sea after Jesus left the district of Tyre and Sidon and went into that of the Decapolis. Luke announces the mission to the Gentiles but tells its story only in the Acts of the Apostles.

[23] The term "apostles" *(hoi apostoloi)* refers to the Twelve (see 9:1, 12) from the point of view of their being sent by Jesus as missionaries. As the gospel indicated when the community of the Twelve was constituted, "When day came, he called his disciples to himself, and from them he chose Twelve, whom he also named apostles." (6:13)

[24] The connection between the bread Jesus gives and the manna provided in the desert is most explicit in John's gospel, in Jesus' discourse (see 6:31–33) after the breaking of the bread (6:1–15).

[25] Luke's source, Mark 6:44, also referred to "men" *(andres),* but in Mark, the breaking of bread with 5,000 men (6:34–44) reflects an early stage in the development of the church community within the Jewish world. Later in Mark's gospel, this early stage is supplemented by the breaking of bread with 4,000 people (8:1–9), this time in Gentile territory, reflecting a later stage when the church community included both men and women. Luke did not situate the mission to the Gentiles in the gospel's story of Jesus, but in Acts, in the story of the apostolic church, and so did not refer to Mark's second story where Jesus breaks the bread among the Gentiles. Like Luke, Matthew did not include the mission to the Gentiles in the life of Jesus, but he did tell both stories of the breaking of bread (Matthew 14:13–21; 15:32–38). In telling the stories, Matthew referred to 5,000 men *(andres)* and 4,000 *(andres),* but added each time "not counting women and children" (Matthew 14:21; 15:38), thereby making the breaking of bread, or eucharist, inclusive.

[26] The translation in the NRSV is no better, "Make them sit down in groups of about fifty each." It may be that the unlikelihood of having a large gathering of symposia in a desert place leads translators to

accommodate the meaning of the text to the physical situation. From a literary point of view, however, situating symposia in a desert place is extremely meaningful, associating the early Christian breaking of the bread with Israel's desert experience of the manna.

27 Mark, however, did have symposia in mind. Literally, Jesus' orders for the preparation asked that all recline by symposia *(anaklinai pantas sumposia sumposia)*. The RNAB reads "have them sit down in groups."

28 In the Jewish tradition, blessings were always for persons. God blessed human beings, and human beings blessed God in return. Human beings could also bless one another. Mark's story in 6:30–44, which reflects a tradition close to the Christian community's Jewish origins, has Jesus pronouncing a blessing, but not blessing the bread and fish. In Mark 8:1–9, Jesus gives thanks with regard to the bread but he blesses the fish, indicating the story was handed down in a Gentile Christian milieu. Luke reflects the same kind of traditional milieu when Jesus blesses the bread and the fish at Bethsaida (9:16).

## Chapter III

1 The journey's opening statement defines the journey thematically: "When the days for his being taken up were fulfilled, he resolutely determined to journey to Jerusalem." (9:51) The Greek term for "being taken up" is *analempsis,* the same that is used in Acts in the verb form to describe the ascension (see Acts 1:2, 11, 22). In the transfiguration story, the same event is referred to as Jesus' "exodus *[exodos]* that he was going to accomplish in Jerusalem" (9:31).

2 Commentators tend to focus on Jesus' actual arrival at Jerusalem, ending the journey at either 19:27 or 19:44. Literarily, however, the journey continues through 19:48. Luke explicitly situates the preparations for Jesus' entry into Jerusalem (19:28–40) as part of the journey: "After he had said this, he proceeded on his journey up to Jerusalem." (19:28) In 19:41, Jesus was still drawing near. In 19:45, Jesus entered the temple area and proceeded to cleanse the temple (19:45–48), and from this we might argue that the journey narrative ends at 19:44, except that, literarily, 19:45–48 is part of the story unit begun with 19:28 and including Jesus' lament over Jerusalem (19:41–44).

The unit (19:28 – 48), which ends with a concluding summary of Jesus' ministry in the temple (19:47 – 48), brings a major section of the journey narrative to a close. The next section, which presents Jesus' teaching in the temple, opens with a summary reference to the same ministry (20:1) and closes with a concluding summary of Jesus' activity in the temple (21:37 – 38) which parallels the one in 19:47 – 48.

**3** For a historical critical approach to the story, see Fitzmyer, *The Gospel According to Luke X-XXIV,* 891 – 95; for a literary and theological approach, see Eugene LaVerdiere, *Luke,* 151 – 53.

**4** The introduction includes two stories in which Jesus sends disciples ahead of him to prepare the way for his coming (9:51 – 56; 10:1 – 24), each of which is followed by teaching regarding attitudes, behavior and relationships for the journey (9:57 – 62; 10:25 – 37); see LaVerdiere, *Luke,* 141 – 51.

**5** Luke often presents a place as a city *(polis)* when the source or tradition referred to it as a town or village. This is what he does in the case of Nazareth (1:26; 2:4, 39), "the city of Judah" where Zechariah and Elizabeth had their home (1:39); Bethlehem, "the city of David" (2:4); Capernaum (4:31); and Nain (7:11), all of which are introduced as cities. In the present case, he maintained Bethany as a village as he would do for the village of the Samaritans (9:52) and for Emmaus toward the end of the gospel (24:13, 28). Since Jerusalem was the journey's destination, he may have wanted to downplay the importance of places on the way.

**6** The manner of introducing Martha, "a woman named Martha," recalls the way Mary the mother of Jesus was introduced, "a virgin betrothed to a man named Joseph," where emphasis was on Mary neither as an individual person nor as a woman, but more precisely as a virgin (1:27).

**7** While such scribal explicitations in ancient manuscripts are not part of the original text, they do constitute a very early commentary on the text, especially when the story has no parallel in another gospel. Knowing a text by heart from another gospel, a scribe may unintentionally introduce wording from the other gospel. The story of Martha and Mary, however, has no parallel in the other gospels. Consequently, the explicitation comes either from the oral telling of this particular story or from the scribe's own personal understanding of it.

[8] The Greek verb "to stay" *(meno)*, a term associated with early Christian hospitality, implies making one's home with someone. The same verb is used in the story of the disciples of Emmaus inviting Jesus "to stay" with them (24:29), as well as in the story of Zacchaeus when Jesus announces he must stay at his house (19:5).

[9] See France Beydon, *"A temps nouveau, nouvelles questions: Luc 10, 38-42,"* Foi et Vie 88 (1989): 25 – 32.

[10] The translation, "listening to him speak," is unfortunate, blurring any previous references to "the word" of Jesus, which was the word of God (see 5:1).

[11] The Twelve were also distracted from prayer, which is extremely close to listening and attending to the word.

[12] See France Beydon, *"A temps nouveau."*

[13] For a historical-critical approach to the story, see Fitzmyer, *The Gospel According to Luke X-XXIV,* 941 – 53. For a literary and theological approach, see LaVerdiere, *Luke,* 164 – 68. See also E. Springs Steele, "Luke 11:37-54 — A Modified Hellenistic Symposium?" *Journal of Biblical Literature* 103/3 (1984): 379 – 94.

[14] See Eugene LaVerdiere, *When We Pray* (Notre Dame: Ave Maria Press, 1983), 111 – 27.

[15] See Luke 14:12, where Jesus distinguished between a lunch *(ariston)* and a dinner *(deipnon)*.

[16] The title *kurios* was used in 10:38 – 42 as well as in the introduction of the Lord's Prayer (11:1).

[17] The reference to the cup and the dish may have been inspired by Mark's parenthesis in 7:3 – 4: "For the Pharisees and, in fact, all Jews, do not eat without carefully washing their hands, keeping the tradition of the elders. And on coming from the marketplace they do not eat without purifying themselves. And there are many other things that they have traditionally observed, the purification of cups and jugs and kettles [and beds]."

[18] For blessings and woes, see the sermon on the plain in Luke 6:20 – 23 and 6:24 – 26.

[19] In 7:30, Luke included "scholars of the law" among those who were not baptized by John the Baptist and rejected the plan of God for themselves. Then in 10:25 it is "a scholar of the law" who stood up to test Jesus about what was needed to inherit eternal life. Jesus had answered him with a question concerning the law, and when the lawyer tried to justify himself Jesus told him the story of the good Samaritan and ended by telling him to imitate the Samaritan (10:25 – 37).

[20] For a historical-critical approach to the story, see Fitzmyer, *The Gospel according to Luke X-XXIV*, 1038 – 59. For a literary and theological approach, see LaVerdiere, *Luke*, 190 – 95.

[21] There are many examples of Luke composing a story with traditional elements coming from distinct sources. A good example is his account of the Last Supper (22:7 – 13, 14 – 38), as we shall see futher on. Another is the story of the call of Simon Peter and his partners (5:1 – 11).

[22] By presenting this third meal at the home of a Pharisee as climactic, Luke indicates that he thought of these meals as a unit, even though they are told in different parts of the gospel. Each of the meals represents a development in relation to the previous one. Of the three taken at the home of a Pharisee, this third meal represents a climax. To appreciate it, we consequently need to pay attention not only to its general context in the journey narrative but to the two previous meals at the home of a Pharisee.

[23] In the previous section (10:38 — 13:21), Jesus was referred to either by a pronoun, or in direct address by the title "Lord" or "Teacher."

[24] The issue of healing on the sabbath came up in 6:6 – 11 and 13:10 – 17. The first part of the meal may have been inspired by those stories.

[25] For a historical-critical approach to the story of Zacchaeus, see Fitzmyer, *The Gospel According to Luke X-XXIV* 1218 – 27; for a literary and theological approach, see LaVerdiere, *Luke*, 222 – 25.

[26] In the story of Jesus' Galilean ministry, Luke included a meal (5:27 – 39; 7:36 – 50; 9:10 – 17) in each of the three sections (5:1 — 6:11; 6:12 – 8:56; 9:1 – 50) coming after the introduction (4:14 – 44). The

same symmetry is not found in the story of Jesus' geographical journey to Jerusalem, where the four meals (10:38 – 42; 11:37 – 54; 14:1 – 24; 19:1 – 10) do not correspond to the four parts of the journey (10:38 — 13:21; 13:22 — 17:10; 17:11 — 19:27; 19:28 – 48) coming after the introduction (9:51 — 10:37).

[27] In Mark's gospel, Luke's source for the story of the blind beggar, the healing took place as Jesus was leaving Jericho. Luke may have changed the time of the healing to when Jesus was entering to make room for the story of Zacchaeus. The Zacchaeus event took place as Jesus was making his way through Jericho.

[28] In Luke's gospel, it is important not only to hear the gospel but to see it. In the prologue, the shepherds not only heard the gospel of Jesus from the angel (2:10 – 11) but went to see it (2:15 – 16). Having seen the gospel of Jesus, they would then make it known (2:17). When John the Baptist sent two of his disciples to ask if Jesus was the one who was to come, Jesus sent them back to tell John what they had both seen and heard (7:18 – 23).

[29] For the popular view of tax collectors as sinners and for the nature of their sin, we have the ministry of John the Baptist in 3:12 – 13: "Even tax collectors came to be baptized and they said to him, 'Teacher, what shall we do?' He answered them, 'Stop collecting more than is prescribed.'"

[30] For the law, see Exodus 21:37: "When a man steals an ox or a sheep and slaughters or sells it, he shall restore five oxen for the one ox, and four sheep for the one sheep." See also Numbers 5:5 – 10.

## Chapter IV

[1] For a historical-critical approach to the Last Supper, see Fitzmyer, *The Gospel According to Luke X-XXIV* 1376 – 1435; for a literary and theological approach, see LaVerdiere, *Luke,* 252 – 62. See also Jerome Neyrey, *The Passion According to Luke. A Redaction Study of Luke's Soteriology* (New York: Paulist Press, 1985), 5 – 48.

[2] See 4:22, 34, 36, 41; 5:21; 7:16, 19 – 20, 39, 49; 8:25; 9:7 – 9, 18 – 21.

[3] See Johannes Munck, *"Discours d'adieu dans le Nouveau Testament and dans la litterature biblique,"* *Aux sources de la tradition chretienne* (Paris: Delachaux & Niestle, 1950), 155 – 70; Eugene LaVerdiere, "A Discourse at the Last Supper," *The Bible Today* (March 1974): 1540 – 48; W. Kurz, "Luke 22:14 – 38 and Greco-Roman and Biblical Farewell Addresses," *Journal of Biblical Literature* 104 (1985): 251 – 68.

[4] See Arthur Voobus, *The Prelude to the Lukan Passion Narrative* (Stockholm: Estonian Theological Society in Exile, 1968).

[5] The central contention of Raymond Brown's commentary on the infancy narratives in Matthew and Luke was precisely this, "that the infancy narratives are worthy vehicles of the Gospel message; indeed, each is the essential Gospel story in miniature." *The Birth of the Messiah* (Garden City NY: Doubleday, 1977), 8.

[6] See Joel B. Green, "Preparation for Passover (Luke 22:7 – 13): A Question of Redactional Technique," *Novum Testamentum* 29/4 (1987): 305 – 19. The study shows that in this passage Luke's only source was Mark 14:12 – 16, and that all the changes Luke introduced into the passage were for stylistic or theological reasons.

[7] Mark had introduced Judas Iscariot more directly as "one of the Twelve" — *ho heis ton dodeka* (14:10). Luke introduces him with an oblique reference to the Twelve as "being of the number of the Twelve" — *onta ek tou arithmou ton dodeka,* suggesting that he may have been of their number but was no longer really one of them. Later, however, Luke does follow Mark 14:43 in referring to Judas as "one of the Twelve" — *heis ton dodeka* (22:47).

[8] The feasts of Passover and Unleavened Bread have a long and complicated history antedating that of Israel. At first, the two feasts were independent of one another, the first being a nomadic festival and the second an agrarian one. The nomadic feast of Passover became associated with the agrarian feast of Unleavened Bread in the course of Israel's settlement in Canaan, and it soon became related to the great events of Israel's deliverance and exodus from Egypt. The nomadic feast of Passover, corresponding to Israel's earlier history, would very likely have been absorbed by that of Unleavened Bread when Israel became mainly sedentary and agrarian. However, Passover was more intimately related to the foundations of Israel and the deliverance

from Egypt and for this reason it continued to dominate the combined feast's theology.

In New Testament times, as Luke noted, the feast was called Passover. The celebration of Unleavened Bread was part of it as an important but secondary element. This can be seen from Mark and Matthew, both of whom referred first to Passover (Mark 14:1; Matthew 26:2) and then related the feast of Unleavened Bread to it (Mark 14:1, 12; Matthew 26:17). For Luke, however, the feast of Unleavened Bread was primary and Passover secondary, perhaps in order to highlight the radical newness of the Lord's Supper and the new covenant, emphasizing once again the need to beware of the leaven of the Pharisees (see Luke 12:1 and the meal in 11:37 – 54; see also Mark 8:15; Matthew 16:6).

[9] Peter and John are often mentioned together, along with James in Luke (5:1 – 11; 8:51; 9:28) and by themselves in Acts (3:1, 3, 11; 4:13, 19; 8:14).

[10] See Luke 6:13 – 16 and Acts 1:13.

[11] See Joachim Jeremias, *The Eucharistic Words of Jesus,* trans. Norman Perrin (Philadelphia: Fortress Press, 1977), 15 – 88. After weighing the arguments for and against, Jeremias concluded that the Last Supper was very likely a Jewish Passover meal. But here is his final word on the matter: "It should be emphasized, however, that the Last Supper would still be surrounded by the atmosphere of the Passover even if it should have occurred on the evening before the feast." (p. 88)

[12] Jeremias, *The Eucharistic Words of Jesus,* 89 – 105.

[13] Jeremias, *The Eucharistic Words of Jesus,* 106 – 37; see also I. Howard Marshall, *Last Supper and Lord's Supper* (Grand Rapids: William B. Eerdmans, 1980).

[14] The Hebrew word *seder,* meaning "order," appears only once in the Bible in a reference to "disorder" (Job 10:22). Later in rabbinical times, it was applied to the "order" of readings for the three-year Jewish cycle, to the major divisions of the Mishnah, to the "order" of prayer and worship, as also to the "order" of the Jewish ceremonial meal taken in homes on the first night of Passover. In the time of Jesus, the Passover was a sacred meal with the participants sharing in the sacrificial lamb in memory of the people's deliverance from bondage. As a

Christian Passover, the eucharist also is a sacred sacrificial meal shared as the memorial of the people's deliverance from bondage by the blood of Christ. On the Jewish feast of Passover and the feast of Unleavened Bread, see Samuel Sandmel, *Judaism and Christian Beginnings* (New York: Oxford University Press, 1978), 213 – 14.

[15] Good examples of the inclusive use of *anthropos* can be seen in Jesus' sayings, for example, "A good person *[anthropos]* out of the store of goodness in his [or her] heart produces good, but an evil person out of a store of evil produces evil." (Luke 6:45) Sayings such as this apply to both women and men.

[16] The reference to the disciples' being met by someone carrying a water jar is found also in Mark 14:13 – 14 but has no parallel in Matthew. In Mark as well as Luke, the disciples were to follow the person *(auto)* into the house he or she entered. It is true that the Greek pronoun *auto* (dative case) is masculine, but this comes from grammatical agreement with the masculine noun *anthropos* and has nothing to do with the person's sex. Greek, like many other languages, both ancient and modern, but unlike English, is very sensitive to gender. Gender is a matter not of sex but of grammar.

[17] Luke's gospel is noted for pairing stories of men and women. For the old prophet Simeon (2:25 – 35), there is the old prophetess Anna (2:36-38). For the man *(anthropos)* finding the lost sheep (15:4 – 7), there is the woman *(gune)* finding the lost coin (15:8 – 10). The parable of the mustard seed compares the kingdom of God to a mustard seed that a man *(anthropos)* took and planted in the garden (13:18 – 19). It is followed by the parable of the yeast which compares the kingdom of God to a yeast that a woman *(gune)* took and mixed in three measures of flour (13:20 – 21). In a culture where the roles of men and women were more sharply distinguished than they are today, making bread was a woman's role. Planting a mustard seed, however, could just as easily be done by a woman as by a man. The use of *anthropos* in the parable of the mustard seed respects the distinction between the man and the woman, but does not emphasize it.

[18] In modern times, Luke's attitude would be described as inclusive but not reactionary, an indication that the conflicts still evident in the Pauline era and to a lesser extent in the time of Mark had been resolved. From Paul's letters, we see how difficult it was for the early Christians to integrate women into the community, as was required by

their baptism (see Galatians 3:26–28). From Mark, we see how the need to include women had to be recalled and insisted upon (see Mark 7:24–30). From Luke-Acts, we see that it could be done without too much difficulty and that it had become normal to do so.

[19] According to Mark, darkness came over the whole land from the sixth hour *(genomenes horas hektes)* until the ninth hour *(eos horas enates)* when Jesus gave a loud cry and breathed his last (see Mark 15:33–37). In their story of Jesus' death, Mark and Luke presuppose not the Jewish day, which started at sundown, but the Roman day, which began at dawn.

[20] Luke's account, "It was now about noon [the sixth hour] and darkness came over the whole land until three in the afternoon [the ninth hour]," also presupposes the Roman reckoning from dawn to dawn.

[21] Mark uses the term *dei* in a theological sense in 8:31; 9:11; 13:7, 10, 14. Luke, on the other hand, used it 18 times in the gospel and 24 times in Acts.

[22] For Luke's use of *dei* with reference to a meal, see 15:32; 19:5; 22:37; 24:26, 44, besides in 22:7.

[23] For Luke, the Last Supper and Lord's Supper was therefore sacrificial independently of one's view on the authenticity of 22:19b–20.

[24] Luke's ecclesial emphasis was already noted in the story of the meal at the house of Levi (5:27–39), where the Pharisees' concern was not so much that Jesus ate with tax collectors and sinners but that his disciples did.

[25] Luke refers to "the disciples" 38 times in the course of the gospel; the last time is in the story of Jesus' prayer at the Mount of Olives (22:39, 45).

[26] Luke refers to the apostles only six times in the gospel (6:13; 9:10; 11:49; 17:5; 22:14; 24:10), but 28 times in Acts; the last time is in 16:4.

[27] For the structure of 22:15–20, see J. H. Petzer, "Luke 22:19b–20 and the Structure of the Passage," *Novum Testamentum* 26 (1984): 249–52. Petzger shows how 22:15–20 is divided into two parallel

parts, 22:15–18 and 22:19–20, each of which is itself divided into two parallel parts, one on eating bread, 22:15–16 and 22:19, the other on drinking the cup, 22:17–18 and 22:20. Each of the four small sub-units is also divided into two parts, one presenting a sign, 22:15–16a, 17–18a, 19a, 20a, and the other providing its "explanation," 22:16b, 18b, 19b, 20b.

[28] In Mark and Matthew, Jesus' statement about not drinking again the fruit of the vine follows the liturgical text. Drinking it new in the kingdom of God consequently refers not to the eucharistic banquet of the church but to its fulfillment in the heavenly banquet.

[29] Seeing the parallelism between the two statements, one referring to eating and one referring to drinking, and both referring to their fulfillment in the kingdom of God, is very important. The tendency is rather to dissociate the second statement, whose source is Mark 14:25, from the first, which Luke personally developed, and connect it with the following statements concerning the bread and the cup (22:19–20). This blurs both the distinction and the relationship between the Last Supper and the Lord's Supper as presented by Luke.

[30] Because the Lukan statements about this being the Last Supper precede the liturgical text from the Lord's Supper, Jesus' eating and drinking in the kingdom of God refer directly to the fulfillment of the Last Supper in the eucharistic banquet of the church. The eucharistic banquet is thus the first realization of the meal in the kingdom of God. Indirectly, it also refers to the eucharist's own fulfillment in the heavenly banquet.

[31] The first statement, concerning eating the Passover, is patterned on Mark's statement in 14:25, which bears on drinking the cup. Luke's second statement, the one concerning the cup, whose source is Mark 14:25, is patterned on Luke's second statement concerning the cup in 22:20a. Unlike Mark 14:25 and Matthew 26:29, where Jesus merely comments on the meal, Luke 22:17 shows Jesus actually engaging in the meal: "Then he took a cup, gave thanks, and said, 'Take this and share it among yourselves.'" The same is implied in 22:15, when Jesus says, "I have eagerly desired to eat this Passover with you before I suffer." Mark's statement began with Jesus' reference to the future: "Amen I say to you, I shall not drink again the fruit of the vine . . ." (Mark 14:25).

[32] The absolute use of the term "to suffer" *(pathein)* with reference to the passion and death of Christ is typical of Luke's writing (see 24:46; Acts 1:3; 3:18; 17:3; 26:23).

[33] Peter's discourse in the household of Cornelius refers to such meals when referring "to us, the witnesses chosen by God in advance, who ate and drank with him after he rose from the dead" (Acts 10:41).

[34] The words from verse 19b, "which will be given for you; do this in memory of me," and all of verse 20 are absent in a few manuscripts of Luke, but present in the vast majority. Although some scholars have maintained that the shorter form without verses 19b-20 is the authentic text, the majority consider the longer form, including verses 19b-20, to be authentically Lukan (see Fitzmyer, *The Gospel According to Luke x-xxiv*, 1387 – 89).

[35] In 1 Corinthians 11:25, the repetition of "Do this in memory of me" may have been introduced by Paul for emphasis. At Corinth, the Christians did come together for a meal, but their meal was not in memory of Christ. It consequently was not the Lord's Supper (see 1 Corinthians 11:20). It is only when they ate the bread and drank the cup in memory of Christ that they proclaimed the death of the Lord until he came (see l Corinthians 11:26).

[36] The reference to "the hand of the betrayer" being with Christ on the table is vague from the point of view of identifying the betrayer. However, since the hand is a biblical symbol for power (see Deuteronomy 26:8) the statement itself is extremely forceful, announcing that the power of the betrayer, not just the betrayer, was actually there with Christ on the table of mutual solidarity.

[37] On that occasion, Jesus responded by taking a child and placing it by his side, thereby associating the child with himself. Then he said, "Whoever receives this child in my name receives me, and whoever receives me receives the one who sent me," and concluded, "For the one who is least among all of you is the one who is the greatest." (Luke 9:46 – 48; see Mark 9:34 – 37)

[38] For 22:25 – 27, Luke's source is Mark 10:42 – 45. Unlike Mark, however, Luke is not harshly critical of the kings of the Gentiles or of those who exercise authority. Luke's point is that their manner of ruling and of exercising authority must have no place among the apostles.

[39] In the parable on the attitude of a servant, however, the term used is not precisely "servant" *(diakonos* or *ho diakonon)* but "slave" *(doulos)*, one in the ownership of the master. In the parable, a slave *(doulos)* has the role of a servant at table *(diakonos)*.

[40] Luke first used the Greek term *peirasmos*, meaning temptation, trial or test, to describe the three "temptations" of Jesus in 4:1 – 12: "When the devil had finished every temptation *(peirasmon)*, he departed from him for a time" (4:13). The Greek word for "time" *(kairos)* refers to "the opportune time," not to duration. A better translation would have been "until the right time." For the devil, "the right time" came with Christ's passion, but the apostles were not overwhelmed by the test, thanks to the Father, to whom they prayed, "and do not subject us to the final test *[peirasmon]"* (11:2 – 4).

[41] Jesus indicated similar concern for Martha and for Jerusalem, calling them by name and repeating the name: "Martha, Martha, you are anxious and worried about many things" (10:41); "Jerusalem, Jerusalem, you who kill the prophets and stone those sent to you, how many times I yearned to gather your children together as a hen gathers her brood under her wings, but you were unwilling!" (13:34)

[42] Peter's prayer recalls another prayer when Jesus first called him: "Depart from me, Lord, for I am a sinful man." (5:8) On that occasion Peter asked Jesus to depart from him. At the Last Supper, he pledged not to depart from Jesus.

[43] Many may assume that the cock crowed at dawn, which would indicate several more hours of solidarity with Jesus. The cock actually crows all night long. In effect, Christ was telling Peter that in no time at all Peter would deny Christ repeatedly.

[44] In Mark, the instructions for the Twelve were "to take nothing for the journey but a walking stick — no food, no sack, no money in their belts." They were, however, to wear sandals but not a second tunic (Mark 6:8 – 9). The instructions in Luke seem closer to the ancient tradition, which is also reflected in Matthew 10:9 – 10. Mark seems to have adapted the tradition to evoke the instructions for eating the Passover: "This is how you are to eat it: with your loins girt, sandals on your feet and staff in hand." (Exodus 12:11)

### Chapter V

[1] Without Judas, the Twelve were now the Eleven (see also 24:9). In Acts, Luke would sometimes refer to the Eleven (Acts 1:26; 2:14) when he wanted to distinguish Peter from the others, highlighting his unique mission of strengthening the apostolic community (see 22:32). In Acts 1:15–26, Peter assumes leadership in reconstituting their number of apostles, and in Acts 2:14–41, in his first Pentecost discourse, he spoke for all of them. In 6:2, Peter's role is not distinguished from the others, hence the reference to the Twelve.

[2] For a historical-critical approach to the breaking of the bread at Emmaus, see Fitzmyer, *The Gospel According to Luke X-XXIV*, 1553–72; for a literary and theological approach, see LaVerdiere, *Luke,* 282–88.

[3] Mary Magdalene and Joanna were first introduced in 8:1–3. To indicate the greatness of Mary Magdalene's conversion, Luke mentioned that seven demons had gone out from her. To indicate that some of the first Christians were well-placed socially, he mentioned that Joanna was the wife of Herod's steward Chuza. Along with Mary the mother of James (see Mark 15:40; 16:1) and others, they had followed Jesus from Galilee and witnessed the crucifixion (23:49) and the burial of Jesus (23:55–56).

[4] Good examples of carefully crafted introductions in Luke include Luke 1:5–7 and its presentation of Zechariah and Elizabeth in the annunciation of the conception and birth of John the Baptist (1:5–25), and the introduction of the first meal story (5:27–39) with the call of Levi (5:27–28).

[5] For the relationship of "the first day of the week" to the "Lord's Day" *(kuriake hemera),* see Thomas J. Talley, *The Origins of the Liturgical Year* (New York: Pueblo Publishing Company, 1986), 13–18. Talley's purpose in these pages was to determine whether Luke followed the Jewish, the Roman or the Hellenistic way of determining the beginning and the end of the day. See also Power, *The Eucharistic Mystery,* 74–75. For the meaning of "the first day of the week" as the day of the new creation, see Eugene LaVerdiere, "The Origins of Sunday in the New Testament," *Sunday Morning: a Time for Worship,* ed. Mark Searle (Collegeville: The Liturgical Press, 1982), 11–27.

[6] The journey began in 9:51, "When the days for his being taken up were fulfilled, he resolutely determined to journey to Jerusalem," and was repeatedly referred to as it unfolded (see 9:57; 10:38; 13:22; 17:11; 18:35; 19:1, 28, 41, 45).

[7] A Greek stadion equalled 607 English feet or 185 meters.

[8] Four sites have been proposed for the Emmaus in Luke's story: Khirbet Imwas (Nicopolis), el-Qubeibeh, Qaloniyeh, and Abu Ghosh. Of these, Khirbet Imwas, which preserves the name Emmaus, is situated 161 stadia from Jerusalem on the road to Joppa. See *The Interpreter's Dictionary of the Bible*, 1962 ed., s.v. "Emmaus," by K. W. Clark. *The Anchor Bible Dictionary*, 1992 ed., s.v. "Emmaus," by J. F. Strange, for some reason considers Nicopolis a distinct site from Khirbet Imwas, but is otherwise quite good. A number of ancient manuscripts, including the Codex Sinaiticus, reveal an early textual change from 60 to 160 stadia, accommodating Luke's text to geographical realities.

[9] A brief summary of the Emmaus story included in an early second-century addition to Mark's gospel focuses entirely on Jesus' changed appearance: "After this he appeared in another form *[en hetera morphe]* to two of them walking along on the way to the country. They returned and told the others; but they did not believe them either." (Mark 16:12–13) Shifting the focus from the disciples, whose eyes were prevented from recognizing, to Jesus, who appeared in another form, results in a very different reading of the Lukan story.

[10] Theophilus may have been a particular person, very likely Luke's patron for publishing and disseminating the work, but in 1:4 (see also Acts 1:1), Theophilus represents every reader of Luke-Acts.

[11] The repetition of a phrase or key words, such as we find in Luke 24:16 and 24:31, is referred to as a literary inclusion. Its purpose is to outline a unit, as here where it includes or outlines the body of the story. It may also indicate the unit's basic theme, in this case the recognition of Jesus, the risen Lord.

[12] Referring to this passage in the early third century, Origen reflects the prevailing view that Cleopas' companion was Simon (Peter). But then, since Simon is mentioned in 24:34, it was necessary to end the story with 24:32 (see *Contra Celsum* 2. 62. 68 and 2. 184. 190). In our own

time, some suggest that the companion is Cleopas's wife, identifying her with the wife of Clopas (John 19:25). But Cleopas, whose name is a short form of Cleopatros, the masculine name corresponding to Cleopatra, is not the same as Clopas, which is a grecized form of a semitic name (see J. Fitzmyer, *The Gospel According to Luke X-XXIV*, 1563). Besides, if the companion had been Cleopas's wife, Luke would normally have given her name, as he did in the case of Priscilla, the wife of Aquila (see Acts 18:2, 18, 26).

[13] For a discussion of Luke-Acts' presentation of Jesus as a prophet, see David P. Moessner, *Lord of the Banquet, The Literary and Theological Significnce of the Lukan Travel Narrative* (Minneapolis: Fortress Press, 1989).

[14] An ancient Jewish commentary, the *Midrash Rabbah,* preserving an even older tradition, collected the many passages where God saved his people on the third day and used these to interpret the story of Abraham and the sacrificial offering of his son Isaiah, an event which took place "on the third day" (Genesis 22:4). The texts cited included Hosea 6:2, Genesis 42:18, Exodus 19:16, Joshua 2:16, Jonah 2:1, Ezra 8:32 and Esther 5:1, all of which refer either to the third day or to a time span of three days. See Rabbi H. Freedman and Maurice Simon, eds., *Midrash Rabbah I* (London: The Soncino Press, 1939), 491.

[15] The necessity expressed in the term *dei* is not based on logic or cause and effect but on God's freely willing it as part of human history.

[16] The verb describing Jesus' position at table is *kataklino* (to recline). In the New Testament, the verb is used exclusively in Luke and always in relation to a dinner or banquet, as for the dinner in the house of a Pharisee (7:36; 14:8) and for the breaking of bread at Bethsaida (9:14, 15). Another verb, *katakeimai,* also meaning "to recline," was used for the feast at the house of Levi (5:25, 29) and again for the dinner in the house of a Pharisee (7:39; see Mark 14:3).

[17] The parallel, however, does not imply that in Luke's time the eucharist was structured as it would be by the time of Justin in the mid-second century. From Luke, we would infer that if the eucharist had a formal structure, it was that of the symposium where the dialogue or discourse did not precede but followed the dinner. Hospitality-type meals, however, had little formal structure. In those cases, the dialogue or discourse both preceded and followed the meal, as in the

breaking of the bread at Bethsaida (9:10 – 17), the meals at the home of Martha (10:38 – 42) and at the home of Zacchaeus (19:1 – 10), the meals with the full community gathered in Jerusalem (14:36 – 53) and with Paul at Troas (Acts 20:7 – 12) and here in the story of Emmaus.

[18] The Greek word for "appeared," *ophthe*, is the same that was used in the primitive Antiochene creed Paul quoted in 1 Corinthians 15:3 – 5 and which he himself used in the following verses. The verb is an aorist passive form of *horao*, meaning "to see." In the Septuagint, the same form is used exclusively to announce that the Lord (God), the angel of the Lord and the glory of the Lord appeared. Its use here for the appearance to Simon and elsewhere in the New Testament associates the appearances of the risen Lord with divine appearances in the Old Testament. Like the appearances of God, that of the risen Lord cannot be described, distinguishing them from any apparitions that have been reported in the course of church history.

[19] The verb here translated as "he was made known" *(egnosthe)*, like the verb *ophthe*, is an aorist passive form, taking into consideration that the knowledge comes as a free disclosure.

[20] For a historical-critical approach to the meal with the whole community assembled in Jerusalem, see Fitzmyer, *The Gospel According to Luke X-XXIV*, 1572 – 93; for a literary and theological approach, see LaVerdiere, *Luke*, 288 – 92.

[21] Luke included *koinonia* among the four basic characteristics of the Christian community: "They devoted themselves to the teaching of the apostles and to the communal life *[koinonia]*, to the breaking of the bread and to the prayers." (Acts 2:42)

[22] For a study of the traditional apostolic preaching in Luke 24, see Paul Schubert, "The Structure and Significance of Luke 24," *Neutestamentliche Studien fur Rudolf Bultmann* (Berlin: Topelmann, 1954), 165 – 86.

[23] Jesus told them, "Stay *[menete]* in the same house and eat and drink what is offered to you." (10:7) The verb *meno* expresses meal hospitality. It was also used in the story of Zacchaeus (19:5) and in that of Emmaus (24:29).

[24] The shortest form of the greeting is in 1 Thessalonians, "Grace to you and peace" (1:1). The form found in most of the letters is, "Grace to

you and peace from God our Father and the Lord Jesus Christ" (Romans 1:7; 1 Corinthians 1:3; 2 Corinthians 1:2; Galations 1:3; Ephesians 1:2, Philippians 1:2; 2 Thessalonians 1:2).

[25] Paul referred to peace in his final greeting to the Romans, "May the God of hope fill you with all joy and peace in believing, so that you may abound in hope by the power of the holy Spirit."

[26] The Greek term is not *phantasma* but *pneuma,* which is best translated as "spirit." The term "spirit" invites reflection on possible spiritualizing tendencies in the Lukan communities, similar to those in the Johannine community. Responding to such tendencies, the Lukan Jesus insisted on the reality of his risen body, showing that the assembly was a matter of flesh *(sarx)* as well as spirit *(pneuma).* By asking for food, Jesus showed that the body's hunger had to be attended to.

[27] In this way, Luke would be responding to incipient docetic or protognostic tendencies in his communities. Those with such tendencies played down or ignored the physical needs of others, which Jesus manifestly did not do. Recall that when the apostles wanted him to send a large crowd away he asked them to give them food (9:12 – 13).

[28] At the Last Supper, Jesus told the apostles that the leader among them must be as the servant (22:26), and he referred to himself "as the one who serves" (22:27).

[29] John 21:9 refers to fish cooked over a charcoal fire.

[30] The Christian Bible, following the Septuagint, has a different order, with the Pentateuch (Law) coming first, the Wisdom literature second, and the Prophets third. With this order, the Christian Old Testament is prophetically oriented to the New Testament.

[31] Luke first referred to this theme of promise and fulfillment in the preface for Luke-Acts, stating that like many before him he would write "a narrative of the events that have been fulfilled among us" (1:1).

[32] In Acts, Jesus again refers to "the promise of the Father" (1:4) and interprets it as the "power of the holy Spirit" (1:8).

[33] Acts frequently refers to the promises made to Abraham and their fulfillment in the mission of Jesus (2:39; 3:24 – 26; 13:32; 26:6). The

connection between the promise to Abraham and Jesus' blessing is explicitly made in Acts 3:24–26: "Moreover, all the prophets who spoke, from Samuel and those afterwards, also announced these days. You are the children of the prophets and of the covenant that God made with your ancestors when he said to Abraham, 'In your offspring all the families of the earth shall be blessed.' For you first, God raised up his servant and sent him to bless you by turning each of you from your evil ways."

[34] Similar concluding summaries are found in the gospel's prologue (1:80; 2:40, 52) and in Acts (see, for example, 1:14; 5:42; 6:7; 12:24; 28:30–31).